Reading Companion
for
Fifty Classics

James P. Stobaugh

For Such a Time as This Ministries
Hollsopple, Pennsylvania

Reading Companion for Fifty Classics

READING COMPANION FOR FIFTY CLASSICS
Copyright © 2004 by James P. Stobaugh
Published by For Such a Time as This Ministries
Printed in the United States of America
Book design by James Butti
Cover design by James Butti

Printed in the United States of America.

10 9 8 7 6 5 4 3 2 1 13 12 11 10 09 08 07 06 05 04

Contents

3

Appendixes

Preface

For several years I have wished to write an omnibus companion to the classics. Their reclamation into American rhetoric is critical to our success as a civilization.

This companion is neither a substitute for an English course nor an exhaustive list of classics in general. It does not presume to be anything other than a brief overview and introduction of fifty classics. The reader, with justification, could take this author to task for his selections. No doubt he has omitted many good books; nonetheless, this paltry offering may help some teachers become better instructors of at least these timeless chosen pieces.

For each title the author presents a short description, objective questions, quotations with vocabulary gleanings, and challenging discussion questions. In the book's first part are student chapters; in the second part are teacher chapters (with answers).

Appendixes provide a glossary of literary terms, biographies of authors, an index of authors, and a two-group listing of books to fit the age and maturity of readers. Nevertheless, it is wise for teachers to examine proposed books and make selections to match their specific students.

This whole-book companion is a wonderful addition to an anthology-driven curriculum although it is not designed to replace a full-fledged English course. It also is a helpful supplement to the *SAT and College Preparation Course for the Christian Student* (1998). Most youths, while pursuing a regimented reading program, appreciate a guide to superior classics.

Reading Companion for Fifty Classics will aid teachers in challenging their charges. It will also help students drink from the rich resources of literature and become more able to critique and improve the cultures they meet today.

My prayer is that this book will encourage thoughtful Christians to be taking every thought captive to the gospel (cf. 2 Corinthians 10:4) and, like the apostles, to be turning the world upside down (Acts 17:6).

James P. Stobaugh

Acknowledgments

I wish to thank Mrs. Judy Kovalik and Dr. David Garber for their editorial assistance, and Mr. Jim Butti for his design and layout work. Finally and most of all, I want to thank my best friend and editor, my wife, Karen. "Come, let us glorify the Lord and praise his name forever" (cf. Psalm 34:3).

Classics
for the Student

Agamemnon

Aeschylus

 Not much is known about Aeschylus, the first of the three great masters of Greek tragedy. He was born at Eleusis, near Athens, in 525 B.C., the son of Euphorion. *Agamemnon* is one of three tragedies on the same topic. The three tragedies are called the Oresteia Trilogy.

In 458 B.C. *Agamemnon* returns to Argos from the Trojan War and is killed by his wife, Clytemnestra, and his first cousin Aegisthus. The Oresteia Trilogy, then, is a study in justice. With all its vivid, groundbreaking language and its universal popularity, it was the Star Wars Trilogy of its age.

Objective Test

_____ *Agamemnon* begins with (A) a guard waiting for a signal announcing the fall of Troy to the Greek armies, (B) a recapitulation of the fall of Troy, or (C) the death of Aeneas.

_____ A beacon flashes, and he joyfully runs to tell the news to (A) Hektor, (B) Apollinus, or (C) Queen Clytemnestra.

_____ When he is gone, the Chorus—made up of (A) the old men of Argos, (B) widows of fallen soldiers, or (C) the gods—enters and tells the story of how the Trojan prince Paris stole Helen, the wife of the Greek king Menelaus, leading to ten years of war between Greece and Troy.

_____ Then the Chorus recalls how—to obtain a favorable wind for the Greek fleet—(A) Clytemnestra's husband, Agamemnon

9

(Menelaus's brother), sacrificed their son to the goddess Artemis; (B) Clytemnestra's husband, Agamemnon (Menelaus's brother), sacrificed their daughter to the goddess Artemis, or (C) Clytemnestra's husband, Agamemnon (Menelaus' brother), sacrificed their daughter to the god Zeus.

_____ Clytemnestra (A) murders her husband, (B) throws a party to honor her husband, or (C) kills Paris.

Suggested Vocabulary Words

A. Thus upon mine unrestful couch I lie, Bathed with the dews of night, unvisited / By dreams—ah me!—for in the place of sleep / Stands Fear as my familiar, and repels / The soft repose that would mine eyelids seal. / And if at whiles, for the lost <u>balm</u> of sleep, I medicine my soul with melody / Of <u>trill</u> or song—anon to tears I turn, <u>Wailing</u> the woe that broods upon this home, / Not now by honour guided as of old. (lines 16–24)

B. And so he steeled his heart—ah, well-a-day—Aiding a war for one false woman's sake, / His child to slay, / And with her spilt blood make / An offering, to speed the ships upon their way! / Lusting for war, the bloody <u>arbiters</u> / Closed heart and ears, and would nor hear nor heed / The girl-voice plead, *Pity me, Father!* nor her prayers, Nor tender, virgin years. (lines 268–274)

C. Shamed, silent, <u>unreproachful</u>, stretching hands / That find her not, and sees, yet will not see, That she is far away! / And his sad fancy, <u>yearning</u> o'er the sea, Shall <u>summon</u> and recall / Her wraith, once more to queen it in his hall. And sad with many memories, / The fair cold beauty of each <u>sculptured</u> face—And all to hatefulness is turned their grace, / Seen blankly by <u>forlorn</u> and hungering eyes! And when the night is deep, Come visions, sweet and sad, and bearing pain (lines 486–498)

D. Lastly, whate'er be due to men or gods, / With joint <u>debate</u>, in public council held, We will decide, and <u>warily</u> <u>contrive</u> / That all which now is well may so abide: / For that which haply needs the healer's art, That will we medicine, <u>discerning</u> well / If cautery or knife befit the time. (Lines 980–984)

Discussion Questions

A. Is Clytemnestra's murder of her husband justified?

B. Although Shakespeare's tragedies employ some comic relief, Greek tragedies are altogether tragic: every event leads the characters toward imminent disaster. Discuss how Aeschylus accomplishes this.

C. What function does Aegisthus's character have in the play?

And Then There Were None

Agatha Christie

 First, there were ten—a strange collection of strangers invited as weekend guests to an island off the coast of England. Their host, an odd millionaire unknown to all of them, is nowhere to be found. All the guests have a deplorable past that they are unwilling to reveal. One by one they die. Before the weekend is gone, there will be none.

Objective Test

_____ When the guests arrive on the island, they are told (A) to go home, (B) that they will all be murdered, or (C) that the host will join them tomorrow.

_____ That evening, as all the guests gather after an excellent dinner, they hear a recorded voice (A) accusing each of them of a specific murder committed in the past and never uncovered, (B) welcoming the guests to the house, or (C) asking them to help.

_____ As they discuss what to do, (A) Vera dies, (B) Bob dies, or (C) Tony Marston dies.

_____ The next morning (A) Vera is dead, (B) Mrs. Rogers is dead, or (C) General MacArthur is dead.

_____ The murderer was (A) Tony, (B) Vera, or (C) the Judge.

Suggested Vocabulary Words

A. There was a silence—a comfortable <u>replete</u> silence. Into that silence came The Voice. Without warning, inhuman, <u>penetrating</u> . . . *"Ladies and gentlemen! Silence, please! . . .* You are charged with the following <u>indictments</u>." (ch. 3)

B. But—<u>incongruous</u> as it may seem to some—I was <u>restrained</u> and <u>hampered</u> by my <u>innate</u> sense of justice. The innocent must not suffer. (Epilogue)

Discussion Questions

A. How does Christie build suspense?

B. Do you agree with the Judge's decision to kill all these people?

C. How do the weaknesses of each character hasten their end?

D. Did you guess who the murderer was before the novel ended?

Animal Farm

George Orwell

 *A nimal farm* is a great fable turned into a novel. Its simple plot camouflages a much deeper, darker message. The story is about a farm run by a mean farmer, who is later run out of the farm by the animals. The animals take control of the farm and find that it isn't as easy to run as they thought.

Objective Test

_____ Old Major, a prize-winning boar, gathers the animals of the Manor Farm (A) to warn them of a great slaughter, (B) for a meeting in the big barn, or (C) to lead a revolt.

_____ He tells them (A) about a dream he has had, (B) to prepare for winter, or (C) that he will die.

_____ He tells the animals that they must (A) run away, (B) create a workers' paradise, or (C) kill all the rats.

_____ He teaches them (A) to speak French, (B) to run fast, or (C) a song called "Beasts of England."

_____ Ultimately the community-run government is taken over by (A) pigs who look more and more like the men they replaced, (B) horses who carry big whips, or (C) cows who try to bring consensus.

Suggested Vocabulary Words

A. The pigs had an even harder struggle to <u>counteract</u> the lies put about by Moses, the tame raven. Moses, who was Mr. Jones's special pet, was a spy and a tale-bearer, but he was also a clever talker. He claimed to know of the existence of a mysterious country called Sugarcandy Mountain, to which all animals went when they died. It was situated somewhere up in the sky, a little distance beyond the clouds, Moses said. In Sugarcandy Mountain it was Sunday seven days a week, clover was in season all the year round, and lump sugar and linseed cake grew on the hedges. The animals hated Moses because he told tales and did no work, but some of them believed in Sugarcandy Mountain, and the pigs had to argue very hard to <u>persuade</u> them that there was no such place. (ch. 2)

B. The animals were not badly off throughout that summer, in spite of the hardness of their work. If they had no more food than they had had in Jones's day, at least they did not have less. The <u>advantage</u> of only having to feed themselves, and not having to support five <u>extravagant</u> human beings as well, was so great that it would have taken a lot of failures to outweigh it. And in many ways the animal method of doing things was more <u>efficient</u> and saved labour. Such jobs as weeding, for instance, could be done with a thoroughness impossible to human beings. And again, since no animal now stole, it was unnecessary to fence off pasture from <u>arable</u> land, which saved a lot of labour on the upkeep of hedges and gates. Nevertheless, as the summer wore on, various unforeseen shortages began to make themselves felt. (ch. 6)

C. At the beginning, when the laws of Animal Farm were first formulated, the retiring age had been fixed for horses and pigs at twelve, for cows at fourteen, for dogs at nine, for sheep at seven, and for hens and geese at five. Liberal old-age pensions had been agreed upon. As yet no animal had actually retired on pension, but of late the subject had been discussed more and more. Now that the small field beyond the orchard had been set aside for barley, it was rumoured that a corner of the large pasture was to be fenced off and turned into a grazing-ground for <u>superannuated</u> animals. (ch. 9)

D. There was the same hearty cheering as before, and the mugs were emptied to the dregs. But as the animals outside gazed at the scene, it seemed to them that some strange thing was happening. What was it that had <u>altered</u> in the faces of the pigs? Clover's old dim eyes flitted from one face to another. Some of them had five chins, some had four, some had three. But what was it that seemed to be melting and changing? (ch. 10)

Discussion Questions

A. This book is a parody of what actual cultural/political revolution?

B. In what chapter does the plot turn in mood and meaning?

C. What style does Orwell employ in this book?

D. To a Christian, when, if ever, is a revolution necessary?

E. How does Orwell use his narrative point of view to produce irony?

The Autobiography of Benjamin Franklin

Benjamin Franklin

S peaking to his "Dear Son," Benjamin Franklin began what is one of the most famous autobiographies in world history. At the age of sixty-two, Franklin wrote his reminiscences for the benefit of his son, William Franklin (1731–1813). The book was composed in sections, the first part dealing with Franklin's first twenty-four years. He finished this in 1771. Then, with the end of the American Revolution, he resumed his writing in 1783 and finished it in 1789. Ironically, though, the *Autobiography* covers his life only until 1757. There is no mention even of the American Revolution. Full of anecdotes and wisdom, *The Autobiography of Benjamin Franklin* remains a timeless classic.

Objective Test

_____ Franklin was the first American (A) to express openly his discontent with England, (B) to be considered an equal to European scientists, or (C) to send a telegraph message to England.

_____ Franklin was (A) the youngest son of seventeen children, (B) the oldest of four children, or (C) an only child.

_____ Franklin did not enter the ministry because (A) he did not feel called, (B) he preferred to be a lawyer, or (C) after considering the paltry salary that ministers received, his father made him work at his shop.

17

_____ At age twelve Franklin (A) was apprenticed to his brother James, (B) traveled to Georgia, or (C) invented the Franklin Stove.

_____ Franklin founded (A) the *Philadelphia Enquirer,* (B) the *Pennsylvania Gazette*, or (C) the Spectator Society.

_____ Franklin practiced (A) twelve virtues, (B) seven virtues, or (C) thirteen virtues.

_____ Franklin was fluent in (A) Italian, German, and English; (B) Spanish, French, and English; or (C) French, Spanish, Italian, and English.

_____ While postmaster of Philadelphia, Franklin (A) reorganized the fire department, (B) founded a hospital, or (C) experimented with electricity.

_____ In 1732 he published (A) his memoirs, (B) *Poor Richard's Almanac*, or (C) a book of verse.

Suggested Vocabulary Words

A. Having emerged from the poverty and obscurity in which I was born and bred, to a state of affluence and some degree of reputation in the world, and having gone so far through life with a considerable share of felicity, the conducing means I made use of, which with the blessing of God so well succeeded, my posterity may like to know, as they may find some of them suitable to their own situations, and therefore fit to be imitated. (part 1)

B. It was written in 1675, in the home-spun verse of that time and people, and addressed to those then concerned in the government there. It was in favor of liberty of conscience, and in behalf of the Baptists, Quakers, and other sectaries that had been under persecution, ascribing the Indian wars, and other distresses that had befallen the country, to that persecution, as so many judgments of God to punish so heinous an offense, and exhorting a repeal of those uncharitable laws. (part 1)

C. At his table he liked to have, as often as he could, some sensible friend or neighbor to converse with, and always took care to start some <u>ingenious</u> or useful topic for <u>discourse</u>, which might tend to improve the minds of his children. (part 1)

D. I continu'd this method some few years, but gradually left it, retaining only the habit of expressing myself in terms of modest <u>diffidence.</u> (part 2)

E. In his house I lay that night, and the next morning reach'd Burlington, but had the <u>mortification</u> to find that the regular boats were gone a little before my coming, and no other expected to go before Tuesday, this being Saturday; wherefore I returned to an old woman in the town, of whom I had bought gingerbread to eat on the water, and ask'd her advice. (part 2)

F. My ideas at that time were, that the sect should be begun and spread at first among young and single men only; that each person to be initiated should not only declare his assent to such creed, but should have exercised himself with the thirteen weeks' examination and practice of the virtues as in the before-mention'd model; that the existence of such a society should he kept a secret, till it was become considerable, to prevent <u>solicitations </u>for the admission of improper persons, but that the members should each of them search among his acquaintance for <u>ingenuous</u>, well-disposed youths, to whom, with <u>prudent</u> caution, the scheme should be gradually communicated these proverbs, which contained the wisdom of many ages and nations, I assembled and form'd into a connected discourse prefix'd to the *Almanack* of 1757, as the <u>harangue</u> of a wise old man to the people attending an auction. (part 3)

G. In 1751, Dr. Thomas Bond, a particular friend of mine, conceived the idea of establishing a hospital in Philadelphia (a very <u>beneficent</u> design, which has been ascrib'd to me, but was originally his), for the reception and cure of poor sick persons, whether inhabitants of the province or strangers. He was <u>zealous</u> and active in endeavoring to <u>procure </u>subscriptions for it, but the proposal being a <u>novelty</u> in America, and at first not well understood, he met with but small success. (part 4)

Discussion Questions

A. Based on this quote, and other passages, describe Franklin's faith journey:

> Before I enter upon my public appearance in business, it may be well to let you know the then state of my mind with regard to my principles and morals, that you may see how far those influenc'd the future events of my life. My parents had early given me religious impressions, and brought me through my childhood piously in the Dissenting way. But I was scarce fifteen, when, after doubting by turns of several points, as I found them disputed in the different books I read, I began to doubt of Revelation itself. Some books against Deism fell into my hands; they were said to be the substance of sermons preached at Boyle's Lectures. It happened that they wrought an effect on me quite contrary to what was intended by them; for the arguments of the Deists, which were quoted to be refuted, appeared to me much stronger than the refutations; in short, I soon became a thorough Deist. My arguments perverted some others, particularly Collins and Ralph; but, each of them having afterwards wrong'd me greatly without the least compunction, and recollecting Keith's conduct towards me (who was another freethinker), and my own towards Vernon and Miss Read, which at times gave me great trouble, I began to suspect that this doctrine, tho' it might be true, was not very useful.

B. Discuss Franklin's quest for moral perfection.

C. Who was General Braddock, and what advice did he receive from Franklin?

D. What writing style does Franklin employ?

E. Is the *Autobiography* a rags-to-riches story or a self-serving, egotistical story of a man's self-absorption?

Brave New World

Aldous Huxley

 Huxley's vision of the future in his astonishing 1931 novel *Brave New World* continues to intrigue readers into the twenty-first century. Huxley's world is one in which Western civilization has been maintained through the most efficient scientific and psychological engineering, where people are genetically designed to be useful to the ruling class.

Objective Test

_____ The Bokanovsky and Podsnap Processes (A) do not work, (B) allow the Hatchery to produce thousands of nearly identical human embryos, (C) are a new project, or (D) produce identical sheep.

_____ Alpha, Beta, Gamma, Delta, and Epsilon refer to (A) classes of people, (B) college fraternities, (C) new weapons, or (D) the Director's pets.

_____ Lenina Crowne, an employee at the factory, describes (A) how the embryos are used to create new specimens, (B) how to make stronger horses, (C) how she aborts unborn infants, or (D) how she vaccinates embryos destined for tropical climates.

_____ Hypnopaedic is (A) a way to teach young people, (B) the end of the world, (C) a fear of water, or (D) a nonsense world to describe human psychology.

_____ The new order is called (A) the Universe, (B) the Brave New World, (C) the New Order, or (D) the World-State Society.

Suggested Vocabulary Words

A. The Director opened a door. They were in a large bare room, very bright and sunny; for the whole of the southern wall was a single window. Half a dozen nurses, trousered and jacketed in the regulation white viscose-linen uniform, their hair aseptically hidden under white caps, were engaged in setting out bowls of roses in a long row across the floor. Big bowls, packed tight with blossom. Thousands of petals, ripe-blown and silkily smooth, like the cheeks of innumerable little cherubs, but of cherubs, in that bright light, not exclusively pink and Aryan, but also luminously Chinese, also Mexican, also apoplectic with too much blowing of celestial trumpets, also pale as death, pale with the posthumous whiteness of marble. (ch. 2)

B. An almost naked Indian was very slowly climbing down the ladder from the first-floor terrace of a neighboring house—rung after rung, with the tremulous caution of extreme old age. His face was profoundly wrinkled and black, like a mask of obsidian. The toothless mouth had fallen in. At the corners of the lips, and on each side of the chin, a few long bristles gleamed almost white against the dark skin. The long unbraided hair hung down in grey wisps round his face. His body was bent and emaciated to the bone, almost fleshless. Very slowly he came down, pausing at each rung before he ventured another step. (ch. 7)

C. Lenina alone said nothing. Pale, her blue eyes clouded with an unwonted melancholy, she sat in a corner, cut off from those who surrounded her by an emotion which they did not share. She had come to the party filled with a strange feeling of anxious exultation. "In a few minutes," she had said to herself, as she entered the room, "I shall be seeing him, talking to him, telling him" (for she had come with her mind made up) "that I like him—more than anybody I've ever known. And then perhaps he'll say . . ." (ch. 12)

D. When morning came, he felt he had earned the right to inhabit the lighthouse; yet, even though there still was glass in most of the windows, even though the view from the platform was so fine. For the very reason why he had chosen the lighthouse had become almost instantly a reason for going somewhere else. He had decided to live there because the view was so beautiful, because, from his vantage point, he seemed to be looking out on to the incarnation of a divine being. But who was he to be <u>pampered</u> with the daily and hourly sight of loveliness? Who was he to be living in the visible presence of God? All he deserved to live in was some filthy sty, some blind hole in the ground. Stiff and still aching after his long night of pain, but for that very reason inwardly reassured, he climbed up to the platform of his tower, he looked out over the bright sunrise world which he had regained the right to inhabit. On the north the view was bounded by the long chalk ridge of the Hog's Back, from behind whose eastern extremity rose the towers of the seven skyscrapers which constituted Guildford. Seeing them, the Savage made a <u>grimace</u>; but he was to become <u>reconciled</u> to them in course of time; for at night they twinkled gaily with geometrical <u>constellations,</u> or else, flood-lighted, pointed their <u>luminous</u> fingers (with a gesture whose significance nobody in England but the Savage now understood) solemnly towards the plumbless mysteries of heaven. (ch. 18)

Discussion Questions

A. What narrative point of view does Aldous Huxley employ? Why?

B. This novel is about the creation of a utopia. Explain.

C. The Controller has a meeting with John, the Savage, in the climactic confrontation of the book. John laments that the world has paid a high price for happiness by giving up art and science. The Controller adds religion to this list and says, "God isn't compatible with machinery and scientific medicine and universal happiness." What does the Controller mean?

D. Agree or disagree with this analysis by a critic: "For Huxley, it is plain, there is no need to travel into the future to find the brave new world; it already exists, only too palpably, in the American Joy City, where the declaration of dependence begins and ends with the single-minded pursuit of happiness."

E. Scholar Peter Bowering concludes:

In the World-State man has been enslaved by science, or as the hypnopaedic platitude puts it, "Science is everything." But, while everything owes its origin to science, science itself has been paradoxically relegated to the limbo of the past along with culture, religion, and every other worthwhile object of human endeavor. It is ironic that science, which has given the stablest equilibrium in history, should itself be regarded as a potential menace, and that all scientific progress should have been frozen since the establishment of the World-State.

This is called postmodernism. Define *postmodernism*.

The Brothers Karamazov

Fyodor Dostoyevsky

 Dostoyevsky's last and greatest novel, *The Brothers Karamazov,* is both a crime drama and a pedantic debate over truth. In fact, no novel—since Plato's *Republic*—so fervently addresses the issue. The worthless landowner Fyodor Pavlovich Karamazov is murdered. His sons—the atheist intellectual Ivan, the hot-blooded Dmitry, and the saintly novice Alyosha—are all at some level involved. As one critic explains, "Bound up with this intense family drama is Dostoyevsky's exploration of many deeply felt ideas about the existence of God, the question of human freedom, the collective nature of guilt, the disastrous consequences of rationalism.

The novel is also richly comic: the Russian Orthodox Church, the legal system, and even the author's most cherished causes and beliefs are presented with a note of irreverence, so that orthodoxy and radicalism, sanity and madness, love and hatred, right and wrong—all are no longer mutually exclusive. Rebecca West considered it "the allegory for the world's maturity, but with children to the fore. Rebecca West considered it "the allegory for the world's maturity," but with children to the fore. The new translations do full justice to Dostoyevsky's genius, especially in the use of the spoken word, ranging over every mode of human expression.

Objective Test

_____ Karamazov has (A) three sons, (B) four sons, or (C) six sons.

_____ Father and son quarrel over (A) an estate, (B) money and a woman, or (C) the cause of the Russian Revolution.

_____ One of Karamazov's sons loves to (A) farm, (B) shoot pool, or (C) discuss philosophy.

_____ Ivan really loves (A) Maria, (B) Katerina, or (C) Grushenka.

_____ The character who represents the religious impulse of nineteenth century Russia is (A) Karamazov, (B) Alyosha, or (C) Ivan.

Suggested Vocabulary Words

A. At the time of Yefim Petrovitch's death, Alyosha had two more years to complete at the <u>provincial</u> gymnasium. The <u>inconsolable</u> widow went almost immediately after his death for a long visit to Italy with her whole family, which consisted only of women and girls. (part 1, book 1, ch. 4)

B. As he hastened out of the hermitage <u>precincts</u> to reach the monastery in time to serve at the Father Superior's dinner, he felt a sudden <u>pang</u> at his heart, and stopped short. He seemed to hear again Father Zossima's words, foretelling his approaching end. What he had foretold so exactly must <u>infallibly</u> come to pass. Alyosha believed that <u>implicitly</u>. But how could he go? (part 1, book 2, ch. 7)

C. "Quite so, quite so," cried Ivan, with <u>peculiar</u> eagerness, obviously <u>annoyed</u> at being interrupted, "in anyone else this moment would be only due to yesterday's impression and would be only a moment. But with Katerina Ivanovna's character, that moment will last all her life. What for anyone else would be only a promise is for her an everlasting burdensome, grim perhaps, but <u>unflagging</u> duty. And she will be <u>sustained</u> by the feeling of this duty being fulfilled. Your life, Katerina Ivanovna, will henceforth be spent in painful <u>brooding</u> over your own feelings, your own heroism, and your own suffering; but in the end that suffering will be softened and will pass into sweet <u>contemplation</u> of the fulfillment of a bold and proud design. Yes, proud it certainly is, and desperate in any case, but a triumph for you. And the consciousness of it will at last be a source of complete satisfaction and will make you resigned to everything else." (part 2, book 4, ch. 5)

D. "After a month of hopeless love and moral <u>degradation</u>, during which he betrayed his <u>betrothed</u> and <u>appropriated</u> money entrusted to his honour, the prisoner was driven almost to frenzy, almost to madness by continual jealousy—and of whom? His father! And the worst of it was that the crazy old man was alluring and <u>enticing</u> the object of his affection by means of that very three thousand roubles, which the son looked upon as his own property, part of his inheritance from his mother, of which his father was cheating him. Yes, I admit it was hard to bear! It might well drive a man to madness. It was not the money, but the fact that this money was used with such revolting cynicism to ruin his happiness!" (part 3, book 12, ch. 7)

Dscussion Questions

A. Why do you think that novels celebrating Christian values were being written in Russia in the nineteenth century, when no such novels were being written in America?

B. Why does Dostoyevsky tease the reader with Dimitri's innocence or guilt?

C. While *The Brothers Karamazov* is not a religious text, it has at its core the theme of redemption. Explain.

D. Why would some critics argue that this is the greatest novel ever written?

The Chosen

Chaim Potok

 *The Chosen* is basically the story of two cultures colliding. On one level it is the story of Orthodox Judaism versus Hasidic Judaism. On the other hand, it embraces life at many different levels. In fact, it also celebrates human virtues like respect and loyalty.

Objective Test

_____ Reuven Malter is (A) the narrator, (B) antagonist, (C) a foil, or (D) a Gentile.

_____ He is the son of David Malter, (A) a Hasidic Jew, (B) a dedicated scholar and humanitarian, (C) an Israeli army general, or (D) a converted Christian.

_____ Danny Saunders, the other protagonist, is (A) a brilliant Hasid with a love of baseball, (B) a rabbi, (C) a brilliant Hasid with a photographic memory and a passion for psychoanalysis, or (D) a Zionist.

_____ Danny is the son of Reb Saunders, (A) an Israeli army general, (B) the respected head of a great Hasidic dynasty, (C) the author of a famous book written on the Torah, or (D) a psychology professor.

_____ Danny ultimately (A) is killed by a freak accident, (B) converts to Christianity, (C) becomes a Hasidic leader, or (D) enters Columbia University.

Suggested Vocabulary Words

A. I had spent five days in a hospital and the world around seemed <u>sharpened</u> now and <u>pulsing</u> with life. (ch. 5)

B. A span of life is nothing. But the man who lives that <u>span</u>, he is something. (ch. 13)

C. It makes us aware of how <u>frail</u> and tiny we are and of how much we must depend upon the Master of the Universe. (ch. 18)

D. We shook hands and I watched him walk quickly away, tall, lean, bent <u>forward</u> with eagerness and hungry for the future, his metal capped shoes tapping against the sidewalk. (last chapter)

Discussion Questions

A. Should Danny have become a psychotherapist even though it violated his father's wishes?

B. Do you like the ending of the book?

C. If you were making a movie of this book, who would you want to play Danny? Reuven?

D. Potok is a master storyteller. In some ways "what he does not write" is important as "what he does write." Explain.

E. What role do women have in this novel?

F. Why does Potok tell the story from Reuven's rather than Danny's point of view?

The Civil War

Shelby Foote

Newsweek magazine described Foote's three-volume masterpiece this way: "Foote is a novelist who temporarily abandoned fiction to apply the novelist's shaping hand to history: his model is not Thucydides but the *Iliad*, and his story, innocent of notes and formal biography, has a literary design." This great historical work has the distinction of being the best single work on the American Civil War. It is well worth the effort to read all three volumes.

Objective Test: True or False

_____ Jefferson Davis welcomed the Civil War.

_____ Abraham Lincoln was elected in 1860 by a landslide vote.

_____ Initially Abraham Lincoln, while favoring the prohibition of slavery in new territories, opposed the abolition of slavery in the present states.

_____ Robert E. Lee was offered the command of all Union forces.

_____ Stonewall Jackson performed admirably in the Seven Days Campaign.

_____ The South won the Battle of Shiloh.

_____ Lee's greatest tactical victory was the Battle of Chancellorsville.

_____ J. E. B. Stuart was the brilliant Union commander of cavalry.

_____ One reason the South lost Gettysburg was that the North had a new, secret weapon.

_____ New Orleans was captured by the North before Vicksburg.

_____ Lincoln was pleased and irritated by General Meade's victory at Gettysburg. On one hand, the South was soundly defeated. On the other hand, Meade neglected to pursue and to destroy Lee's army.

_____ General Banks lost the Red River campaign.

_____ General Albert Sidney Johnston saved Petersburg.

_____ Hood led an ill-fated expedition to capture Nashville.

_____ The most brilliant cavalry officer of the War, Nathan Bedford Forrest, was a West Point graduate.

Suggested Vocabulary Words

A. Perhaps by now McClellan had learned to abide the <u>tantrums</u> and <u>exasperations</u> of his former friend and sympathizer. (vol. 1)

B. McClellan was quite aware of the danger of <u>straddling</u> what he called "the <u>confounded</u> Chickahominy." (vol. 1)

C. In addition to retaining the services of Seward and Chase, both excellent men at their <u>respective</u> posts, he had managed to turn aside the <u>wrath</u> of the <u>Jacobins</u> without increasing their bitterness toward himself or <u>incurring</u> their open hatred. . . . <u>Paradoxically,</u> because of the way he had done it . . . (vol. 2)

D. Stuart had accepted the <u>gambit</u>. . . . (vol. 3)

E. Poor as the plan was in the first place, mainly because of its necessary surrender of the <u>initiative</u> to the enemy, it was rendered even poorer—in fact <u>inoperative</u>—by the speed in which Sherman moved through the supposedly <u>impenetrable</u> swamps. (vol. 3)

Discussion Questions

A. As you read this book, did you feel that Shelby Foote, a native of Memphis, Tennessee, was prejudiced in favor of the Confederacy? Defend your answer.

B. What were the causes of the American Civil War?

C. Why was the loss of Vicksburg, Mississippi, such a grievous blow to the Confederacy?

D. Do you believe that Forrest ordered, or even condoned, the massacre of Black troops at Fort Pillow? Defend your answer.

E. Even though McClellan had access to Lee's strategic plan, he still managed merely to stop, not destroy, Lee as he advanced northward. Why?

F. What sort of man was Stonewall Jackson?

G. What do you think would have happened if the South had won the Battle of Gettysburg?

The Count of Monte Cristo

Alexandre Dumas

 Like so many of Dumas's novels, *Count of Monte Cristo* is set at the end of the Napoleonic era, which the French regard as one of the most exciting and tumultuous periods of modern times. It is a story of Edmond Dantès, a charismatic young seaman falsely accused of treason. The story of his cruel imprisonment, miraculous escape, and carefully engineered revenge keeps the reader spellbound.

Objective Test

_____ At the age of (A) eighteen, (B) nineteen, (C) twenty-one, or (D) twenty-four, Edmond Dantès has the perfect life.

_____ He is about to become the captain of a ship, and (A) he is engaged to a beautiful woman, (B) he has inherited a fortune, (C) he has won the lottery, or (D) he is appointed a magistrate.

_____ Two people resent his success, however. The treasurer of his ship, Danglers, and (A) Pierre, (B) Marcus, (C) Fernand, or (D) Jacques.

_____ Caderousse is (A) Dantès's good friend, (B) angry that Dantès is so much better off than he is, (C) the jailer, or (D) sick.

_____ Dantès is accused of (A) larceny, (B) murder, (C) grand theft, or (D) treason.

_____ The Deputy Public Prosecutor, Villefort, sees through the plot to

33

frame Dantès and is prepared to set him free. At the last moment, though, Dantès jeopardizes his freedom by revealing the name of the man to whom he is supposed to deliver Napoleon's letter. He is (A) Villefort's brother, (B) Villefort's father-in-law, (C) Villefort's uncle, or (D) Villefort's father.

_____ While in prison Dantès is tutored by (A) an Italian priest, (B) Leonardo da Vinci, (C) an imprisoned professor, or (D) a death-row inmate.

_____ Before he dies, The priest tells Dantès about a (A) treasure map, (B) secret code, (C) treasure in Monte Cristo, or (D) new cure for cancer.

_____ Dantès collects the fortune and (A) retires happily, (B) ruins his enemies, (C) invests in the stock market, or (D) closes the prison.

_____ Dantès falls in love with (A) Haydee, (B) Mary, (C) Susan, or (D) Evangeline.

Suggested Vocabulary Words

A. Now, in spite of the mobility of his countenance, the command of which, like a finished actor, he had carefully studied before the glass, it was by no means easy for him to assume an air of judicial severity. Except the recollection of the line of politics his father had adopted, and which might interfere, unless he acted with the greatest prudence, with his own career, Gerard de Villefort was as happy as a man could be. (ch. 7)

B. "Then," answered the elder prisoner, "the will of God be done!" and as the old man slowly pronounced those words, an air of profound resignation spread itself over his careworn countenance. Dantès gazed on the man who could thus philosophically resign hopes so long and ardently nourished with an astonishment mingled with admiration. (ch. 16)

C. He had a very clear idea of the men with whom his lot had been cast. . . . It spared him <u>interpreters</u>, persons always <u>troublesome</u> and frequently <u>indiscreet</u>, gave him great <u>facilities</u> of communication, either with the vessels he met at sea, with the small boats sailing along the coast, or with the people without name, country, or occupation, who are always seen on the <u>quays</u> of seaports, and who live by hidden and mysterious means which we must suppose to be a direct gift of providence, as they have no visible means of support. It is fair to assume that Dantès was on board a smuggler. (ch. 22)

D. It would be difficult to describe the state of <u>stupor</u> in which Villefort left the Palais. Every <u>pulse</u> beat with <u>feverish</u> excitement, every nerve was <u>strained</u>, every vein swollen, and every part of his body seemed to suffer distinctly from the rest, thus multiplying his agony a thousand-fold. He made his way along the <u>corridors</u> through force of habit; he threw <u>aside</u> his <u>magisterial</u> robe, not out of <u>deference</u> to <u>etiquette</u>, but because it was an <u>unbearable</u> burden, a <u>veritable</u> garb of Nessus, <u>insatiate</u> in torture. Having <u>staggered</u> as far as the Rue Dauphine, he perceived his carriage, awoke his sleeping coachman by opening the door himself, threw himself on the cushions, and pointed towards the Faubourg Saint-Honoré; the carriage drove on. The weight of his fallen fortunes seemed suddenly to crush him; he could not foresee the <u>consequences</u>; he could not contemplate the future with the <u>indifference</u> of the hardened criminal who merely faces a <u>contingency</u> already familiar. God was still in his heart. "God," he <u>murmured</u>, not knowing what he said,—"God—God!" Behind the event that had <u>overwhelmed</u> him he saw the hand of God. The carriage rolled rapidly onward. Villefort, while turning restlessly on the cushions, felt something press against him. He put out his hand to remove the object; it was a fan which Madame de Villefort had left in the carriage; this fan awakened a <u>recollection</u> which darted through his mind like lightning. He thought of his wife. (ch. 111)

Discussion Questions

A. If you can, watch several movie versions of this book and compare them with the book itself.

B. In what way, metaphorically, does Dantès die in prison?

C. Discuss how Valentine de Villefort and Haydee function as foils.

D. What does the Bible say about unforgivingness and revenge?

E. Contrast Dantès and Heathcliff (in *Wuthering Heights*). Contrast them both to Jean Valjean in *Les Misérables*.

The Crucible

Arthur Miller

The Crucible is set in a time in which the church and the state are one, and the religion is a strict, austere form of Puritanism. Sin and the status of an individual's soul are matters of public concern. Within this setting a tragedy unfolds.

Objective Test

_____ In the Puritan New England town of Salem, Massachusetts, a group of girls (A) dance in the forest with a black slave named Tituba, (B) run away with a slave named Tituba, or (C) skip school and hang around Rev. Parris's house.

_____ A crowd gathers in the Parris home while rumors are filling the town, rumors of (A) a new outbreak of cholera, (B) the British invasion, or (C) witchcraft.

_____ Miller implies that the girls are pretending there are witches to (A) cause excitement, (B) deflect attention from themselves, or (C) make some money.

_____ John Proctor refuses to participate in this activity and calls their bluff. He is (A) reprimanded, (B) dunked, or (C) hanged.

_____ Abigail loves (A) Proctor, (B) Rev. Parris, or (C) Ishmael.

Suggested Vocabulary Words

A. I look for John Proctor that took me from my sleep and put knowledge in my heart! I never knew what <u>pretense</u> Salem was, I never knew the lying lessons I was taught by all these Christian women and their <u>covenanted</u> men! And now you bid me tear the light out of my eyes? I will not, I cannot! You loved me, John Proctor, and whatever sin it is, you love me yet!

B. You must understand, sir, that a person is either with this court or he must be counted against it, there be no road between. This is a sharp time, now, a <u>precise</u> time—we live no longer in the dusky afternoon when evil mixed itself with good and <u>befuddled</u> the world. Now, by God's grace, the shining sun is up, and them that fear not light will surely praise it.

Discussion Questions

A. Discuss the McCarthy trials of the 1950s.

B. Is John Proctor a realistic character? Does he seem more a product of the 1950s than a character living in the seventeenth century?

C. Why doesn't Proctor pretend to be guilty so that he can live?

D. Would you forgive John Proctor if you were Elizabeth Proctor?

E. What is Abigail's motivation?

F. Later, after the play was written, Arthur Miller said: "In my play, Danforth seems about to conceive of the truth, and surely there is a disposition in him at least to listen to arguments that go counter to the line of the prosecution. There is no such swerving in the record, and I think now, almost four years after writing it, that I was wrong in mitigating the evil of this man and the judges he represents. Instead, I would perfect his evil to its utmost and make an open issue, a thematic consideration of it, in the play." Do you agree with Miller? Say why or why not.

Daisy Miller

Henry James

 Daisy Miller is a young, beautiful, liberated American girl traveling in Europe. Many find her irresistible; others completely reject her. Because she does not conform to the social etiquette of her European setting, she is eventually rejected by high society.

Objective Test

_____ Daisy, her mother, and brother Randolph are (A) traveling in Asia, (B) visiting Chicago, (C) fishing in Mexico, or (D) visiting Europe.

_____ Winterbourne, who lives in Geneva, is (A) related to Daisy, (B) attracted to her charm but repelled by her straightforward manner, (C) returning home with Daisy, or (D) instantly in love with Daisy.

_____ Daisy falls in love with (A) Giovanelli, (B) Winterbourne, (C) Maurice, or (D) Peter.

_____ Winterbourne finds Daisy and Giovanni at (A) the park, (B) in the Colosseum, (C) at home, or (D) in the theater.

_____ Daisy (A) marries Giovanni (B) marries Winterbourne (C) dies, or (D) returns home.

Suggested Vocabulary Words

A. I hardly know whether it was the <u>analogies</u> or the differences that were <u>uppermost</u> in the mind of a young American, who, two or three years ago, sat in the garden of the "Trois Couronnes," looking about him, rather idly, at some of the graceful objects I have mentioned. It was a beautiful summer morning, and in whatever fashion the young American looked at things, they must have seemed to him charming. He had come from Geneva the day before by the little steamer, to see his aunt, who was staying at the hotel—Geneva having been for a long time his place of residence. But his aunt had a headache—his aunt had almost always a headache—and now she was shut up in her room, smelling camphor, so that he was at liberty to wander about. He was some seven-and-twenty years of age; when his friends spoke of him, they usually said that he was at Geneva "studying." When his enemies spoke of him, they said—but, after all, he had no enemies; he was an extremely <u>amiable</u> fellow, and <u>universally</u> liked. What I should say is, simply, that when certain persons spoke of him they affirmed that the reason of his spending so much time at Geneva was that he was extremely devoted to a lady who lived there—a foreign lady—a person older than himself. Very few Americans—indeed, I think none—had ever seen this lady, about whom there were some <u>singular</u> stories. But Winterbourne had an old <u>attachment</u> for the little <u>metropolis</u> of <u>Calvinism</u>; he had been put to school there as a boy, and he had afterward gone to college there—circumstances which had led to his forming a great many youthful friendships. Many of these he had kept, and they were a source of great satisfaction to him. (part 1)

B. Daisy evidently had a natural talent for performing introductions; she mentioned the name of each of her companions to the other. She strolled alone with one of them on each side of her; Mr. Giovanelli, who spoke English very cleverly—Winterbourne afterward learned that he had practiced the idiom upon a great many American <u>heiresses</u>—addressed her a great deal of very polite nonsense; he was extremely <u>urbane</u>, and the young American, who said nothing, reflected upon that <u>profundity</u> of Italian cleverness which enables people to appear more gracious in <u>proportion</u> as they are more acutely disappointed. Giovanelli, of course, had counted upon something more intimate; he had not bargained for a party of three. But he kept his temper in a manner which suggested far-stretching intentions. Winterbourne flattered himself that he had taken his measure. "He is not a gentleman," said the young American; "he is only a clever imitation of one. He is a music master, or a penny-a-liner, or a third-rate artist. Damn his good looks!" Mr. Giovanelli had certainly a very pretty face; but Winterbourne felt a superior indignation at his own lovely fellow countrywoman's not knowing the difference between a spurious gentleman and a real one. Giovanelli chattered and jested and made himself wonderfully agreeable. It was true that, if he was an imitation, the imitation was brilliant. "Nevertheless," Winterbourne said to himself, "a nice girl ought to know!" And then he came back to the question whether this was, in fact, a nice girl. Would a nice girl, even allowing for her being a little American flirt, make a rendezvous with a presumably low-lived foreigner? The rendezvous in this case, indeed, had been in broad daylight and in the most crowded corner of Rome, but was it not impossible to regard the choice of these circumstances as a proof of extreme cynicism? Singular though it may seem, Winterbourne was vexed that the young girl, in joining her amoroso, should not appear more impatient of his own company, and he was vexed because of his inclination. It was impossible to regard her as a perfectly well-conducted young lady; she was wanting in a certain indispensable delicacy. It would therefore simplify matters greatly to be able to treat her as the object of one of those sentiments which are called by romancers "lawless passions." That she should seem to wish to get rid of him would help him to think more lightly of her, and to be able to think more lightly of her would make her much less perplexing. But Daisy, on this occasion, continued to present herself as an inscrutable combination of audacity and innocence. (part 2)

Discussion Questions

A. How credible a person is Daisy?

B. Is the ending satisfactory?

C. If Daisy Miller is representing America in Europe, as some critics suggest, what is James saying?

D. Would you assign this book to a high school class?

David Copperfield

Charles Dickens

David Copperfield was Dickens's favorite novel and a thinly veiled autobiographical one too. *David Copperfield* is a typical Dickens's story of an innocent orphan making his way in an uncaring world. As usual, Dickens draws a gallery of memorable characters into the protagonist's life, such as happy Mr. Micawber and the evil Uriah Heep.

Objective Test

_____ David Copperfield (A) is born in a workhouse, (B) is abused by his stepfather, or (C) enjoys his early childhood with his mother and their kindly servant, Peggotty.

_____ But when his mother marries the cruel Mr. Murdstone, he is (A) forced to work in a factory, (B) sent to live with an aunt, or (C) sent away to Salem House, a run-down London boarding school or where the boys are beaten by Mr. Creakle.

_____ David's mother dies, and David is (A) forced to go to work at Murdstone's wine warehouse, (B) David returns home to live, or (C) is disowned.

_____ Who adopts David? (A) Mr. Murdstone, (B) Miss Trotwood, or (C) Old Peggotty.

_____ Uriah Heep is (A) an evil law clerk, (B) a robber, or (C) a friend to David.

Suggested Vocabulary Words

A. And yet my thoughts were <u>idle</u>; not intent on the calamity that weighed upon my heart, but idly <u>loitering</u> near it. I thought of our house shut up and hushed. I thought of the little baby, who, Mrs. Creakle said, had been <u>pining</u> away for some time, and who, they believed, would die too. I thought of my father's grave in the churchyard, by our house, and of my mother lying there beneath the tree I knew so well. I stood upon a chair when I was left alone, and looked into the glass to see how red my eyes were, and how sorrowful my face. I considered, after some hours were gone, if my tears were really hard to flow now, as they seemed to be, what, in connection with my loss, it would affect me most to think of when I drew near home—for I was going home to the funeral. I am sensible of having felt that a <u>dignity</u> attached to me among the rest of the boys, and that I was important in my <u>affliction</u>. (ch. 9)

B. While I advanced in friendship and <u>intimacy</u> with Mr. Dick, I did not go backward in the favour of his <u>staunch</u> friend, my aunt. She took so kindly to me, that, in the course of a few weeks, she shortened my adopted name of Trotwood into Trot; and even encouraged me to hope, that if I went on as I had begun, I might take equal rank in her <u>affections</u> with my sister Betsey Trotwood. (ch. 15)

C. He was a little light-haired gentleman, with <u>undeniable</u> boots, and the stiffest of white cravats and shirt-collars. He was buttoned up, mighty trim and tight, and must have taken a great deal of pains with his whiskers, which were accurately curled. His gold watch-chain was so <u>massive</u>, that a fancy came across me, that he ought to have a sinewy golden arm, to draw it out with, like those which are put up over the goldbeaters' shops. He was got up with such care, and was so stiff, that he could hardly bend himself; being obliged, when he glanced at some papers on his desk, after sitting down in his chair, to move his whole body, from the bottom of his spine, like Punch. (ch. 23)

D. It feel as if it were not for me to record, even though this manuscript is intended for no eyes but mine, how hard I worked at that <u>tremendous</u> short-hand, and all improvement <u>appertaining</u> to it, in my sense of responsibility to Dora and her aunts. I will only add, to what I have already written of my perseverance at this time of my life, and of a patient and continuous energy which then began to be matured within me, and which I know to be the strong part of my character, if it have any strength at all, that there, on looking back, I find the source of my success. I have been very fortunate in worldly matters; many men have worked much harder, and not succeeded half so well; but I never could have done what I have done, without the habits of punctuality, order, and diligence, without the determination to concentrate myself on one object at a time, no matter how quickly its successor should come upon its heels, which I then formed. (ch. 42)

Discussion Questions

A. What was the narrative point of view? Why did Dickens choose this narrative technique?

B. Dickens is a masterful descriptive writer. Using the following description from chapter 23, discuss the way Dickens describes characters. "He was a little light-haired gentleman, with undeniable boots, and the stiffest of white cravats and shirt-collars. He was buttoned up, mighty trim and tight, and must have taken a great deal of pains with his whiskers, which were accurately curled. His gold watch-chain was so massive, that a fancy came across me, that he ought to have a sinewy golden arm, to draw it out with, like those which are put up over the goldbeaters' shops. He was got up with such care, and was so stiff, that he could hardly bend himself; being obliged, when he glanced at some papers on his desk, after sitting down in his chair, to move his whole body, from the bottom of his spine, like Punch."

C. G. K. Chesterton said, "[Dickens's] books are full of baffled villains stalking out or cowardly bullies kicked downstairs. But the villains and the cowards are such delightful people that the reader always hopes the villain will put his head through a side window and make a last remark; or that the bully will say one more thing, even from the bottom of the stairs." What does Chesterton mean? Do you agree?

Don Quixote

Miguel de Cervantes

 Don Quixote is a worn-out, older Spanish gentle-man who sets off on a great imagined quest to win honor and glory in the name of his imaginary damsel-in-distress, Dulcinea. Don Quixote is much more; he is larger than life. He represents Cervantes's satire of the sixteenth-century Spanish aristocracy. Don Quixote longs for a world that does not exist—a world of beauty and achievement. He naively seeks to bring order into this Renaissance world by Middle Age chivalry. But Don Quixote, nearly blind figuratively and literarily, with the best of intentions, harms everyone around him.

As the novel progresses, Don Quixote, with the help of his modern, loyal squire, Sancho, who is able to see things as they are, slowly distinguishes between reality and the pictures in his head. Even though he ceases to attack windmills, he never loses his conviction that fair Dulcinea is his salvation from all heartache.

Objective Test

_____ At one point Don Quixote freed some prisoners. They responded by (A) thanking him, (B) attacking him, (C) giving him a prize, or (D) ignoring him.

_____ The name of Don Quixote's squire was (A) Sancho, (B) Pere, (C) Jacques, or (D) Maurice.

_____ Sancho sought to learn more from his master than he was able to learn. What did he really want to learn? (A) Don Quixote's middle name, (B) how to be heroic knight, (C) how to ride a horse with eloquence, or (D) the source of Don Quixote's income.

_____ Dulcinea was really (A) a princess, (B) a prostitute, (C) a neighbor, or (D) an ordinary, local girl who was not remotely interested in Don Quixote.

_____ Windmills, to Don Quixote, were (A) dragons, (B) ships, (C) giants, or (D) opposing knights.

Suggested Vocabulary Words

A. You must know, then, that the above-named gentleman whenever he was at leisure (which was mostly all the year round) gave himself up to reading books of <u>chivalry</u> with such <u>ardor</u> and <u>avidity</u> that he almost entirely neglected the pursuit of his field-sports, and even the management of his property; and to such a pitch did his eagerness and <u>infatuation</u> go that he sold many an acre of land to buy books of chivalry to read, and brought home as many of them as he could get. (part 1, ch. 1)

B. He approved highly of the giant Morgante, because, although of the giant breed which is always <u>arrogant</u> and ill-conditioned, he alone was <u>affable</u> and well-bred. (part 1, ch. 1)

C. Thus setting out, our new-fledged adventurer paced along, talking to himself and saying, "Who knows but that in time to come, when the <u>veracious</u> history of my famous deeds is made known, the sage who writes it, when he has to set forth my first sally in the early morning, will do it after this fashion? 'Scarce had the <u>rubicund</u> Apollo spread o'er the face of the broad spacious earth the golden threads of his bright hair, scarce had the little birds of painted plumage attuned their notes to hail with <u>dulcet</u> and <u>mellifluous</u> harmony the coming of the rosy Dawn, that, deserting the soft couch of her jealous spouse, was appearing to mortals at the gates and balconies of the Manchegan horizon, when the renowned knight Don Quixote of La Mancha, quitting the lazy down, mounted his celebrated steed Rocinante and began to traverse the ancient and famous Campo de Montiel;'" which in fact he was actually traversing. "Happy the age, happy the time," he continued, "in which shall be made known my deeds of fame, worthy to be moulded in brass, carved in marble, limned in pictures, for a memorial for ever. And thou, O sage magician, whoever thou art, to whom it shall fall to be the chronicler of this wondrous history, forget not, I entreat thee, my good Rocinante, the constant companion of my ways and wanderings." Presently he broke out again, as if he were love-stricken in earnest, "O Princess Dulcinea, lady of this captive heart, a grievous wrong hast thou done me to drive me forth with scorn, and with <u>inexorable</u> <u>obduracy</u> banish me from the presence of thy beauty. O lady, deign to hold in remembrance this heart, thy vassal, that thus in anguish pines for love of thee." (part 1, ch. 2)

D. Seeing what was going on, Don Quixote said in an angry voice, "Discourteous knight, it ill becomes you to <u>assail</u> one who cannot defend himself; mount your steed and take your lance" (for there was a lance leaning against the oak to which the mare was tied), "and I will make you know that you are behaving as a coward." The farmer, seeing before him this figure in full armor <u>brandishing</u> a lance over his head, gave himself up for dead, and made answer meekly, "Sir Knight, this youth that I am chastising is my servant, employed by me to watch a flock of sheep that I have hard by, and he is so careless that I lose one every day, and when I punish him for his carelessness and <u>knavery</u> he says I do it out of <u>niggardliness</u>, to escape paying him the wages I owe him, and before God, and on my soul, he lies." (part 1, ch. 4)

E. Such was the end of the Ingenious Gentleman of La Mancha, whose village Cide Hamete would not indicate precisely, in order to leave all the towns and villages of La Mancha to contend among themselves for the right to adopt him and claim him as a son, as the seven cities of Greece contended for Homer. The <u>lamentations</u> of Sancho and the niece and housekeeper are omitted here, as well as the new <u>epitaphs</u> upon his tomb. (part 2, ch. 74)

Discussion Questions

A. In what way was Don Quixote a parody of the struggle between Renaissance thought and medieval thought?

B. Examine Cervantes's life and discuss how much personal disappointment colored the sarcasm that *Don Quixote* exhibited.

C. *Don Quixote* generated new interest in 1960s America. Why?

D. Respond to the following criticism by Vladimir Nabokov:

> Both parts of *Don Quixote* form a veritable encyclopedia of cruelty. From that viewpoint it is one of the most bitter and barbarous books ever penned. And its cruelty is artistic. The extraordinary commentators who talk through their academic caps or birettas of the humorous and humane mellowly Christian atmosphere of the book, or a happy world where "all is sweetened by the humanities of love and good fellowship," and particularly those who talk of a certain "kindly duchess" who "entertains the Don" in the second Part—these gushing experts have probably been reading some other book or are looking through some rosy gauze at the brutal world of Cervantes' novel.

E. Critic Joseph Wood Krutch argued that *Don Quixote* strove "for that synthesis of the comedy and tragedy of life which we recognize as the distinguishing mark of the modern novel." Agree or disagree.

F. In what ways, if any, was Don Quixote a Christlike figure?

G. Several years ago, the story of *Don Quixote* was adapted as the musical play *Man of La Mancha*. In this version, at Quixote's deathbed, Sancho promises to continue Don Quixote's mission. Do you think Cervantes would have been pleased with this ending?

Emma

Jane Austen

In this reader's opinion, *Emma* is the best of Jane Austen. Emma, the person, defies archetypal categories. She transcends her time and place and will remain one of the most remarkable protagonists in Western literature.

Objective Test

_____ Emma is persuaded that (A) she will someday be rich, (B) that she will never marry, or (C) that she will die in childbirth.

_____ Emma then embarks on a series of (A) matchmaking plans, (B) trips, or (C) jobs.

_____ Emma is trying to place her friend Harriet with Mr. Elton, but it does not work out because (A) Harriet is too poor, (B) Mr. Elton is terminally ill, or (C) Mr. Elton really likes Emma and feels that Harriet is below him socially.

_____ Emma has a very close friend who speaks frankly with her. His name is (A) Mr. Knightley, (B) Mr. Martin, or (C) Mr. Elton.

_____ Ultimately Emma marries (A) Mr. Churchill, (B) Mr. Martin, or (C) Mr. Knightley.

Suggested Vocabulary Words

A. Harriet Smith's <u>intimacy</u> at Hartfield was soon a settled thing. Quick and decided in her ways, Emma lost no time in inviting, encouraging, and telling her to come very often; and as their acquaintance increased, so did their satisfaction in each other. As a walking companion, Emma had very early foreseen how useful she might find her. In that respect Mrs. Weston's loss had been important. Her father never went beyond the shrubbery, where two divisions of the ground sufficed him for his long walk, or his short, as the year varied; and since Mrs. Weston's marriage her exercise had been too much confined. (vol. 1, ch. 4)

B. In short, she sat, during the first visit, looking at Jane Fairfax with twofold complacency; the sense of pleasure and the sense of rendering justice, and was determining that she would dislike her no longer. When she took in her history, indeed, her situation, as well as her beauty; when she considered what all this elegance was destined to, what she was going to sink from, how she was going to live, it seemed impossible to feel any thing but compassion and respect; especially, if to every well-known particular entitling her to interest, were added the highly probable circumstance of an attachment to Mr. Dixon, which she had so naturally started to herself. In that case, nothing could be more pitiable or more honourable than the sacrifices she had resolved on. Emma was very willing now to acquit her of having seduced Mr. Dixon's actions from his wife, or of any thing mischievous which her imagination had suggested at first. If it were love, it might be simple, single, successless love on her side alone. She might have been unconsciously sucking in the sad poison, while a sharer of his conversation with her friend; and from the best, the purest of motives, might now be denying herself this visit to Ireland, and resolving to divide herself effectually from him and his connections by soon beginning her career of laborious duty. (vol. 2, ch. 2)

C. As long as Mr. Knightley remained with them, Emma's fever continued; but when he was gone, she began to be a little tranquillized and subdued—and in the course of the sleepless night, which was the tax for such an evening, she found one or two such very serious points to consider, as made her feel, that even her happiness must have some alloy. Her father—and Harriet. She could not be alone without feeling the full weight of their separate claims; and how to guard the comfort of both to the utmost, was the question. With respect to her father, it was a question soon answered. She hardly knew yet what Mr. Knightley would ask; but a very short parley with her own heart produced the most solemn resolution of never quitting her father.—She even wept over the idea of it, as a sin of thought. While he lived, it must be only an engagement; but she flattered herself, that if divested of the danger of drawing her away, it might become an increase of comfort to him.— How to do her best by Harriet, was of more difficult decision;—how to spare her from any unnecessary pain; how to make her any possible atonement; how to appear least her enemy?—On these subjects, her per- plexity and distress were very great—and her mind had to pass again and again through every bitter reproach and sorrowful regret that had ever surrounded it.—She could only resolve at last, that she would still avoid a meeting with her, and communicate all that need be told by let- ter; that it would be inexpressibly desirable to have her removed just now for a time from Highbury, and—indulging in one scheme more— nearly resolve, that it might be practicable to get an invitation for her to Brunswick Square.—Isabella had been pleased with Harriet; and a few weeks spent in London must give her some amusement.—She did not think it in Harriet's nature to escape being benefited by novelty and variety, by the streets, the shops, and the children.—At any rate, it would be a proof of attention and kindness in herself, from whom every thing was due; a separation for the present; an averting of the evil day, when they must all be together again. (book 3, ch. 14)

Discussion Questions

A. Compare Emma to other protagonists in Jane Austen's novels.

B. Where is the climax in the novel?

C. What is the purpose of so many parlor scenes?

D. Most critics think that *Emma* is superior to other works by Austen because she develops her characters better. What do you think?

E. Do you feel that Emma is a nineteenth-century feminist?

F. Pretend that you are casting the roles of this novel for a dramatic version. Who would you choose to play the major roles?

The Fairie Queen

Edmund Spenser

The Faerie Queene—as you probably know by now—is the longest narrative poem in the English language. It makes Milton's formidable *Paradise Lost* to be like a walk in the park! Still, it is full of action and one of the seminal masterpieces of English literature, and it has influenced scholars since its completion in 1596. Nonetheless, its epic length, its wealth of incident and detail, and the complexity of its allegory and richness of its topical allusions make it one of the hardest texts to understand. By the way, letters *u* and *v* are rather interchangeable in Spenser's deliberately antique English—used to evoke a world of mystery.

Objective Test

_____ *The Faerie Queene* is (A) an allegory, (B) a massive prose work, or (C) originally written in Latin.

_____ As the poet examines the two virtues—holiness and chastity—in books 1 and 3, he follows the journeys of two knights, (A) Pilgrim and Christian, (B) Richard and David, or (C) Redcrosse and Britomart.

_____ In a magic mirror, Britomart sees (A) her future husband, (B) her death, or (C) her salvation.

_____ Spenser reveres (A) King Philip, (B) Queen Elizabeth, or (C) Joan of Arc.

_____ He attacks (A) Protestantism, (B) the French, or (C) Roman Catholicism.

Suggested Vocabulary Words

A. Scarsely had *Phoebus* in the <u>glooming</u> East / Yet harnessed his firie-footed teeme, / Ne reard aboue the earth his flaming creast, / When the last deadly smoke aloft did steeme, / That signe of last outbreathed life did seeme, / Vnto the watchman on the castle wall; / Who thereby dead that <u>balefull</u> Beast did deeme, / And to his Lord and Ladie lowd gan call, / To tell, how he had seene the Dragons fatall fall. (book 1, canto 12)

B. For all so soone, as *Guyon* thence was gon / Vpon his voyage with his trustie guide, / That wicked band of <u>villeins</u> fresh begon / That castle to assaile on euery side, / And lay strong siege about it far and wide. / So huge and <u>infinite</u> their numbers were, / That all the land they vnder them did hide; / So fowle and vgly, that exceeding feare / Their visages imprest, when they approched neare. (book 2, canto 11)

C. Who backe returning, told as he had seene, / That they were doughtie knights of <u>dreaded</u> name; / And those two Ladies, their two loues vnseene; / And therefore wisht them without blot or blame, / To let them passe at will, for dread of shame. / But *Blandamour* full of <u>vainglorious</u> spright, / And rather stird by his discordfull Dame, / Vpon them gladly would haue prov'd his might, / But that he yet was sore of his late lucklesse fight. (book 4, canto 3)

Discussion Questions

A. Contrast this long narrative poem with Virgil's *Aeneid.*

B. Define courtly love and discuss how Spenser uses it in his epic poem.

C. Give evidence that Spenser dislikes the Roman Catholic Church.

D. Suppose you are retained by a famous publishing company to decide whether or not *The Fairie Queen* should be republished in contemporary setting and English. What would you advise? Does it have any present relevance?

Giants in the Earth

O. E. Rølvaag

Giants in the Earth is one of the most moving immigrant stories in American literature. It is not for the faint-hearted. This is hardly the stuff one sees in *Little House on the Prairie*!

Objective Test

_____ Per Hansa and his family (A) move to California to pan for gold, (B) get lost, or (C) are attacked by Native Americans.

_____ With other Norwegian immigrant families, they (A) establish a small settlement along Spring Creek, (B) reach the Oregon Territory, or (C) turn back.

_____ They live in a (A) log cabin, (B) teepee, or (C) sod house.

_____ Per Hansa's wife, Beret, (A) is homesick for Norway, (B) is killed by Native Americans, or (C) dies in childbirth.

_____ Per (A) strikes it rich in gold, (B) dies in a blizzard, or (C) leaves Beret.

Suggested Vocabulary Words

A. It bent <u>resiliently</u> under the <u>trampling</u> feet; it did not break, but it complained aloud every time—for nothing like this had ever happened to it before. (book 1, ch. 1)

B. How could human beings continue to live here while that magic ring <u>encompassed</u> them? And those who were strong enough to break through were only being <u>enticed</u> still farther to their destruction. (book 2, ch. 3)

C. For you and me, life out here is nothing; but there may be others so <u>constructed</u> that they don't fit into this life at all; and yet they are finer and better souls than either one of us. (book 1, ch. 4)

Discussion Questions

A. How well does the author develop his characters?

B. Does Beret's religious conversion seem realistic to you?

C. Did you like the ending? How would you change it?

D. Does Per love Beret?

The Grapes of Wrath

John Steinbeck

 This novel is epic in its scope but manages nonetheless to tell the story of one family. It follows the movement of thousands of men and women and the effect of the Depression on the nation. Yet *The Grapes of Wrath* is also the story of one Oklahoma farm family, the Joads, who lose their farm and are forced to travel west to California, looking for work. Their migration is a quintessential journey from ignorance to knowledge, hopelessness to hope.

Objective Test

_____ Tom Joad has recently (A) left the army, (B) been fired from a job, or (C) been released from prison.

_____ Jim is (A) a former preacher, (B) a rich landowner, (C) another dust-bowl farmer, or (D) Tom's brother.

_____ To find work the whole family travels to (A) Texas, (B) South America, (C) Chicago, or (D) California.

_____ As they travel across country, older members of the family (A) return to Oklahoma, (B) stop and homestead, (C) die, or (D) join the army.

_____ When they reach California, they (A) find work, (B) find fewer jobs than they had heard, (C) return home, or (D) take a boat to New York City.

Suggested Vocabulary Words

A. But we've been here for <u>generations</u>. Besides, where'll we go? (ch. 5)

B. Fella like that bust the <u>holiness</u>. But when they're all workin' together, not one fella for another fella, but one fella kind of <u>harnessed</u> to the whole shebang—that's right, that's holy. (ch. 8)

C. "We're Joads. We don't look up to nobody. Grampa's grampa, he fit in the <u>Revolution</u>. We was farm people till the debt. And then—them people. They done somepin to us. (ch. 22)

Discussion Questions

A. Does the novel end in hope or hopelessness?

B. What is Jim Casey's role?

C. Do you think the vulgar language was necessary to the theme, plot, or tone of the story?

D. How would the novel be different if a California grower wrote the novel?

The Great Gatsby

F. Scott Fitzgerald

Generations of readers have enjoyed the story of the wealthy Jay Gatsby and his love for the inimitable Daisy Buchanan. Fitzgerald's subtly biting criticism of the excesses and superficiality of the 1920s remains one of the greatest American classics of the twentieth century.

Objective Test

_____ The narrator in this book is (A) Jay Gatsby, (B) Nick Carraway, (C) Tom Buchanan, or (D) Daisy Buchanan.

_____ Nick's neighbor is (A) Jay Gatsby, (B) Nick Carraway, (C) Tom Buchanan, or (D) Daisy Buchanan.

_____ Nick's cousin is (A) Jay Gatsby, (B) Nick Carraway, (C) Tom Buchanan, or (D) Daisy Buchanan.

_____ The book is primarily about the life of (A) Jay Gatsby, (B) Nick Carraway, (C) Tom Buchanan, or (D) Daisy Buchanan.

_____ Nick meets Jordan Baker at (A) a Gatsby party, (B) the shore, (C) the opera, or (D) Yale.

_____ Gatsby tells Jordan (A) he has a terminal disease, (B) he knew Daisy in Louisville in 1917 and is deeply in love with her, (C) Tom is no good, or (D) how to play the stock market.

_____ Nick brings Gatsby and Daisy together by (A) inviting them both to tea, (B) passing notes back and forth, (C) making a video of Daisy, or (D) staying out of everything.

_____ Tom is bothered because (A) Daisy is spending too much money, (B) Jay is richer than he, (C) Daisy obviously likes Gatsby, or (D) Nick is interfering.

_____ While driving Gatsby's car, Tom accidentally kills (A) his mistress, (B) his best pet, (C) Jay, or (D) Daisy.

_____ At the end of the novel (A) Gatsby and Daisy get married, (B) Tom dies, (C) Gatsby is killed, or (D) Nick and Daisy marry.

Suggested Vocabulary Words

A. In my younger and more <u>vulnerable</u> years my father gave me some advice that I've been turning over in my mind ever since. (ch. 1)

B. There was the boom of a bass drum, and the voice of the orchestra leader rang out suddenly above the <u>echolalia</u> of the garden. (ch. 3)

C. "We've met before," <u>muttered</u> Gatsby. His eyes glanced <u>momentarily</u> at me, and his lips parted with an <u>abortive</u> attempt at a laugh. Luckily the clock took this moment to tilt dangerously at the pressure of his head, whereupon he turned and caught it with trembling fingers, and set it back in place. Then he sat down, <u>rigidly</u>, his elbow on the arm of the sofa and his chin in his hand. (ch. 5)

D. It was a <u>random</u> shot, and yet the reporter's instinct was right. Gatsby's <u>notoriety</u>, spread about by the hundreds who had accepted his hospitality and so become authorities on his past, had increased all summer until he fell just short of being news. Contemporary legends such as the "underground pipe-line to Canada." attached themselves to him, and there was one <u>persistent</u> story that he didn't live in a house at all, but in a boat that looked like a house and was moved secretly up and down the Long Island shore. Just why these inventions were a source of satisfaction to James Gatz of North Dakota, isn't easy to say. (ch. 6)

E. After a little while Mr. Gatz opened the door and came out, his mouth ajar, his face flushed slightly, his eyes leaking isolated and unpunctual tears. He had reached an age where death no longer has the quality of ghastly surprise, and when he looked around him now for the first time and saw the height and splendor of the hall and the great rooms opening out from it into other rooms, his grief began to be mixed with an awed pride. I helped him to a bedroom up-stairs; while he took off his coat and vest I told him that all arrangements had been deferred until he came. (ch. 9)

Discussion Questions

A. If you were producing this book as a movie, which actor would you have play Gatsby? Tom? Daisy? Nick? Why?

B. The characters all represent 1920 American "types." Discuss the type represented by each main character: Jay, Nick, Daisy, Tom, and Jordan.

C. Why does Fitzgerald wait until chapter 4 to begin the plot?

D. In what way is this novel autobiographical?

E. Discuss how Fitzgerald uses symbolism in this novel.

Hard Times

Charles Dickens

Hard Times was originally written for a magazine called *Household Words* in 1850. It occurs during the Industrial Revolution in a fictional place called Coketown. This novel is more or less a polemic against the economic theory of Utilitarianism, called the "terrible mistake," which argued for an Adam Smith hands-off policy for industry. But the novel, Dickens's shortest, is also the tragic story of Louisa Gradgrind and her father.

Objective Test

_____ Thomas Gradgrind, is (A) a wealthy philanthropist who lives in Liverpool, England, (B) a wealthy, retired merchant in the industrial city of Coketown, England, or (C) a banker in London, England.

_____ He felt strongly that (A) government should have a hands-off policy, (B) government should help the poor, or (C) poor people are inevitable.

_____ Ultimately, in his view, self-interest would (A) corrupt the country, (B) take care of the most people with the least effort, or (C) be unchristian.

_____ Gradgrind realizes the liability of his worldview because of (A) the situation of his workers, (B) the example of America, or (C) the problems his daughter faces.

_____ Gradgrind (A) gives up his philosophy of facts and devotes his

political power to helping the poor, (B) joins a union, or
(C) fires his workers.

Suggested Vocabulary Words

A. "I trust, sir," rejoined Mrs. Sparsit, with decent <u>resignation</u>, "it is
not necessary that you should do anything of that kind. I hope I have
learnt how to <u>accommodate</u> myself to the changes of life. If I have
acquired an interest in hearing of your <u>instructive</u> experiences, and can
scarcely hear enough of them, I claim no merit for that, since I believe
it is a general sentiment." (book 1, ch. 7)

B. Herein, too, the sense of even thinking unselfishly aided him.
Before he had so much as closed Mr. Bounderby's door, he had reflected that at least his being obliged to go away was good for her, as it
would save her from the chance of being brought into question for not
withdrawing from him. Though it would cost him a hard <u>pang</u> to leave
her, and though he could think of no similar place in which his <u>condem-
nation</u> would not pursue him, perhaps it was almost a relief to be forced
away from the <u>endurance</u> of the last four days, even to unknown difficulties and distresses. (book 2, ch. 6)

C. Every night, Sissy went to Rachael's lodging, and sat with her in
her small neat room. All day, Rachael toiled as such people must toil,
whatever their anxieties. The smoke-serpents were <u>indifferent</u> who was
lost or found, who turned out bad or good; the melancholy mad elephants, like the Hard Fact men, abated nothing of their set routine,
whatever happened. Day and night again, day and night again. The
<u>monotony</u> was unbroken. Even Stephen Blackpool's disappearance was
falling into the general way, and becoming as monotonous a wonder as
any piece of machinery in Coketown. (book 3, ch. 5)

D. Here was Mr. Gradgrind on the same day, and in the same hour,
sitting thoughtful in his own room. How much of <u>futurity</u> did he see?
Did he see himself, a white-haired <u>decrepit</u> man, bending his hitherto
inflexible theories to appointed circumstances; making his facts and figures <u>subservient</u> to Faith, Hope, and Charity; and no longer trying to
grind that Heavenly trio in his dusty little mills? Did he catch sight of

himself, therefore much despised by his late political associates? Did he see them, in the era of its being quite settled that the national dustmen have only to do with one another, and owe no duty to an <u>abstraction</u> called a People, "taunting the honourable gentleman" with this and with that and with what not, five nights a-week, until the small hours of the morning? Probably he had that much <u>foreknowledge</u>, knowing his men. (book 3, ch. 9)

Discussion Questions

A. Compare this novel to Upton Sinclair's *The Jungle*.

B. What form and structure does Dickens employ in this novel?

C. Discuss two themes in *Hard Times*.

D. What is the point of view in this novel? Why does Dickens choose to write *Hard Times* this way?

E. Who is the protagonist?

The House of the Seven Gables

Nathaniel Hawthorne

In his introduction, Hawthorne claims to be writing a romance. And so he is. Parsimonious Colonel Pyncheon builds a mansion on ill-gotten ground, setting the stage for years of generational suffering. Years later, a country cousin and an enigmatic young boarder reverse the tide of misfortunes surrounding the house having seven gables.

Objective Test

_____ In the late 1600s, a local farmer named Matthew Maule builds a house on prime land near a generous spring, but the land is coveted by (A) Cotton Mather, (B) Colonel Pyncheon, or (C) Uncle Venner.

_____ Maule is hanged for (A) witchcraft, (B) robbery, (C) murder, or (D) treason.

_____ Pyncheon is behind Maule's conviction. Maule curses the Colonel, who then (A) drops dead, (B) says he is sorry, (C) is unimpressed and hires Maule's own son to build him a new mansion with seven gables on the property, or (D) places a curse on Maule's family.

_____ Later, Colonel Pyncheon is (A) forced to join the army, (B) overcome with grief, (C) killed in battle, or (D) found dead in his study.

_____ A descendent named (A) Mary, (B) Alice, (C) Hepzibah, or

(D) Abigail is forced to open a small store in her house to keep from starving.

_____ A visiting cousin is named (A) Hepzibah, (B) Phoebe, (C) Clifford, or (D) Judge Hughes.

_____ The "curse" is broken when (A) Phoebe marries, (B) Hepzibah does penance, (C) the Judge dies, or (D) the house burns.

_____ Who is worried that he will be blamed for the murder and flees with Hepzibah? (A) Clifford, (B) Judge Pyncheon, (C) Leon, or (D) Maule.

_____ Holgrave falls in love with (A) Hepzibah, (B) Phoebe, (C) Mary, or (D) Abigail.

_____ Clifford, Hepzibah, Phoebe, Holgrave, and Uncle Vanner all (A) live in Seven Gables, (B) move to Boston, or (C) move to the country estate.

Suggested Vocabulary Words

A. The aspect of the venerable mansion has always affected me like a human countenance, bearing the traces not merely of outward storm and sunshine, but expressive also, of the long lapse of mortal life, and accompanying vicissitudes that have passed within. Were these to be worthily recounted, they would form a narrative of no small interest and instruction, and possessing, moreover, a certain remarkable unity, which might almost seem the result of artistic arrangement. But the story would include a chain of events extending over the better part of two centuries, and, written out with reasonable amplitude, would fill a bigger folio volume, or a longer series of duodecimos, than could prudently be appropriated to the annals of all New England during a similar period. (ch. 1)

B. In proof of the authenticity of this legendary renown, Hepzibah could have exhibited the shell of a great egg, which an ostrich need hardly have been ashamed of. Be that as it might, the hens were now scarcely larger than pigeons, and had a queer, rusty, withered aspect, and a gouty kind of movement, and a sleepy and melancholy tone throughout all the <u>variations</u> of their clucking and cackling. It was evident that the race had <u>degenerated</u>, like many a noble race besides, in consequence of too strict a watchfulness to keep it pure. (ch. 6)

C. By this time the sun had gone down, and was tinting the clouds towards the <u>zenith</u> with those bright <u>hues</u> which are not seen there until some time after sunset, and when the horizon has quite lost its richer brilliancy. The moon, too, which had long been climbing overhead, and <u>unobtrusively</u> melting its disk into the <u>azure</u>,—like an <u>ambitious</u> <u>demagogue</u>, who hides his <u>aspiring</u> purpose by assuming the <u>prevalent</u> hue of popular sentiment,—now began to shine out, broad and oval, in its middle pathway. These silvery beams were already powerful enough to change the character of the <u>lingering</u> daylight. (ch. 14)

D. The artist looked paler than ordinary; there was a thoughtful and severe <u>contraction</u> of his forehead, tracing a deep, vertical line between the eyebrows. His smile, however, was full of genuine warmth, and had in it a joy, by far the most <u>vivid</u> expression that Phoebe had ever witnessed, shining out of the New England <u>reserve</u> with which Holgrave habitually masked whatever lay near his heart. It was the look wherewith a man, brooding alone over some fearful object, in a dreary forest or <u>illimitable</u> desert, would recognize the familiar aspect of his dearest friend, bringing up all the peaceful ideas that belong to home, and the gentle current of every-day affairs. And yet, as he felt the necessity of responding to her look of inquiry, the smile disappeared. (ch. 20)

Discussion Questions

A. What is the role of "fate" in this novel?

B. Who is the protagonist? Supply your reasoning.

C. Is the hypnotism in this novel crucial to Hawthorne's purposes, or is it merely a distraction?

D. Compare Phoebe in *The House of the Seven Gables* with Hester Prynne in *The Scarlet Letter*.

E. Discuss the mood of this novel and how Hawthorne creates it.

Intruder in the Dust

William Faulkner

 S et in Faulkner's fictional Yoknapatawpha County, the novel is both a murder mystery and an anti-Northern diatribe. Chick Mallison, a twelve-year-old boy, is one of the most memorable characters in American literature. This is a novel full of irony, mystery, and adventure.

Objective Test: True or False

_____ When a twelve-year-old white boy, Chick Mallison, falls through the ice and is rescued by old Lucas Beauchamp, Lucas is insulted by Chick's racist comments.

_____ In turn, Chick resents being indebted to a black man.

_____ Four years later Lucas is arrested for murdering Vinson Gowrie and is taken to jail, where a crowd of Vinson's friends are expected to lynch Lucas.

_____ He tells Chick to get Chick's grandfather, Gavin Stevens, to defend him.

_____ Aided by the young black Aleck Sander and the seventy-year-old spinster Eunice Habersham, Chick digs up Vinson's grave.

_____ They find the body of Vinson.

_____ They convince Gavin and the sheriff to reopen the grave, but the bodies of both Vinson and Montgomery are found in nearby quicksand.

_____ Back in town, Lucas explains that Crawford Gowrie murdered the two men.

_____ Crawford is arrested and then commits suicide in jail, but Lucas is lynched anyhow.

_____ Determined to accept no charity from a white, he pays Gavin a two-dollar fee in coins and demands a receipt. He becomes "tyrant over the whole county's white conscience."

Suggested Vocabulary Words

A. [They] whetted knives or already moved about the pens; . . . [the hogs were] not quite startled, not alarmed but just alerted as though sensing already even though only dimly their rich and immanent destiny.

B. By nightfall the whole land would be hung with their spectral intact tallow-colored carcasses immobilized by the heels in attitudes of frantic running as though full tilt at the center of the earth.

C. It took but one glance to see . . . [that] they had an affinity and rapport with rabbits.

D. He knew the true reason was that he could no more imagine himself contradicting the man striding on ahead of him.

E. . . . but a savage gash half gully and half road mounting a hill with an air solitary independent and intractable.

Discussion Questions

A. The idea that a black man standing over a dead white man must be guilty of murder is an important moment in the novel. Why?

B. In Faulkner's writing, the mentality of the Southern man becomes startlingly clear. At one point Chick's Uncle Gavin Stevens, a lawyer, explains that blacks and whites in the South were all assigned roles and expected to play the part:

That's why we must resist the North: not just to preserve ourselves nor even the two of us as one to remain one nation
because that will be the inescapable by-product of what we will
preserve: which is the very thing that three generations ago we
lost a bloody war in our own back yards so that it remain intact:
the postulate that Sambo is a human being living in a free country and hence must be free. That's what we are really defending:
the privilege of setting him free ourselves.

Respond to this theory.

C. Faulkner ends the novel with the business of paying the bill as
Lucas settles his debt, so that he is not indebted to any man. A movie
made a few years after the book, ended by Uncle John calling Lucas
"the conscience of the town," to which Chick corrected him and called
him "the conscience of us all." Which ending do you like better?

D. Why is Chick so humiliated to be helped by Lucas?

The Invisible Man

H. G. Wells

This was an exciting, terrifying story, really. An obscure scientist invents a way to become invisible and tries the formula on himself. Now he can go anywhere, menace anyone—sight unseen. The problem is that he cannot become visible again—and apparently this makes him insane.

The story is simple. A stranger arrives in a village, where he books a private room in the local bed and breakfast. He never removes bandages that cover his face, so no one knows he is invisible. Meanwhile, he is rude and obnoxious. But most of the village never sees him because he remains confined to his room, working on mysterious experiments. The reader, though, knows that the reason he is so shy is that he is invisible. However, he desperately wants to be visible again. He has failed and made some very bad choices.

Objective Test

_____ In the first scene in the book the invisible man arrives |
(A) home from a long journey, (B) at Mrs. Hall's boarding house, (C) at a scientific convention, or (D) hot and tired.

_____ Mr. Henfrey suspects that the invisible man is (A) wanted by the police, (B) burned in an accident, (C) friendly, or (D) sick.

_____ How does Wells let the reader know that the invisible man has broken into the parsonage? (A) The invisible man tells the pastor, (B) the reader just knows, or (C) both the pastor and his wife know someone is in the room whom they cannot see.

_____ The invisible man is forced to rob his father. This has tragic consequences because (A) it is not his father's money and his father commits suicide, (B) the invisible man is caught, (C) the old man has no more money, or (D) the invisible man uses the money to buy drugs.

_____ The invisible man (A) escapes to Algiers, (B) moves to another English town, (C) is killed by Kemp and others, or (D) literally disappears.

Suggested Vocabulary Words

A. And with that much introduction, that and a ready acquiescence to terms and a couple of sovereigns flung upon the table, he took up his quarters in the inn. (ch. 1)

B. "You don't say so!" said Hall, who was a man of sluggish apprehension. (ch. 2)

C. The first to appear was the proprietor of the Cocoanut Shy, a burly man in a blue jersey. (ch. 12)

D. His meditation became profound. (ch. 18)

E. He laughed, and put his hand to the locked door. "Barred out of my own bedroom, by a flagrant absurdity!" he said. (ch. 18)

F. "Is there such a thing as an invisible animal? In the sea, yes. Thousands! millions! All the larvae, all the little nauplii and tornarias, all the microscopic things, the jelly-fish. In the sea there are more things invisible than visible! I never thought of that before. And in the ponds too. All those little pond-life things,—specks of colourless translucent jelly! But in air? No! (ch. 18)

G. Oliver, my professor, was a scientific bounder, a journalist by instinct, a thief of ideas,—he was always prying! And you know the knavish system of the scientific world. I simply would not publish, and let him share my credit. I went on working, I got nearer and nearer making my formula into an experiment, a reality. . . . Kemp gave a cry of <u>incredulous</u> amazement. (ch. 19)

H. What I want, Kemp, is a goal-keeper, a helper, and a hiding-place, an arrangement whereby I can sleep and eat and rest in peace, and unsuspected. I must have a <u>confederate</u>. With a confederate, with food and rest—a thousand things are possible. (ch. 24)

I. Mr. Heelas stood up, exclaiming vaguely and <u>vehemently</u> at all these wonderful things. (ch. 28)

Discussion Questions

A. One critic who dislikes the book said, "There's one obvious reason for the novel's lack of potency: it is a victim of its own success. The invisible man's story has become embedded in our culture and offers no surprises." Respond to this critic.

B. *The Invisible Man* has a distinctly antiscience message. What is it?

C. This novel is full of suspense. Give an example.

D. Explain how Wells uses Kemp as a foil (someone or something that acts as a contrast for another).

F. What narrative technique does Wells employ? Why?

G. Compare the Invisible Man to Hyde (in Robert Louis Stevenson's *Dr. Jekyll and Mr. Hyde*).

H. In the movie *League of Extraordinary Gentlemen* (2003), the protagonist gathered a group of superhumans to save the world from a nefarious villain named the Fantom. He gathered heroes/villains from literature to help him. The invisible man (from this book) was counted among this number. What does it say about our culture that we have to use villains to save us from other villains?

Jane Eyre

Charlotte Brontë

Charlotte Brontë characterizes the heroine of her 1847 novel as being as poor and plain as herself. Presenting a plain heroine was a gutsy move in a market that wanted to be titillated by the extraordinary. The author drew upon her own experience to depict Jane's struggles at Lowood, an oppressive boarding school, and her troubled career as a governess. This orphan girl, forced to make her way alone in the world, from Lowood School to Thornfield, the estate of the majestically moody Mr. Rochester, has become one of the most memorable eighteenth-century protagonists.

Objective Test

_____ How does Jane relate to the Reeds? (A) She will not be bullied, (B) she is intimidated, (C) she is disrespectful, or (D) she is neutral.

_____ During her interview at Thornfield, Jane is curious when she (A) hears a dog bark, (B) sees a wild woman, (C) hears loud laughter, or (D) sees no children.

_____ Jane saves Rochester's life by (A) giving him a home remedy, (B) keeping him from falling out of his window, (C) speaking up as he walks into a glass door, or (D) putting out a fire.

_____ Eventually Rochester asks Jane to marry him. The wedding is disrupted when someone protests (A) that Rochester has not obtained a license, (B) that Jane is not of the right social class, (C) that Rochester is already married, or (D) that the priest is not credentialed.

_____ Rochester claims that he married his insane wife because (A) his father misled him, (B) he really loved her, (C) she had a lot of money, or (D) he was too tired of dating.

_____ Ultimately Jane marries Rochester when he is a broken man because she (A) feels sorry for him, (B) loves him, (C) needs a home, or (D) is tired of being a governess.

Suggested Vocabulary Words

A. "What do you want?" I asked, with awkward <u>diffidence</u>. (ch. 2)

B. John had not much affection for his mother and sisters, and an <u>antipathy</u> to me. (ch. 2)

C. This will be thought cool language by persons who entertain solemn doctrines about the angelic nature of children, and the duty of those charged with their education to conceive for them an <u>idolatrous</u> devotion: but I am not writing to flatter parental <u>egotism</u>, to echo cant, or prop up humbug; I am merely telling the truth. I felt a <u>conscientious solicitude</u> for Adele's welfare and progress, and a quiet liking for her little self: just as I cherished towards Mrs. Fairfax a thankfulness for her kindness, and a pleasure in her society <u>proportionate</u> to the tranquil regard she had for me, and the moderation of her mind and character. (ch. 12)

D. I rose up suddenly, terror-struck at the <u>solitude</u> which so ruthless a judge haunted,—at the silence which so awful a voice filled. My head swam as I stood erect. I perceived that I was sickening from excitement and <u>inanition</u>; neither meat nor drink had passed my lips that day, for I had taken no breakfast. (ch. 22)

E. This was said with a careless, abstracted <u>indifference</u>, which showed that my solicitude was, at least in his opinion, wholly <u>superfluous</u>. (ch. 23)

F. He replied not: he seemed serious—<u>abstracted</u>; he sighed; he half-opened his lips as if to speak: he closed them again. I felt a little embarrassed. Perhaps I had too rashly over-leaped conventionalities; and he, like St. John, saw impropriety in my inconsiderateness. I had indeed made my proposal from the idea that he wished and would ask me to be his wife: an expectation, not the less certain because unexpressed, had buoyed me up, that he would claim me at once as his own. But no hint to that effect escaping him and his countenance becoming more overcast, I suddenly remembered that I might have been all wrong, and was perhaps playing the fool unwittingly; and I began gently to withdraw myself from his arms—but he eagerly snatched me closer.

Discussion Questions

A. Jane was an entirely new character in the reticent Victorian Age. Why did the public find her so appealing?

B. Was Jane a social revolutionary?

C. Why did Brontë choose first-person narration to tell her story?

D. How does Brontë use the weather to mirror Jane's moods?

E. Compare Charlotte Brontë's parlor scenes with those found in Jane Austen's novels.

F. A critic wrote, "Not one of the main incidents on which its action turns is but incredible. It is incredible that Rochester should hide a mad wife on the top floor of Thornfield Hall, and hide her so imperfectly that she constantly gets loose and roams yelling about the house, without any of his numerous servants and guests suspecting anything: it is incredible that Mrs. Reed, a conventional if disagreeable woman, should conspire to cheat Jane out of a fortune because she had been rude to her as a child of ten: it is supremely incredible that when Jane Eyre collapses on an unknown doorstep after her flight from Rochester it should be on the doorstep of her only surviving amiable relations." Respond to this critic.

Julius Caesar

William Shakespeare

Julius Caesar is not Shakespeare's best play, but it is full of action and memorable dialogue. In this historical tragedy of political betrayal, Shakespeare recounts the famous assassination of Julius Caesar by his republican opponents.

Objective Test

_____ The play begins with (A) the assassination of Julius Caesar, (B) Caesar's triumphant ride into Rome, (C) the battle between Antony and Brutus, or (D) the invasion of the Goths (Germans).

_____ Brutus and his friends fear (A) that Caesar will create a dictatorship, (B) that Caesar will let the masses rule, (C) that the Senate will take over, or (D) that Mark Antony will replace Caesar as emperor.

_____ Caesar's wife Calpurnia (A) is delighted to join her husband on the throne, (B) stays in Capri, (C) begs Caesar not to go to the senate, or (D) goes with him to the senate.

_____ After Caesar is assassinated, a civil war results between (A) Octavius and Brutus against Cassius and Antony, (B) Antony and Brutus against Cassius and Octavius, (C) Brutus and Cassius against Octavius and Antony, or (D) Claudius against Antony.

_____ At the end of the play Brutus (A) dies in battle, (B) commits suicide, (C) wins a great victory, or (D) flees to Egypt.

Suggested Vocabulary Words

A. You are dull, Casca, and those sparks of life / that should be in a Roman you do want, / or else you use not. You look pale and gaze / and put on fear and cast yourself in wonder / to see the strange <u>impatience</u> of the heavens. / But if you would consider the true cause / why all these fires, why all these <u>gliding</u> ghosts, / why birds and beasts from quality and kind, / why old men, fools, and children calculate, / why all these things change from their <u>ordinance</u>, / their natures, and preformed faculties / to monstrous quality, why, you shall find / that heaven hath <u>infused</u> them with these spirits / to make them instruments of fear and warning / unto some monstrous state. / Now could I, Casca, name to thee a man / most like this <u>dreadful</u> night, / that thunders, lightens, opens graves, and roars / as doth the lion in the Capitol, / a man no mightier than thyself or me / in personal action, yet <u>prodigious</u> grown / and fearful, as these strange <u>eruptions</u> are. (act 1, scene 3)

B. Romans, countrymen, and lovers! Hear me for my / cause, and be silent, that you may hear. Believe me / for mine honor, and have respect to mine honor, that / you may believe. <u>Censure</u> me in your wisdom, and / awake your senses, that you may the better judge. / If there be any in this assembly, any dear friend of / Caesar's, to him I say that Brutus' love to Caesar / was no less than his. If then that friend demand / why Brutus rose against Caesar, this is my answer: / —Not that I loved Caesar less, but that I loved / Rome more. Had you rather Caesar were living and / die all slaves, than that Caesar were dead to live / all freemen? As Caesar loved me, I weep for him; / as he was fortunate, I rejoice at it; as he was / <u>valiant</u>, I honor him; but as he was <u>ambitious</u>, I / slew him. There is tears for his love, joy for his / fortune, honor for his valor, and death for his / ambition. Who is here so base that would be a / bondman? If any, speak, for him have I offended. / Who is here so rude that would not be a Roman? If / any, speak, for him have I offended. Who is here so / vile that will not love his country? If any, speak, / for him have I offended. I pause for a reply. (act 3, scene 2)

C. Thou hast described / a hot friend cooling. Ever note, Lucilius, / when love begins to sicken and decay / it useth an enforced ceremony. / There are no tricks in plain and simple faith; / but hollow men, like horses hot at hand, / make gallant show and promise of their <u>mettle</u>; /

but when they should endure the bloody spur, / they fall their crests and like deceitful <u>jades</u> / ~~sink in the trial.~~ Comes his army on? (act 4, scene 2)

D. This was the noblest Roman of them all. / All the <u>conspirators,</u> save only he, / did that they did in envy of great Caesar; / he only, in a general honest thought / and common good to all, made one of them. / His life was gentle, and the elements / so mix'd in him that Nature might stand up / and say to all the world, "This was a man!" (act 5, scene 5)

Discussion Questions

A. React to Brutus's words "Not that I loved Caesar less, but that I loved Rome more" (act 3, scene 2).

B. How does Shakespeare use prophecies and omens to build suspense?

C. How does this play reflect on Elizabethan English politics?

D. Who is the protagonist?

E. If you were casting this play, which contemporary actors would you cast as Julius Caesar? Mark Antony? Brutus? Calpurnia?

The Jungle

Upton Sinclair

 This novel, which many consider mediocre, nonetheless had a profound impact on American culture. Perhaps no fictional novel has directly impacted American social policy as much as *The Jungle.* Sinclair's 1906 landmark novel is widely credited with awakening the public fury that led to the passage of the Pure Food and Drug Act (1906), a watershed in consumer protection and government legislation.

Objective Test

_____ Jurgis Rudkus and Ona Lukoszaite have recently immigrated to Chicago from (A) Russia, (B) Poland, (C) Romania, or (D) Lithuania.

_____ They hold their wedding feast in an area of Chicago known as (A) Packingtown, (B) Cedar Grove, (C) Oak Park, or (D) Shelbyville.

_____ After the reception, Jurgis and Ona discover that they (A) have over $100 in gifts, (B) owe more than $100, (C) receive an anonymous gift of $100, or (D) must give the best man $100.

_____ Jurgis (A) decides to go home, (B) borrows money, (C) vows that he will simply work harder to make more money, or (D) kills the owner of the bar.

_____ Jurgis works in a (A) cotton mill, (B) meatpacking facility, (C) steel mill, or (D) bar.

_____ Jurgis's wife gives birth to a healthy boy, whom she and Jurgis name Antanas, after Jurgis's late father, but (A) she is forced to return to work only seven days later, (B) the baby dies, (C) the baby needs special medicine, or (D) Jurgis loses his job.

_____ After being injured and then fired from his job, Jurgis (A) joins the church, (B) regrets coming to America, (C) starts to drink alcohol, or (D) falls and dies.

_____ Jurgis's wife, Ona, (A) dies in childbirth, (B) leaves him, (C) marries someone else, or (D) joins the church.

_____ Eventually Jurgis (A) dies in despair, (B) lives on the street, (C) gets a job in another meatpacking plant, or (D) returns home.

_____ At the end of the novel, Jurgis (A) joins a political party, (B) leaves his wife, (C) marries again, or (D) returns home.

Suggested Vocabulary Words

A. Their good luck, they felt, had given them the right to think about a home; and sitting out on the doorstep that summer evening, they held consultation about it, and Jurgis took occasion to broach a weighty subject. Passing down the avenue to work that morning he had seen two boys leaving an advertisement from house to house; and seeing that there were pictures upon it, Jurgis had asked for one, and had rolled it up and tucked it into his shirt. (ch. 4)

B. Such were the cruel terms upon which their life was possible, that they might never have nor expect a single instant's respite from worry, a single instant in which they were not haunted by the thought of money. (ch. 10)

C. The other asked him what had led him to safebreaking—to Jurgis a wild and appalling occupation to think about. (ch. 17)

D. "Ask the woman," said the farmer, nodding over his shoulder. The "woman" was more tractable, and for a dime Jurgis secured two thick sandwiches and a piece of pie and two apples. (ch. 22)

E. Jeweled images are made of him, <u>sensual</u> priests burn incense to him, and modern pirates of industry bring their dollars, wrung from the toil of helpless women and children, and build temples to him, and sit in cushioned seats and listen to his teachings <u>expounded</u> by doctors of dusty divinity." (ch. 31)

Discussion Questions

A. Compare the immigrant protagonist in this novel with Antonia in *My Antonia*, by Willa Cather.

B. How accurate is Sinclair's image of late-nineteenth-century industrial America?

C. Marija, Ona's cousin, is one of the most striking characters in the novel. She is the character we think will most likely succeed. Her sad ending, then, becomes a metaphor for one theme of this novel. Explain.

D. Did Sinclair go too far in his description of the meatpacking plant? Judging from other reports, do you think he exaggerated? Would the owners of the meatpacking facility write a different version of the story?

E. Jurgis is the protagonist. In literature, he is a typical figure who gains wisdom through hard times. At the end he is converted to socialism. Does Sinclair adequately develop this character?

F. Scholar Van Wyck Brooks writes, "The conversion of Jurgis to socialism, at the end of the book, was really impossible after his soul had been 'murdered,' as one was told, and the story of his life was quite unreal when, after the death of his wife and his child, he became a hobo, a scab, and a crook. He was as unreal, in fact, as his friend Duane, the fancy man, or the young millionaire who invites him to his house in Chicago, a figure of pure melodrama in which Sinclair reverted to his early pulp-writing. Sinclair's characters, as a rule, were puppets." Is Jurgis's conversion credible?

G. Write a report on the socialist movement in American history.

H. Does Sinclair's obvious prejudice toward a political viewpoint damage the artistic components of this novel? How?

Kidnapped

Robert Louis Stevenson

 Most critics would agree that *Kidnapped* is not of the same quality as *Treasure Island* or *The Strange Case of Dr. Jekyll and Mr. Hyde.* Yet this unpretentious novel is nonetheless a well-written, action-packed adventure tale. Stevenson originally wrote it to amuse his own children.

Objective Test

_____ David is a young man from (A) England, (B) Wales, (C) Scotland, or (D) Boston.

_____ He is (A) an orphan, (B) adopted by a rich sea captain, (C) on board a ship, or (D) the King's son.

_____ In fact, David (A) is dying of cancer, (B) has no funds at all, (C) has a wealthy uncle, or (D) is forced to work in a factory.

_____ David is kidnapped on the ship (A) *Robert E. Lee,* (B) *Testament,* (C) *Comedy of Errors,* or (D) *Covenant.*

_____ After much adventure David (A) is shipwrecked in New Guinea, (B) becomes a very wealthy young man, (C) hides a treasure in Cuba, or (D) returns to France.

Suggested Vocabulary Words

A. There was now no doubt about my uncle's <u>enmity</u>; there was no doubt I carried my life in my hand, and he would leave no stone unturned that he might <u>compass</u> my destruction. But I was young and spirited, and like most lads that have been country-bred, I had a great opinion of my <u>shrewdness</u>. I had come to his door no better than a beggar and little more than a child; he had met me with <u>treachery</u> and violence; it would be a fine <u>consummation</u> to take the upper hand, and drive him like a herd of sheep. (ch. 5)

B. He was smallish in <u>stature</u>, but well set and as <u>nimble</u> as a goat; his face was of a good open expression, but sunburnt very dark, and heavily freckled and pitted with the small-pox; his eyes were unusually light and had a kind of dancing madness in them, that was both <u>engaging</u> and alarming; and when he took off his great-coat, he laid a pair of fine silver-mounted pistols on the table, and I saw that he was belted with a great sword. His manners, besides, were <u>elegant</u>, and he pledged the captain handsomely. Altogether I thought of him, at the first sight, that here was a man I would rather call my friend than my enemy. (ch. 9)

C. Doubtless it was a great relief to walk <u>disencumbered</u>; and perhaps without that relief, and the <u>consequent</u> sense of liberty and lightness, I could not have walked at all. I was but new risen from a bed of sickness; and there was nothing in the state of our affairs to <u>hearten</u> me for much <u>exertion</u>; traveling, as we did, over the most dismal deserts in Scotland, under a cloudy heaven, and with divided hearts among the travelers. (ch. 24)

D. The soldiers let us be; although once a party of two companies and some dragoons went by in the bottom of the valley, where I could see them through the window as I lay in bed. What was much more <u>astonishing</u>, no <u>magistrate</u> came near me, and there was no question put of <u>whence</u> I came or whither I was going; and in that time of excitement, I was as free of all <u>inquiry</u> as though I had lain in a desert. Yet my presence was known before I left to all the people in Balquhidder and the <u>adjacent</u> parts; many coming about the house on visits and these (after the custom of the country) spreading the news among their neighbours. The bills, too, had now been printed. There was one pinned near the foot of my bed, where I could read my own not very <u>flattering</u> portrait and, in larger characters, the amount of the blood money that had been set upon my life. (ch. 25)

Discussion Questions

A. Compare this novel to other novels by Stevenson. Which one do you like the best? Why?

B. Does David handle Ebenezer fairly?

C. What relationship exists between David and Alan?

D. Alan has the "Long John Silver" role in *Kidnapped*. Explain.

The Last of the Mohicans

James Fenimore Cooper

 Written in 1826, *The Last of the Mohicans* was one of the first great novels of American literature, and James Fenimore Cooper's most popular one. The book established the American frontier as a setting for an epic adventure and introduced, in Hawkeye, the quintessential frontier hero.

Objective Test

_____ This book occurs during (A) the American Revolution, (B) the French and Indian War, or (C) the War of 1812.

_____ Alice and Cora set out from Fort Edward to visit their (A) father, (B) brother, (C) cousin, or (D) uncle.

_____ Major Duncan Heyward escorts them through the dangerous forest, as guided by an Indian named Magua. Soon David Gamut joins them. Traveling cautiously, the group encounters (A) Davy Crockett, (B) Daniel Boone, (C) Natty Bumppo, or (D) George Washington.

_____ Natty Bumppo calls himself (A) Bear Claw, (B) Hawkeye, (C) Bobcat Bob, or (D) Cougar Charlie.

_____ Chingachgook and Uncas, Chingachgook's son, are the only surviving members of the (A) Leni-Lenape tribe, (B) Delaware tribe, (C) Mohican tribe, or (D) Sioux tribe.

_____ Hawkeye says that Magua, a Huron, is (A) leading them in the

85

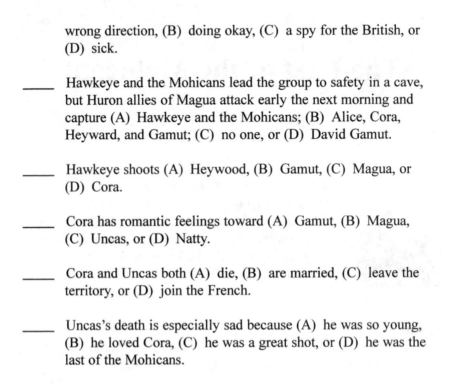

wrong direction, (B) doing okay, (C) a spy for the British, or (D) sick.

_____ Hawkeye and the Mohicans lead the group to safety in a cave, but Huron allies of Magua attack early the next morning and capture (A) Hawkeye and the Mohicans; (B) Alice, Cora, Heyward, and Gamut; (C) no one, or (D) David Gamut.

_____ Hawkeye shoots (A) Heywood, (B) Gamut, (C) Magua, or (D) Cora.

_____ Cora has romantic feelings toward (A) Gamut, (B) Magua, (C) Uncas, or (D) Natty.

_____ Cora and Uncas both (A) die, (B) are married, (C) leave the territory, or (D) join the French.

_____ Uncas's death is especially sad because (A) he was so young, (B) he loved Cora, (C) he was a great shot, or (D) he was the last of the Mohicans.

Suggested Vocabulary Words

A. In a moment of such painful doubt, Duncan did not hesitate to look around him, without consulting that protection from the rocks which just before had been so necessary to his safety. Every effort, however, to detect the least evidence of the approach of their hidden enemies was as fruitless as the inquiry after his late companions. The wooded banks of the river seemed again deserted by everything possessing animal life. The uproar which had so lately echoed through the vaults of the forest was gone, leaving the rush of the waters to swell and sink on the currents of the air, in the unmingled sweetness of nature. A fish-hawk, which, secure on the topmost branches of a dead pine, had been a distant spectator of the fray, now swooped from his high and ragged perch, and soared, in wide sweeps, above his prey; while a jay, whose noisy voice had been stilled by the hoarser cries of the savages, ventured again to open his discordant throat, as though once more in undisturbed possession of his wild domains. Duncan caught from these natural accompaniments of the solitary scene a glimmering of hope; and he began to rally his <u>faculties</u> to renewed exertions, with something like a <u>reviving</u> confidence of success. (ch. 9)

B. "If you judge of Indian <u>cunning</u> by the rules you find in books, or by white <u>sagacity</u>, they will lead you <u>astray</u>, if not to your death," returned Hawkeye, examining the signs of the place with that <u>acuteness</u> which distinguished him. "If I may be permitted to speak in this matter, it will be to say, that we have but two things to choose between: the one is, to return, and give up all thoughts of following the Hurons." (ch. 20)

C. The <u>impatience</u> of the savages who <u>lingered</u> about the prison of Uncas, as has been seen, had overcome their <u>dread</u> of the <u>conjurer's</u> breath. They stole cautiously, and with beating hearts, to a crevice, through which the faint light of the fire was glimmering. For several minutes they mistook the form of David for that of the prisoner; but the very accident which Hawkeye had foreseen occurred. Tired of keeping the <u>extremities</u> of his long person so near together, the singer gradually suffered the lower limbs to extend themselves, until one of his mis-shapen feet actually came in contact with and shoved aside the embers of the fire. At first the Hurons believed the Delaware had been thus deformed by witchcraft. But when David, unconscious of being observed, turned his head, and exposed his simple, mild countenance, in place of the haughty lineaments of their prisoner, it would have exceed-ed the <u>credulity</u> of even a native to have doubted any longer. They rushed together into the lodge, and, laying their hands, with but little ceremony, on their captive, immediately detected the <u>imposition</u>. They arose the cry first heard by the fugitives. It was succeeded by the most frantic and angry <u>demonstrations</u> of vengeance. David, however, firm in his determination to cover the retreat of his friends, was compelled to believe that his own final hour had come. Deprived of his book and his pipe, he was <u>fain</u> to trust to a memory that rarely failed him on such subjects; and breaking forth in a loud and impassioned strain, he endeavored to smooth his passage into the other world by singing the opening verse of a funeral anthem. The Indians were seasonably reminded of his <u>infirmity</u>, and, rushing into the open air, they aroused the village in the manner described. (ch. 27)

D. Chingachgook was a <u>solitary</u> <u>exception</u> to the interest <u>manifested</u> by the native part of the audience. His look never changed throughout the whole of the scene, nor did a muscle move in his <u>rigid</u> countenance, even at the wildest or the most <u>pathetic</u> parts of the <u>lamentation</u>. The cold and senseless remains of his son was all to him, and every other sense but that of sight seemed frozen, in order that his eyes might take their final gaze at those <u>lineaments</u> he had so long loved, and which were now about to be closed forever from his view. (ch. 33)

Discussion Questions

A. How does Cooper treat the Native Americans in his book?

B. How does Cooper create Hawkeye as a hero?

C. What is Heyward's role?

D. How accurate is Cooper's description of the French and Indian War?

Little Women

Louisa Alcott

 *Little Women* has delighted readers for generations. It combines superb characterization with an inspiring story to make this a timeless classic. Meet the March sisters: the inimical Jo, the beautiful Meg, the frail Beth, and the spoiled younger daughter Amy. Watch as they mature into young women.

Objective Test

_____ The novel begins during the (A) summer, (B) fall, (C) winter, or (D) spring.

_____ The girls decide that they will buy presents for (A) their mother, (B) their dad, (C) the poor, or (D) injured soldiers.

_____ Mr. March, the girls' father, is serving as a (A) Union private, (A) Union chaplain, or (B) Confederate General.

_____ That year, the Marches form the Pickwick Club, in which they (A) take canned goods to the poor, (B) sew socks for soldiers, (C) take poor children to the park, or (D) write a family newspaper.

_____ Beth (A) dies, (B) marries Laurie, (C) goes to college, or (D) joins the nursing corps.

Suggested Vocabulary Words

A. Amy rebelled <u>outright</u>, and <u>passionately</u> declared that she had rather have the fever than go to Aunt March. Meg reasoned, pleaded, and commanded, all in vain. Amy protested that she would not go, and Meg left her in <u>despair</u> to ask Hannah what should be done. Before she came back, Laurie walked into the parlor to find Amy sobbing, with her head in the sofa cushions. She told her story, expecting to be <u>consoled</u>, but Laurie only put his hands in his pockets and walked about the room, whistling softly, as he knit his brows in deep thought. Presently he sat down beside her, and said, in his most <u>wheedlesome</u> tone, "Now be a sensible little woman, and do as they say. No, don't cry, but hear what a jolly plan I've got. You go to Aunt March's, and I'll come and take you out every day, driving or walking, and we'll have capital times. Won't that be better than <u>moping</u> here?" (ch. 17)

B. Jo's face was a study next day, for the secret rather weighed upon her, and she found it hard not to look <u>mysterious</u> and important. Meg observed it, but did not trouble herself to make inquiries, for she had learned that the best way to manage Jo was by the law of <u>contraries</u>, so she felt sure of being told everything if she did not ask. She was rather surprised, therefore, when the silence remained unbroken, and Jo assumed a <u>patronizing</u> air, which decidedly aggravated Meg, who in turn assumed an air of dignified reserve and devoted herself to her mother. This left Jo to her own devices, for Mrs. March had taken her place as nurse, and <u>bade</u> her rest, exercise, and amuse herself after her long <u>confinement</u>. Amy being gone, Laurie was her only refuge, and much as she enjoyed his society, she rather dreaded him just then, for he was an <u>incorrigible</u> tease, and she feared he would <u>coax</u> the secret from her. (ch. 21)

C. There were to be no <u>ceremonious</u> performances, everything was to be as natural and homelike as possible, so when Aunt March arrived, she was <u>scandalized</u> to see the bride come running to welcome and lead her in, to find the bridegroom fastening up a garland that had fallen down, and to catch a glimpse of the <u>paternal</u> minister marching upstairs with a <u>grave</u> countenance and a wine bottle under each arm. (ch. 25)

D. "You look like the <u>effigy</u> of a young knight asleep on his tomb," she said, carefully tracing the well-cut <u>profile</u> defined against the dark stone. (ch. 39)

E. Yes, Jo was a very happy woman there, in spite of hard work, much anxiety, and a <u>perpetual</u> racket. She enjoyed it <u>heartily</u> and found the applause of her boys more satisfying than any praise of the world, for now she told no stories except to her flock of enthusiastic believers and admirers. As the years went on, two little lads of her own came to increase her happiness—Rob, named for Grandpa, and Teddy, a happy-go-lucky baby, who seemed to have <u>inherited</u> his papa's sunshiny temper as well as his mother's lively spirit. How they ever grew up alive in that whirlpool of boys was a mystery to their grandma and aunts, but they <u>flourished</u> like dandelions in spring, and their rough nurses loved and served them well. (ch. 47)

Discussion Questions

A. Some critics find the young girls to be archetypes, one-dimensional, and static. What do you think?

B. Why does Alcott call her book *Little Women*?

C. Contrast these young women with contemporary young women.

D. How important is the setting to this novel?

Madame Bovary

Gustave Flaubert

 *M*adame Bovary is the story of a beautiful young woman who marries an ordinary country doctor. Through a series of affairs, she attempts to escape the narrow confines of her life, hoping to find in other men the romantic ideal she has always wanted. Her bad choices destroy her, however. The moral vision in this classic is breathtaking, and in its own way, is strong impetus for the reader to embrace moral Theism.

Objective Test

_____ Charles Bovary is (A) a spoiled rich boy, (B) unable to fit in at his new school, (C) injured in a nasty fall, or (D) called to be a pastor.

_____ Bovary is (A) a mediocre and ordinary doctor, (B) a promising surgeon, (C) an important pastor, or (D) an unemployed brick-layer.

_____ Bovary marries (A) Mary, (B) Susan, (C) Emma, or (D) Margaret.

_____ Madame Bovary (A) loves Charles very much, (B) gambles too much, (C) has a conversion experience, or (D) finds that country living does not live up to her romantic expectations.

_____ Madame Bovary's first affair is with (A) Rodolphe, (B) David, (C) Mark, or (D) Gustave.

_____ Dr. Bovary's practice nearly fails when (A) his procedure causes a man to lose his foot, (B) his investments fail, (C) he becomes ill himself, or (D) Madame Bovary spends too much money at the opera.

_____ Madame Bovary has an affair with another man and in the process (A) dies, (B) goes heavily into debt, (C) has a conversion experience, or (D) apologizes to her husband, Charles.

_____ Ultimately, Madame Bovary dies (A) from a disease, (B) in an accident, (C) when Charles shoots her, or (D) by suicide.

_____ The novel ends with (A) Charles killing himself, (B) Charles remarrying, (C) Charles discovering the truth and dying with a broken heart, or (D) Charles returning to medical school.

_____ Berthe is (A) sent to work in a cotton mill, (B) forced to live with an aunt, (C) killed by a falling tree, or (D) just like her mother.

Suggested Vocabulary Words

A. And she detested her <u>instinctively</u>. At first she solaced herself by <u>allusions</u> that Charles did not understand, then by casual observations that he let pass for fear of a storm, finally by open <u>apostrophes</u> to which he knew not what to answer. (part 1, ch. 2)

B. Emma's heart beat rather faster when, her partner holding her by the tips of the fingers, she took her place in a line with the dancers, and waited for the first note to start. But her emotion soon <u>vanished</u>, and, <u>swaying</u> to the rhythm of the orchestra, she glided forward with slight movements of the neck. A smile rose to her lips at certain delicate phrases of the violin, that sometimes played alone while the other instruments were silent; one could hear the clear clink of the <u>louis d'or</u> that were being thrown down upon the card tables in the next room; then all struck again, the cornet-a-piston uttered its <u>sonorous</u> note, feet marked time, skirts swelled and <u>rustled</u>, hands touched and parted; the same eyes falling before you met yours again. (part 1, ch. 8)

C. "Do you think that to be an agriculturist it is necessary to have tilled the earth or fattened fowls oneself? It is necessary rather to know the composition of the substances in question—the geological strata, the atmospheric actions, the quality of the soil, the minerals, the waters, the density of the different bodies, their capillarity, and what not. And one must be master of all the principles of hygiene in order to direct, criticize the construction of buildings, the feeding of animals, the diet of domestics. And, moreover, Madame Lefrançois, one must know botany, be able to distinguish between plants, you understand, which are the wholesome and those that are deleterious, which are unproductive and which nutritive, if it is well to pull them up here and re-sow them there, to propagate some, destroy others; in brief, one must keep pace with science by means of pamphlets and public papers, be always on the alert to find out improvements." (part 2, ch. 8)

D. And fixing her eyes upon an embossed carabine, that shone against its panoply, "But when one is so poor one doesn't have silver on the butt of one's gun. (part 3, ch. 8)

E. The other went on talking agriculture, cattle, pasturage, filling out with banal phrases all the gaps where an allusion might slip in. Charles was not listening to him; Rodolphe noticed it, and he followed the succession of memories that crossed his face. This gradually grew redder; the nostrils throbbed fast, the lips quivered. There was at last a moment when Charles, full of a somber fury, fixed his eyes on Rodolphe, who, in something of fear, stopped talking. But soon the same look of weary lassitude came back to his face. (part 3, ch. 11)

Discussion Questions

A. How did you like the ending? Would you change it?

B. Compare Madame Bovary with Don Quixote.

C. Critic Mark Tunnell expresses sympathy for Madame Bovary:

> We cannot help noticing that Flaubert displayed a marked reluctance to give due weight to what was valid and genuine in

Emma. She was not, as Henry James alleged, a woman who was "naturally depraved." She possessed a number of solid virtues which were deliberately played down by the novelist. It was after all to her credit that she possessed too much sensibility to fit comfortably into the appalling provincial society of Yonville-l'Abbaye and it was her misfortune that she was not big enough to find a way out of the dilemma. We cannot withhold our approval from her attempts to improve her mind or from the pride that she took in her personal appearance and in the running of her house.

Do you agree?

D. Contrast the worldview clashes that occur between Madame Bovary and her husband.

Middlemarch

George Eliot

 Confined by the terms of her late husband's will, an idealistic young Victorian woman throws herself into the struggle for medical reforms advocated by a visionary doctor. Not only is *Middlemarch* Eliot's finest work; it also is probably the best English prose novel ever written. By the way, "George Eliot" is the pseudonym of Mary Ann (or Marian) Evans.

Objective Test

_____ Both and Rosamond and Lydgate think of courtship and marriage (A) in terms of ideals taken directly from conventional storybooks, (B) from a marriage manual, or (C) from the Bible.

_____ Dorothea's husband (A) leaves her, (B) is a millionaire, or (C) dies.

_____ Mary refuses to marry Fred if he (A) becomes a doctor, (B) becomes a pastor, or (C) continues to work at night.

_____ Dorothea has a passion for (A) Chinese checkers, (B) the poor, or (C) medical reform.

_____ *Middlemarch* (A) refuses to present a typical Victorian marriage, (B) tries to advance women's liberation, or (C) has very unhealthy women.

Suggested Vocabulary Words

A. Dorothea by this time had looked deep into the <u>ungauged</u> reservoir of Mr. Casaubon's mind, seeing reflected there in vague <u>labyrinthine</u> <u>extension</u> every quality she herself brought; had opened much of her own experience to him, and had understood from him the scope of his great work, also of attractively labyrinthine extent. For he had been as instructive as Milton's "<u>affable</u> <u>archangel</u>;" and with something of the archangelic manner he told her how he had undertaken to show (what indeed had been attempted before, but not with that <u>thoroughness</u>, justice of comparison, and effectiveness of arrangement at which Mr. Casaubon aimed) that all the mythical systems or erratic mythical fragments in the world were corruptions of a tradition originally revealed. Having once mastered the true position and taken a firm footing there, the vast field of mythical constructions became intelligible, nay, <u>luminous</u> with the reflected light of correspondences." (ch. 3)

B. "What do you think of that for a fine bit of <u>antithesis</u>?" said the German, searching in his friend's face for responding admiration, but going on volubly without waiting for any other answer. "There lies antique beauty, not <u>corpse-like</u> even in death, but arrested in the complete contentment of its sensuous perfection: and here stands beauty in its breathing life, with the consciousness of Christian centuries in its bosom. But she should be dressed as a nun; I think she looks almost what you call a Quaker; I would dress her as a nun in my picture. However, she is married; I saw her wedding-ring on that wonderful left hand, otherwise I should have thought the <u>sallow</u> <u>Geistlicher</u> was her father. I saw him parting from her a good while ago, and just now I found her in that <u>magnificent</u> pose. Only think! he is perhaps rich, and would like to have her portrait taken. Ah! it is no use looking after her—there she goes! Let us follow her home!" (ch. 19)

C. "I am aware of that. The only course is to try by all means, direct and indirect, to <u>moderate</u> and vary his occupations. With a happy <u>concurrence</u> of circumstances, there is, as I said, no immediate danger from that <u>affection</u> of the heart, which I believe to have been the cause of his late attack." (ch. 30)

D. "Close the book now, my dear. We will resume our work to-morrow. I have <u>deferred</u> it too long, and would gladly see it completed. But you observe that the principle on which my selection is made, is to give adequate, and not <u>disproportionate</u> illustration to each of the theses <u>enumerated</u> in my introduction, as at present sketched. You have perceived that distinctly, Dorothea?" (ch. 48)

Discussion Questions

A. Most critics feel that this novel is vastly superior to other Victorian novels (e.g., *Wuthering Heights*). Do you agree? Why? What makes this novel superior?

B. Why were so many British Victorian novels written by women?

C. What actor would you cast for Dorothea?

Les Misérables

Victor Hugo

*L*es Misérables is set during the great 1848 nationalist French revolution. It introduced to Western literature one of its most memorable protagonists, convict Jean Valjean. Hugo related Valjean's emergence from bitter unforgivingness to tranquil peace. A critical foil (contrasting figure) was the obsessive Inspector Javert. Hugo was masterful in his characterizations. The characters retained their epic proportions and personify the major theme of redemption. In the midst of aberrant worldviews such as Naturalism (e.g., Stephen Crane) in America, it is quite refreshing to read of such strong Theism. Hugo has blessed us all with this memorable story of hope.

Objective Test

_____ In 1815, Charles-François-Bienvenu Myriel, Bishop of Digne, is (A) 65 years old, (B) 75 years old, (C) 45 years old, or (D) 55 years old.

_____ Jean Valjean was imprisoned for (A) stealing bread, (B) murder, (C) assaulting the Bishop, or (D) tax evasion.

_____ Inspector Javert is obsessed with capturing Valjean because (A) he feels responsible for his original escape, (B) Valjean hurt Javert's sister, or (C) there is a big reward on Valjean's head.

_____ Valjean takes care of Cosette because (A) she is his granddaughter, (B) she is a handicapped neighbor, (C) he promised Cosette's mom that he would take care of her, or (D) he needs to pretend to be a father.

_____ Cosette falls in love with (A) Jacques, (B) Marius, or
(C) André.

Suggested Vocabulary Words

A. Although this detail has no connection whatever with the real
substance of what we are about to relate, it will not be <u>superfluous</u>, if
merely for the sake of exactness in all points, to mention here the various <u>rumors</u> and remarks which had been in circulation about him from
the very moment when he arrived in the diocese. (vol. 1, ch. 1)

B. Whether this penalty, complicated by successive <u>aggravations</u> for
attempts at escape, had not ended in becoming a sort of <u>outrage perpe-
trated</u> by the stronger upon the feebler, a crime of society against the
individual, a crime which was being committed afresh every day, a
crime which had lasted nineteen years. (vol. 1, ch. 7)

C. This 1815 was a sort of <u>lugubrious</u> April, . . . a <u>recrudescence</u> of
divine right. (vol. 2, ch. 8)

D. And, on abandoning society, he had <u>immured</u> himself in his
habits. The principal one, and that which was <u>invariable</u>, was to keep
his door absolutely closed during the day, and never to receive any one
whatever except in the evening. (vol. 3, ch. 7)

E. The <u>vicissitudes</u> of flight . . . The New Building, which was the
most cracked and <u>decrepit</u> thing to be seen anywhere in the world, was
the weak point in the prison. (vol. 4, ch. 3)

F. These <u>felicities</u> are the true ones. (vol. 5, ch. 2)

Discussion Questions

A. Here is Hugo's description of Jean Valjean's imprisonment:
"Jean Valjean had entered the galleys sobbing and shuddering; he
emerged impassive. He had entered in despair; he emerged gloomy." Do
you think Jean Valjean is unjustly imprisoned?

B. Is there a time when violating the law might be necessary? Is Valjean's crime morally acceptable?

C. Why does the Bishop overlook Jean Valjean's crime?

D. In what way does the Bishop represent Christ?

E. How does Jean Valjean repay the Bishop?

F. Discuss how Inspector Javert develops as a character?

G. Why does Hugo have Javert commit suicide? Is he reconciled with Jean Valjean?

H. What is Cosette's role in this novel?

Moby Dick

Herman Melville

Written by one of America's most controversial authors, *Moby Dick* is a powerful epic. Herman Melville recounts the memorable quest of Captain Ahab, who lost a leg in an earlier battle with the white whale, Moby Dick, and is determined to catch the beast and destroy it. By the time readers meet Ahab, he is a vengeful, terrifying figure. His enemy is not merely a whale; this monster of the deep represents the unknown, the unquantifiable.

Moby Dick has many different levels. On one level it is a simple story, one that can be understood by the young reader. On another level scholars have pondered and debated for years the symbolism and complexity that Melville has woven into this classic.

Objective Test

_____ The narrator is (A) Melville, (B) Ahab, (C) Queequeg, or (D) Ishmael.

_____ Before the *Pequod* sails, Ishmael stops at (A) a chapel, (B) a market, (C) home, or (D) the post office.

_____ Queequeg is (A) the name of Ahab's dog, (B) a Native who is also a master harpooner, (C) second in command, or (D) a New Bedford native.

_____ During the quest thunder destroys the compass. Ahab decides to (A) return home, (B) follow the tides, (C) build another compass, or (D) use his own instincts.

_____ Ahab dies when he (A) is attached to his own line, (B) is eaten by Moby Dick, or (C) falls to the deck of the ship.

Suggested Vocabulary Words

A. What do you see?—Posted like silent <u>sentinels</u> all around the town, stand thousands upon thousands of mortal men fixed in ocean <u>reveries</u>. (ch. 1)

B. Should you ever be athirst in the great American desert, try this experiment, if your caravan happen to be supplied with a <u>metaphysical</u> professor. (ch. 1)

C. Affected by the <u>solemnity</u> of the scene, there was a <u>wondering</u> gaze of <u>incredulous</u> curiosity in his <u>countenance</u>. (ch. 7)

D. In behalf of the dignity of whaling, I would <u>fain</u> advance <u>naught</u> but <u>substantiated</u> facts. But after <u>embattling</u> his facts, an <u>advocate</u> who should wholly <u>suppress</u> a not unreasonable surmise, which might tell <u>eloquently</u> upon his cause—such an advocate, would he not be blame-worthy? (ch. 25)

E. Now, with the <u>subordinate</u> <u>phantoms</u>, what wonder remained soon <u>waned</u> away; for in a whaler wonders soon wane. (ch. 50)

F. "Yes, I may as well," said the surgeon, coolly. "I was about observing, sir, before Captain Boomer's <u>facetious</u> interruption, that spite of my best and severest <u>endeavors</u>, the wound kept getting worse and worse; the truth was, sir, it was as ugly <u>gaping</u> wound as surgeon ever saw; more than two feet and several inches long. (ch. 100)

G. It was a clear steel-blue day. The <u>firmaments</u> of air and sea were hardly separable in that all-pervading azure; only, the <u>pensive</u> air was transparently pure and soft, with a woman's look, and the <u>robust</u> and man-like sea heaved with long, strong, <u>lingering</u> swells, as Samson's chest in his sleep. (ch. 132)

H. While Daggoo and Queequeg were stopping the <u>strained</u> planks; and as the whale swimming out from them, turned, and showed one entire flank as he shot by them again; at that moment a quick cry went up. Lashed round and round to the fish's back; <u>pinioned</u> in the turns upon turns in which, during the past night, the whale had reeled the <u>involutions</u> of the lines around him, the half torn body of the Parsee was seen; his <u>sable</u> raiment frayed to shreds; his <u>distended</u> eyes turned full upon old Ahab. (ch. 135)

Discussion Questions

A. The critic Alfred Kazin writes:

> Ahab . . . is a hero; we cannot insist enough on that. Melville believed in the heroic and he specifically wanted to cast his hero on American lines—someone noble by nature, not by birth, who would have "not the dignity of kings and robes, but that abounding dignity which has no robed investiture." Ahab sinned against man and God, and like his namesake in the Old Testament, becomes "a wicked king." But Ahab is not just a fanatic who leads the whole crew to their destruction; he is a hero of thought who is trying, by terrible force, to reassert man's place in nature. And it is the struggle that Ahab incarnates that makes him so magnificent a voice, thundering in Shakespearean rhetoric, storming at the gates of the inhuman, awful world. Ahab is trying to give man, in one awful, final assertion that his will does mean something, a feeling of relatedness with his world.

Do you agree that Ahab is a "hero?"

B. The critic Richard B. Sewall describes Ahab:

> As Ahab in his whaleboat watches the Pequod founder under the attack of the whale, he realizes that all is lost. He faces his "lonely death on lonely life," denied even "the last fond pride of meanest shipwrecked captains," the privilege of going down with his ship. But here, at the nadir of his fortunes, he sees that in his greatest suffering lies his greatest glory. He dies spitting hate at the whale, but he does not die cynically or in bitterness. The whale conquers—but is "unconquering." The "god bullied

hull" goes down "death glorious." What Ahab feels is not joy or serenity or goodness at the heart of things. But with his sense of elation, even triumph, at having persevered to the end, there is also a note of reconciliation: "Oh now I feel my topmost greatness lies in my topmost grief." This is not reconciliation with the whale, or with the malice in the universe, but it is a reconciliation of Ahab with Ahab. Whatever justice, order, or equivalence there is, he has found not in the universe but in himself.

. . . In finally coming to terms with existence (though too late), he is tragic man; to the extent that he transcends it, finds "greatness" in suffering, he is a tragic hero.

Paraphrase Sewall and agree or disagree with him.

C. Some scholars argue that *Moby Dick* is a transitional novel from the Romanticism of Emerson to the Naturalism of a Stephen Crane. They argue that Ahab is the budding Naturalist who sees the subjective universe come unglued. In one scene Ahab watches a dying whale turn to face the sun. Ahab identifies with the great beast he's slain, for both are fire-worshipers. Both are in a futile struggle with "God." What do you think?

D. The harpooner, Queequeg, a classic foil, is a pagan who rejects Christianity. Obviously, Melville admires this creature. At the Spouter-Inn, Ishmael at first is terrified to be near Queequeg, but he soon concludes that Queequeg is more noble than most of Ishmael's Christian friends. "We cannibals must help these Christians," Queequeg says after he rescues from drowning the very man who had been rude to him moments before. What is Melville trying to say to his reader by creating a character like Queequeg?

E. On one level Moby Dick is a stupid animal. On the other hand, he seems to represent so much more. He appears to be ubiquitous, alternately evil and then good. What do you think?

F. If you were the editor of *Moby Dick*, would you keep the lengthy sections on whaling? Do they make the novel more or less effective?

My Antonia

Willa Cather

 Willa Cather's *My Antonia* is considered one of the most significant American novels of the twentieth century. Set during the great migration west to settle the plains of the North American continent, the narrative follows Antonia Shimerda. She is a pioneer who comes to Nebraska as a child and grows with the country, inspiring a childhood friend, Jim Burden, to write her life story. The novel is important both for its literary aesthetic and as a portrayal of important aspects of American social ideals and history, particularly the centrality of migration to American culture.

Objective Test

_____ The story line of this novel is that Jim Burden, a successful lawyer, (A) talks about his mother, Antonia; (B) remembers growing up in Nebraska; or (C) returns unexpectedly to his Nebraska home.

_____ Burden first arrives in Nebraska at the age of (A) 10, (B) 12, (C) 14, or (D) 16.

_____ He makes the trip west to live with his grandparents because (A) he has always wanted to see the West, (B) his parents have left him, or (C) he is an orphan.

_____ On the train going out west, Jim meets (A) a Bohemian immigrant family traveling in the same direction, (B) Wild Bill Cody, (C) Billy the Kid, or (D) his uncle.

_____ Jim makes friends with (A) Barbara, (B) Nellie, (C) David, or
(D) Antonia.

_____ Antonia's mother (A) dies of cancer, (B) returns to her native
land, (C) commits suicide, or (D) dies of pneumonia.

_____ Jim attends (A) Harvard, (B) the University of Chicago,
(C) Yale, or (D) Stanford.

_____ Antonia (A) dies, (B) has a child out of wedlock, (C) returns to
Bohemia, or (D) visits Jim.

_____ Jim returns home in twenty years to find (A) his home
destroyed, (B) Antonia happily married, or (C) his grandparents
dead.

_____ Antonia (A) stays in Nebraska but remembers Jim, (B) leaves
with Jim, or (C) dies suddenly.

Suggested Vocabulary Words

A. As for Jim, no disappointments have been severe enough to chill
his naturally romantic and <u>ardent</u> <u>disposition</u>. (introduction)

B. <u>Magnified</u> across the distance by the horizontal light, it stood out
against the sun, was exactly contained within the circle of the disk; the
handles, the tongue, the share—black against the <u>molten</u> red. (book 2,
ch. 14)

C. She lent herself to <u>immemorial</u> human attitudes which we recognize by instinct as universal and true. I had not been mistaken. She was
a <u>battered</u> woman now, not a lovely girl; but she still had that something
which fires the imagination, could still stop one's breath for a moment
by a look or <u>gesture</u> that somehow revealed the meaning in common
things. (book 5, ch. 1)

Discussion Questions

A. Who is the protagonist?

B. What is Jim's relationship with Antonia?

C. Does Willa Cather, a woman, effectively present the perspective of Jim, a man?

D. In this novel is Cather agitating for social change?

Old Indian Legends

Zitkala-¨Sa

Native American Zitkala-¨Sa wrote these words as an introduction to her work of retelling these inherited stories:

These legends are relics of our country's once virgin soil. These and many others are the tales the little black-haired aborigine loved so much to hear beside the night fire. For him the personified elements and other spirits played in a vast world right around the center fire of the wigwam. Iktomi, the snare weaver, Iya, the Eater, and Old Double-Face are not wholly fanciful creatures. There were other worlds of legendary folk for the young aborigine, such as "The Star-Men of the Sky," "The Thunder Birds Blinking Zigzag Lightning," and "The Mysterious Spirits of Trees and Flowers." Under an open sky, nestling close to the earth, the old Dakota story-tellers have told me these legends. In both Dakotas, North and South, I have often listened to the same story told over again by a new story-teller. While I recognized such a legend without the least difficulty, I found the renderings varying much in little incidents. Generally one helped the other in restoring some lost link in the original character of the tale. And now I have tried to transplant the native spirit of these tales—root and all—into the English language, since America in the last few centuries has acquired a second tongue. . . . If it be true that much lies "in the eye of the beholder," then in the American aborigine as in any other race, sincerity of belief, though it were based upon mere optical illusion, demands a little respect. After all he seems at heart much like other peoples.

Objective Test

_____ What kills the unwary ducks? (A) Hunger, (B) anger, (C) curiosity, or (D) lightning.

_____ Iktomi calls his god (A) Grandfather, (B) God, (C) Lord, or (D) King.

_____ The moral of the story "The Badgers and the Bear" is that (A) one should work hard and save for winter, (B) one should take care of oneself first, or (D) if one returns evil for good, evil will also soon come to that evildoer.

_____ The avenger is (A) a lion, (B) a spirit, (C) a warrior, or (D) a demon.

_____ Patkasa is easily tricked but gets the last laugh on (A) Dancing Wolf, (B) Iktomi, (C) Sharp Arrow, or (D) Running Brook.

Suggested Vocabulary Words

A. Iktomi is a <u>wily</u> fellow. (legend 1)

B. His black nose was dry and <u>parched</u>. (legend 6)

C. Wordless, like a <u>bashful</u> Indian maid, the <u>avenger</u> ate in silence the food set before him on the ground in front of his crossed shins. (legend 8)

D. Patkasa was always ready to believe the words of <u>scheming</u> people and to do the little favors any one asked of him. However, on this occasion, he did not answer "Yes, my friend." He realized that Iktomi's <u>flattering</u> tongue had made him foolish. (legend 9)

Discussion Questions

A. Do you agree with this statement by the author, Zitkala-"Sa? "The old legends of America belong quite as much to the blue-eyed little patriot as to the black-haired aborigine. And when they are grown tall like the wise grown-ups may they not lack interest in a further study of Indian folklore, a study which so strongly suggests our near kinship with the rest of humanity and points a steady finger toward the great brotherhood of mankind, and by which one is so forcibly impressed with the possible earnestness of life as seen through the teepee door!"

B. Moral fables with animals as characters are quite effective. Why?

C. Some Native Americans claim that the God of their fathers is the same God as the Judeo-Christian God of the European-Americans. Do you agree?

D. Native Americans have been sorely wronged by European Americans. They were betrayed and slaughtered by settlers, lynching gangs, and regiments from the ruling authorities. Today, some Christians are calling for a massive repentance on the part of European-Americans. Do you think it is advisable for contemporary people to confess the sins of their fathers and mothers and to offer some sort of restitution?

Oliver Twist

Charles Dickens

 *Oliver Twist* has long been one of Charles Dickens's best-loved novels. In a wonderfully suspenseful, if predictable, novel, Charles Dickens tells the story of a poor orphan boy in his journey from a harsh workhouse to fame and fortune. In spite of incipient and frequent coincidences, this novel remains one of the great Victorian novels of the nineteenth century.

Objective Test

_____ Oliver Twist is born in (A) a run-down hospital, (B) a tenement, (C) a workhouse, or (D) Ireland.

_____ His mother is (A) found on the street and dies just after Oliver's birth, (B) an unknown relative of Queen Victoria, (C) sick with the flu, or (D) confused and lonely.

_____ After several adventures, Oliver works for (A) Appleby, (B) Fagin, (C) Nancy, or (D) Jack.

_____ While bungling a burglary, Oliver is captured by (A) Nancy, (B) Fagin, (C) Dick, or (D) Mr. Brownlow.

_____ Mr. Brownlow is surprised about (A) Oliver's resemblance to his deceased son, (B) how young Oliver is, (C) how strong Oliver is, or (D) Oliver's resemblance to a daughter.

_____ Bill Sikes and Nancy (A) send Oliver some food, (B) kidnap Oliver and take him back to Fagin, or (C) go to the police.

_____ It is revealed that (A) Oliver's mother left behind a gold locket when she died, (B) Oliver is very rich, or (C) that Oliver has a rare disease.

_____ Monks is (A) a rich man, (B) Oliver's half brother, or (C) a good friend to Oliver.

_____ Rose is actually (A) Fagin's mother, (B) Fagin's sister, (C) Fagin's wife, or (D) Oliver's aunt.

_____ Oliver (A) inherits a fortune, (B) dies suddenly, or (C) decides to live with Fagin.

Suggested Vocabulary Words

A. In great families, when an advantageous place cannot be obtained, either in possession, reversion, remainder, or expectancy, for the young man who is growing up, it is a very general custom to send him to sea. The board, in imitation of so wise and salutary an example, took counsel together on the expediency of shipping off Oliver Twist, in some small trading vessel bound to a good unhealthy port. This suggested itself as the very best thing that could possibly be done with him: the probability being, that the skipper would flog him to death, in a playful mood, some day after dinner, or would knock his brains out with an iron bar; both pastimes being, as is pretty generally known, very favourite and common recreations among gentleman of that class. The more the case presented itself to the board, in this point of view, the more manifold the advantages of the step appeared; so, they came to the conclusion that the only way of providing for Oliver effectually, was to send him to sea without delay. (ch. 4)

B. It is the custom on the stage, in all good murderous melodramas, to present the tragic and the comic scenes, in as regular alternation, as the layers of red and white in a side of streaky bacon. The hero sinks upon his straw bed, weighed down by fetters and misfortunes; in the next scene, his faithful but unconscious squire regales the audience with a comic song. We behold, with throbbing bosoms, the heroine in the grasp of a proud and ruthless baron: her virtue and her life alike in danger, drawing forth her dagger to preserve the one at the cost of the other; and just as our expectations are wrought up to the highest pitch, a whistle is heard, and we are straightway transported to the great hall of the castle; where a grey-headed <u>seneschal</u> sings a funny chorus with a funnier body of <u>vassals</u>, who are free of all sorts of places, from church vaults to palaces, and roam about in company, carolling <u>perpetually</u>. (ch. 17)

C. "By mine," replied Mr. Brownlow. 'Those persons are <u>indemnified</u> by me. If you complain of being deprived of your liberty—you had power and opportunity to retrieve it as you came along, but you deemed it advisable to remain quiet—I say again, throw yourself for protection on the law. I will appeal to the law too; but when you have gone too far to recede, do not sue to me for <u>leniency</u>, when the power will have passed into other hands; and do not say I plunged you down the gulf into which you rushed, yourself." (ch. 49)

D. I would <u>fain</u> linger yet with a few of those among whom I have so long moved, and share their happiness by endeavouring to depict it. (ch. 53)

Discussion Questions

A. How does Dickens develop his most memorable villains, Fagin and the Artful Dodger?

B. How important is the environment to human nature? Do living conditions determine what happens to people? If so, the reader is to believe that those of Dickens's people who are deprived of good influences are doomed, while those who enjoy love and economic wealth are good. Respond to this view.

C. Love is a powerful theme in this novel. Explain.

D. Discuss the use of coincidence in this novel. Was its use excessive?

E. What was the narrative point of view? Why did Dickens choose this narrative technique?

F. Respond to the following by critic Arnold Kettle:

> The plot of *Oliver Twist* is very complicated and very unsatisfactory. It is a conventional plot about a wronged woman, an illegitimate baby, a destroyed will, a death-bed secret, a locket thrown into the river, a wicked elder brother and the restoration to the hero of name and property. That it should depend on a number of extraordinary coincidences (the only two robberies in which Oliver is called upon to participate are perpetrated, fortuitously, on his father's best friend and his mother's sister's guardian!) is the least of its shortcomings. Literal probability is not an essential quality of an adequate plot. Nor is it a criticism that Dickens should have used his plot for the purposes of serial-publication, i.e., to provide a climax at the end of each instalment and the necessary twists and manoeuvres which popular serialization invited. (It is not a fault in a dramatist that he should provide a climax to each act of his play, and the serial instalment is no more or less artificial a convention than the act of a play.) What we may legitimately object to in the plot of *Oliver Twist* is the very substance of that plot in its relation to the essential pattern of the novel.

The Pearl

John Steinbeck

 Kino, a poor Mexican pearl fisherman, finds an extremely valuable pearl. Yet, instead of bringing great rewards, the pearl brings tragedy and misfortune to Kino and his family. Finally, poor Kino in disgust and grief returns the pearl to the ocean.

Objective Test

_____ Kino originally decides to pray for a great pearl because (A) his son was bitten by a scorpion and he needs money for medicine, (B) he needs money for the dentist, (C) he is tired of living so poorly, or (D) his son has a chance to attend the university and he needs money to send him.

_____ Who suggests that the pearl be abandoned? (A) Kino, (B) the son, (C) Juana, or (D) the doctor.

_____ While escaping from his pursuers, (A) Juana is killed, (B) Coyotito is killed, (C) Kino loses the pearl, or (D) Kino falls and is drowned.

_____ The only friends Kino seems to have are (A) Juan and Apolonia, (B) the priest and his housekeeper, (C) Jose and Maria, or (D) the doctor and his wife.

_____ This story is (A) an epic, (B) a narrative poem, (C) a fable, or (D) a parable.

Suggested Vocabulary Words

A. If this story is a <u>parable</u> everyone takes his own meaning from it. (epilogue)

B. Kino watched with the <u>detachment</u> of God while a dusty ant <u>frantically</u> tried to escape the sand trap an ant lion had dug for him. (ch. 1)

C. Kino looked at his neighbors <u>fiercely</u>. . . . Kino's face shone with <u>prophecy</u>. (ch. 3)

D. And once some large animal <u>lumbered</u> away, crackling the undergrowth as it went. (ch. 6)

Discussion Questions

A. How did you feel when Kino throws the pearl back into the ocean? Would you have found a better way to handle this situation?

B. Why does Kino throw the pearl into the ocean?

C. How does Steinbeck use foreshadowing in his book?

D. How does Steinbeck use ants to make some points?

E. How does Steinbeck present the priest in *The Pearl*?

F. Even though Juana knows that the pearl will cause disaster, she returns it to her husband after it was lost. Why would she do this?

G. What does this book tell you about the way the Naturalist Steinbeck sees God?

The Prince

Niccolò Machiavelli

 Perhaps no philosophical book has been misread and misunderstood more than *The Prince*. Simply, Machiavelli wrote a guidebook on leadership for his friend Lorenzo de' Medici. The volume would be similar to contemporary leadership books written by John Maxwell and others. It was the first book of its kind, and it still serves as a model for later politicians and other leaders.

Objective Test

_____ *The Prince* is concerned with (A) totalitarian regimes, (B) democracies, (C) representative democracies, or (D) socialist governments.

_____ Personal virtue makes (A) bad government, (B) good government, (C) strong governments, or (D) sensitive governments.

_____ Likewise, immoral behavior may be necessary to (A) satisfy the majority, (B) stop enemies from taking over the state, (C) rule generously, or (D) rule effectively.

_____ The appearance of virtue may be more important, therefore, than (A) actual evil, (B) actual virtue, (C) a good prime minister, or (D) a strong parliament.

_____ Machiavelli offers advice on (A) how to choose a leader, (B) how to run a military, (C) how to fight a battle, or (D) how to destroy enemies.

Suggested Vocabulary Words

A. But the difficulties occur in a new principality. And firstly, if it be not entirely new, but is, as it were, a member of a state which, taken collectively, may be called composite, the changes arise chiefly from an inherent difficulty which there is in all new principalities; for men change their rulers willingly, hoping to better themselves, and this hope induces them to take up arms against him who rules: wherein they are deceived, because they afterwards find by experience they have gone from bad to worse. This follows also on another natural and common necessity, which always causes a new prince to burden those who have submitted to him with his soldiery and with infinite other hardships which he must put upon his new acquisition. (ch. 3)

B. Therefore it is unnecessary for a prince to have all the good qualities I have enumerated, but it is very necessary to appear to have them. And I shall dare to say this also, that to have them and always to observe them is injurious, and that to appear to have them is useful; to appear merciful, faithful, humane, religious, upright, and to be so, but with a mind so framed that should you require not to be so, you may be able and know how to change to the opposite. (ch. 18)

C. I do not wish to leave out an important branch of this subject, for it is a danger from which princes are with difficulty preserved, unless they are very careful and discriminating. It is that of flatterers, of whom courts are full, because men are so self-complacent in their own affairs, and in a way so deceived in them, that they are preserved with difficulty from this pest, and if they wish to defend themselves they run the danger of falling into contempt. Because there is no other way of guarding oneself from flatterers except letting men understand that to tell you the truth does not offend you; but when every one may tell you the truth, respect for you abates. (ch. 23)

D. But confining myself more to the particular, I say that a prince may be seen happy to-day and ruined to-morrow without having shown any change of disposition or character. This, I believe, arises firstly from causes that have already been discussed at length, namely, that the prince who relies entirely on fortune is lost when it changes. I believe also that he will be successful who directs his actions according to the spirit of the times, and that he whose actions do not accord with the times will not be successful. Because men are seen, in affairs that lead to the end which every man has before him, namely, glory and riches, to get there by various methods; one with caution, another with haste; one by force, another by skill; one by patience, another by its opposite; and each one succeeds in reaching the goal by a different method. One can also see of two cautious men the one <u>attain</u> his end, the other fail; and similarly, two men by different observances are equally successful, the one being cautious, the other <u>impetuous</u>; all this arises from nothing else than whether or not they conform in their methods to the spirit of the times. This follows from what I have said, that two men working differently bring about the same effect, and of two working similarly, one attains his object and the other does not. (ch. 25)

Discussion Questions

A. Contrast Machiavelli's view of leadership with biblical views of leadership.

B. Does Machiavelli think that history makes rulers, or that rulers make history?

C. Machiavelli values stability and productivity above virtue. Respond.

D. Machiavelli, in effect, argues for a secular government separate from a religious government. Explain.

E. Why was Machiavelli popular in Germany during 1932–45?

Pygmalion

George Bernard Shaw

Two old English friends meet one night. One bets the other that he can, with his knowledge of phonetics, convince high London society that, in a matter of months, he will be able to transform the ordinary Eliza Doolittle into a highly refined Victorian English woman.

Objective Test

_____ The names of the two gentlemen who make a bet are (A) Freddy and Alfred, (B) Mark and David, or (C) Professor Higgins and Colonel Pickerings.

_____ Professor Higgins plans to use what to ameliorate (improve) his subject? (A) Poise training, (B) phonetics, or (C) behavior modification.

_____ The subject is (A) Mary, (B) Susan, or (C) Eliza.

_____ The problem is (A) what to do with the subject when the experiment is over, (B) how to change the subject, or (C) how to keep the subject from spending too much money.

_____ At the end of the play Eliza (A) goes back to her former life, (B) is rich, or (C) marries Freddy.

Suggested Vocabulary Words

A. She sits down on the <u>plinth</u> of the column, sorting her flowers, on the lady's right. She is not at all an attractive person. She is perhaps eighteen, perhaps twenty, hardly older. She wears a little sailor hat of black straw that has long been exposed to the dust and soot of London and has seldom if ever been brushed. Her hair needs washing rather badly: its <u>mousy</u> color can hardly be natural. She wears a <u>shoddy</u> black coat that reaches nearly to her knees and is shaped to her waist. She has a brown skirt with a <u>coarse</u> apron. Her boots are much the worse for wear. She is no doubt as clean as she can afford to be; but compared to the ladies she is very dirty. Her features are no worse than theirs; but their condition leaves something to be desired; and she needs the services of a dentist. (act 1)

B. We're all <u>intimidated</u>. Intimidated, maam: thats what we are. What is there for me if I chuck it but the workhouse in my old age? I have to dye my hair already to keep my job as a dustman. If I was one of the deserving poor, and had put by a bit, I could chuck it; but then why should I, acause the deserving poor might as well be millionaires for all the happiness they ever has. They dont know what happiness is. But I, as one of the undeserving poor, have nothing between me and the <u>pauper's</u> uniform but this here blasted three thousand a year that shoves me into the middle class. (act 5)

C. <u>Complications</u> <u>ensued</u>; but they were economic, not romantic. Freddy had no money and no occupation. His mother's <u>jointure</u>, a last relic of the <u>opulence</u> of Largelady Park, had enabled her to struggle along in Earlscourt with an air of <u>gentility</u>, but not to procure any serious secondary education for her children, much less give the boy a profession. A clerkship at thirty shillings a week was beneath Freddy's dignity, and extremely <u>distasteful</u> to him besides. (sequel)

Discussion Questions

A. Eliza Doolittle is a dynamic character who changes significantly through the play. How?

B. If you were to write another act to *Pygmalion*, what would it be?

C. Do you think Eliza marries Fred?

D. Compare the Audrey Hepburn film version called *My Fair Lady* (1956) with *Pygmalion*.

A Raisin in the Sun

Lorraine Hansberry

A Raisin in the Sun, written by Lorraine Hansberry, was a great controversial play of the 1960s. It is the story of an African-American family struggling to make the American dream come true for itself. A pioneering work by a young African-American playwright, the play was a radically new representation of life among black people

Objective Test

_____ *A Raisin in the Sun* shows a few weeks in the life of the Youngers, an African-American family living (A) in South Carolina; (B) on the South Side of Chicago in the 1950s; (C) in Little Rock, Arkansas, in the 1950s; or (D) on the North Side of Pittsburgh in the 1960s.

_____ The family is receiving $10,000 from (A) a life insurance policy, (B) the lottery, (C) an inheritance, or (D) a rich uncle.

_____ The family decides to (A) go to Nigeria, (B) send a member to medical school, (C) buy a house in a white suburb, or (D) invest the money in the stock market.

_____ Their new white neighbors (A) welcome them with open arms, (B) burn a cross in their yard, (C) refuse to let them move, or (D) offer to buy the house from them.

_____ The plays ends with (A) the family members going their separate ways, (B) the family finding strength within itself,

(C) the mother dying, or (D) a youthful family member going to Harvard.

Suggested Vocabulary Words

A. No, thank you very much. Please. Well—to get right to the point I—I am sure you people must be aware of some of the incidents which have happened in <u>various</u> parts of the city when colored people have moved into certain areas—Well—because we have what I think is going to be a <u>unique</u> type of organization in American community life—not only do we deplore that kind of thing—but we are trying to do something about it. We feel—we feel that most of the trouble in this world, when you come right down to it—most of the trouble exists because people just don't sit down and talk to each other. (act 2)

B. You are looking at what a well-dressed Nigerian woman wears— Isn't it beautiful? Enough of this <u>assimilationist</u> junk! (act 2)

C. Be on my side for once! You saw what he just did, Mama! You saw him—down on his knees. Wasn't it you who taught me—to <u>despise</u> any man who would do that[?] Do what he's going to do. (act 3)

Discussion Questions

A. What statement is the author making about the importance of race?

B. How credible are the characters in the play?

C. How significant is the setting for this play?

The Return of the Native

Thomas Hardy

 The native who returns is Clym Yeobright, one of the most memorable pilgrims in Western literature. From Paris he comes back to the English pastoral area of Egdon Heath and, as is soon evident, all is not smooth. He is quickly taken by and marries the evil Eustacia Vye. The suffering that follows is truly terrible.

Objective Test

____ The novel opens with the plot already underway: (A) Diggory Venn has brought Clym Yeobright home; (B) Diggory Venn rides onto the heath with Thomasin Yeobright, whose marriage to Damon Wildeve has been delayed by an error in the marriage certificate; or (C) Diggory Venn is attacked by robbers.

____ Clym marries (A) Eustacia, (B) Thomasin, (C) Penelope, or (D) Daria.

____ Eustacia's dreams of moving to Paris are rejected by Clym, who wants to (A) move to Warsaw, (B) enter the priesthood, (C) open a country store, or (D) start a school in his native country.

____ Evil Eusticia (A) begins an affair with another man, (B) kills Clym, (C) runs away, or (D) burns down their house.

____ Clym's mother, Mrs. Yeobright, tries to visit Eustacia and Clym and is not allowed to enter. Feeling rejected by her son, she (A) leaves in anger, (B) succumbs to heat and snakebite on the walk home and dies, or (C) disinherits Clym.

_____ Blaming himself for the death of his mother, Clym (A) buys a nice gravestone, (B) resolves to be a better husband, (C) separates from Eustacia when he learns of her role in Mrs. Yeobright's death and of her continued relations with Wildeve, or (D) murders Eustacia.

_____ Wildeve and Eustacia try to leave town but (A) are struck by lightning, (B) change their minds, (C) commit suicide, or (D) both drown.

_____ Meanwhile, (A) Thomasin and Diggory marry, (B) Clym finds that his mother did not really die, or (C) the stock market crashes.

_____ Clym becomes a (A) miller, (B) captain, (C) preacher, or (D) farmer.

Suggested Vocabulary Words

A. Her reason for standing so dead still as the <u>pivot</u> of this circle of heath-country was just as <u>obscure</u>. Her extraordinary <u>fixity</u>, her <u>conspicuous</u> loneliness, her <u>heedlessness</u> of night, <u>betokened</u> among other things an <u>utter</u> absence of fear. A tract of country <u>unaltered</u> from that <u>sinister</u> condition which made Caesar anxious every year to get clear of its glooms before the autumnal <u>equinox</u>, a kind of landscape and weather which leads travellers from the South to describe our island as Homer's Cimmerian land, was not, on the face of it, friendly to women. (book 1, ch. 6)

B. Venn felt much astonishment at this <u>avowal</u>, though he did not show it clearly; that exhibition may greet remarks which are one remove from expectation, but it is usually withheld in complicated cases of two removes and upwards. "Indeed, miss," he replied. (book 2, ch. 7)

C. At length Clym reached the margin of a fir and beech plantation that had been enclosed from heath land in the year of his birth. Here the trees, laden heavily with their new and humid leaves, were now suffering more damage than during the highest winds of winter, when the boughs are especially disencumbered to do battle with the storm. The wet young beeches were undergoing amputations, bruises, cripplings, and harsh lacerations, from which the wasting sap would bleed for many a day to come, and which would leave scars visible till the day of their burning. Each stem was wrenched at the root, where it moved like a bone in its socket, and at every onset of the gale convulsive sounds came from the branches, as if pain were felt. In a neighbouring brake a finch was trying to sing; but the wind blew under his feathers till they stood on end, twisted round his little tail, and made him give up his song. (book 3, ch. 6)

D. The lad was in good spirits that day, for the Fifth of November had again come round, and he was planning yet another scheme to divert her from her too absorbing thoughts. For two successive years his mistress had seemed to take pleasure in lighting a bonfire on the bank overlooking the valley; but this year she had apparently quite forgotten the day and the customary deed. He was careful not to remind her, and went on with his secret preparations for a cheerful surprise, the more zealously that he had been absent last time and unable to assist. At every vacant minute he hastened to gather furze-stumps, thorn-tree roots, and other solid materials from the adjacent slopes, hiding them from cursory view. (book 5, ch. 5)

Discussion Questions

A. Discuss how Hardy uses coincidence to advance his plot. Is it appropriate?

B. Is there a clear-cut villain or hero in this novel?

C. What narrative technique does Hardy employ?

D. At the end of *The Return of the Native,* Hardy writes in a foot-note that the marriage of Thomasin and Diggory Venn was not the origi-nally planned ending to the novel. He asks the reader to choose the best ending. What do you think is the best ending?

E. Does Clem get what he deserves?

Sister Carrie

Theodore Dreiser

Americans were shocked by this nineteenth-century novel featuring the rise of an ordinary and even poor woman to social and financial prominence, for no apparent reason. She was not particularly virtuous, nor did she exhibit any other redeeming qualities. Likewise, they saw an upper-middle-class gentleman deteriorate into a street person, again, for no apparent reason.

Objective Test

_____ Sister Carrie tells the story of two characters: (A) Carrie Meeber and George Hurstwood, (B) Sister Carrie and Margaret Thurber, (C) Raymond Beale and Upton Sinclair, or (D) Bob Jones and Agnes Traylor.

_____ Carrie becomes a (A) bag lady, (B) mayor, (C) housewife, or (D) professional actress.

_____ George Hurstwood moves from (A) upper-middle-class prosperity to poverty, (B) poverty to upper-middle-class prosperity, (C) Oak Park to Wheaton, or (D) poverty to unbelievable riches.

_____ What makes all this incredible is that (A) they are both weak people, (B) they both are from Boston, (C) they both were poor at the beginning, or (D) they have no personal virtue that commends them to their fate.

_____ Hurstwood (A) is saved by Carrie, (B) joins the army, (C) commits suicide, or (D) regains his fortune.

Suggested Vocabulary Words

A. Carrie was certainly better than this man, as she was <u>superior</u>, mentally, to Drouet. She came fresh from the air of the village, the light of the country still in her eye. Here was neither <u>guile</u> nor <u>rapacity</u>. There were slight inherited traits of both in her, but they were <u>rudimentary</u>. She was too full of wonder and desire to be greedy. She still looked about her upon the great maze of the city without understanding. Hurstwood felt the bloom and the youth. He picked her as he would the fresh fruit of a tree. He felt as fresh in her presence as one who is taken out of the flash of summer to the first cool breath of spring. (ch. 13)

B. When Carrie reached her own room she had already fallen a <u>prey</u> to those doubts and misgivings which are ever the result of a lack of decision. She could not <u>persuade</u> herself as to the <u>advisability</u> of her promise, or that now, having given her word, she ought to keep it. She went over the whole ground in Hurstwood's absence, and discovered little objections that had not occurred to her in the warmth of the manager's argument. She saw where she had put herself in a <u>peculiar</u> light, namely, that of agreeing to marry when she was already supposedly married. She remembered a few things Drouet had done, and now that it came to walking away from him without a word, she felt as if she were doing wrong. Now, she was comfortably situated, and to one who is more or less afraid of the world, this is an urgent matter, and one which puts up strange, <u>uncanny</u> arguments. "You do not know what will come. There are miserable things outside. People go a-begging. Women are <u>wretched</u>. You never can tell what will happen. Remember the time you were hungry. Stick to what you have." (ch. 23)

C. Oh, Carrie, Carrie! Oh, blind <u>strivings</u> of the human heart! Onward, onward, it saith, and where beauty leads, there it follows. Whether it be the tinkle of a lone sheep bell o'er some quiet landscape, or the <u>glimmer</u> of beauty in <u>sylvan</u> places, or the show of soul in some passing eye, the heart knows and makes answer, following. It is when the feet weary and hope seems vain that the heartaches and the longings arise. Know, then, that for you is neither <u>surfeit</u> nor content. In your rocking-chair, by your window dreaming, shall you long, alone. In your rocking-chair, by your window, shall you dream such happiness as you may never feel. (ch. 47)

Discussion Questions

A. The main characters in this novel normally do not control their own fate. Neither Carrie nor Hurstwood live their lives through random circumstance. Their successes and failures have no moral value; this is a departure from the conventional literature of the period (such as *Wuthering Heights*). There seems to be an insidious, even evil power that is determining their fate. This is part of a Naturalistic worldview. What is Naturalism?

B. In what ways does Naturalism contradict the Bible?

C. What is the significance of this passage:

> And now Carrie had attained that which in the beginning seemed life's object, or at least, such fraction of it as human beings ever attain of their original desires. She could look about on her gowns and carriage, her furniture and bank account. Friends there were, as the world takes it—those who would bow and smile in acknowledgment of her success. For these she had once craved. Applause there was, and publicity—once far off, essential things, but now grown trivial and indifferent. Beauty also—her type of loveliness—and yet she was lonely. In her rocking-chair she sat, when not otherwise engaged—singing and dreaming. (ch. 47)

D. In what ways is the Captain the most moral person in the novel?

The Song of Roland

Turoldus (?)

The great medieval French epic poem *The Song of Roland* is as significant to the French as the Anglo-Saxon *Beowulf* is to the English. Charlemagne's nephew, the warrior Roland, fights bravely to his death in a legendary battle—one of the most memorable in Western literature, and rivaled only by the great fight scenes in Homer's *Iliad.* Against the backdrop of the struggle between Christianity and Islam, *The Song of Roland* remains a vivid portrayal of knightly chivalry and adventure. It is among the first great literary works of French culture and was likely used orally in celebrations long before it was written, perhaps by an obscure monk named Turoldus.

Objective Test

_____ The epic poem begins with Charlemagne's army fighting the (A) Saracens, (B) English, (C) Germans, or (D) French.

_____ Terrified of the might of Charlemagne's army of Franks, the Saracen leader Marsilla sends out messengers to Charlemagne, (A) asking for terms of surrender, (B) bearing his daughter as a ransom, (C) promising to kill Charlemagne and his army, or (D) promising treasure and Marsilla's conversion to Christianity if the Franks will go back to France.

_____ Charlemagne and his men (A) refuse, (B) are tired of fighting and decide to accept this peace offer, (C) surrender, or (D) attack anyway.

_____ Ganelon, Roland's father-in-law, (A) dies to protect his king, (B) flees to Italy, (C) betrays Charlemagne, or (D) kills Roland.

_____ The Saracen army attacks Charlemagne's army, and the Frankish counterattack is led by (A) Roland, (B) Ganelon, (C) Charlemagne, or (D) Marsilla.

Suggested Vocabulary Words

A. The Emperor Karl of gentle France / Hither hath come for our dire mischance. / Nor host to meet him in battle line, / or power to shatter his power, is mine. / Speak, my sages; your counsel lend. (2)

B. And he said to the king, "Be not dismayed: / Proffer to Karl, the haughty and high, / Lowly friendship and fealty; / Ample largess lay at his feet, / Bear and lion and greyhound fleet. (3)

C. With them many a gallant lance, / Full fifteen thousand of gentle France. / The cavaliers sit upon carpets white, / Playing at tables for their delight: / The older and sager sit at the chess, / The bachelors fence with a light address. (8)

D. Ganelon rides under olives high, / And comes the Saracen envoys nigh. / Blancandrin lingers until they meet, / And in cunning converse each other greet. (19)

E. I will not sound on mine ivory horn: / It shall never be spoken of me in scorn, / That for heathen felons one blast I blew; / I may not dishonor my lineage true. (88)

Discussion Questions

A. How does Oliver function in this poem?

B. How does the author build suspense?

C. How convincing a villain is Ganelon?

D. Is Roland's death necessary to the overall purpose of the epic poem?

20,000 Leagues under the Sea

Jules Verne

 **M**onsieur Arronax, Conseil, and Ned Land are interpreters of one of the most fascinating adventures in Western literature. The brilliant and imaginative Jules Verne writes a book describing a voyage easily a hundred years ahead of its time. What an adventure!

Objective Test

_____ The novel begins in (A) 1966, (B) 1876, (C) 1866, or (D) 1820.

_____ For some time past, vessels have been met by (A) a fast-moving object that destroys ships, (B) more hurricanes, (C) a deadly whale, or (D) a new warship.

_____ Captain Nemo is the captain of (A) the amazing submarine *Nautilus*, (B) a frigate, or (C) a new airplane.

_____ Nemo has advanced science significantly in the area of (A) astrophysics, (B) biological science, or (C) oceanic science.

_____ Nemo is motivated by (A) revenge, (B) pacifism, or (C) nationalism.

Suggested Vocabulary Words

A. For some time past vessels had been met by "an enormous thing," a long object, spindle-shaped, occasionally <u>phosphorescent</u>, and infinitely larger and more rapid in its movements than a whale. (part 1, ch. 1)

B. At that moment Commander Farragut was ordering the last moorings to be cast loose which held the *Abraham Lincoln* to the pier of Brooklyn. So in a quarter of an hour, perhaps less, the frigate would have sailed without me. I should have missed this extraordinary, supernatural, and incredible expedition, the recital of which may well meet with some suspicion. (part 1, ch. 4)

C. We had now arrived on the first platform, where other surprises awaited me. Before us lay some picturesque ruins, which betrayed the hand of man and not that of the Creator. There were vast heaps of stone, amongst which might be traced the vague and shadowy forms of castles and temples, clothed with a world of blossoming zoophytes, and over which, instead of ivy, sea-weed and fucus threw a thick vegetable mantle. But what was this portion of the globe which had been swallowed by cataclysms? Who had placed those rocks and stones like cromlechs of prehistoric times? Where was I? Whither had Captain Nemo's fancy hurried me? (part 2, ch. 9)

D. He had made me, if not an accomplice, at least a witness of his vengeance. (part 2, ch. 22)

Discussion Questions

A. Is Nemo an antagonist or the protagonist?

B. How important are the lengthy scientific explanations to this novel?

C. Compare this book to the Walt Disney movie version.

D. What contemporary actor would you have play Captain Nemo?

E. Is Nemo justified in his quest to destroy ships?

Two Years before the Mast

Henry Dana

 The hardships of life at sea transform the sheltered son of a shipowner into a hardened, valiant leader. He is compelled to lead an uprising against his brutal captain. Dana gives a detailed account of everyday ship life. A later edition includes a chapter written by Dana twenty-four years after his initial voyage, where he revisits some of the people, places, and vessels he had encountered on his original journey.

Objective Test

_____ The narrator is (A) a wealthy Harvard boy, (B) a poor New England farmer, (C) an English castaway, or (D) the cousin of the Captain.

_____ One of the final insults inflicted on the sailors is (A) removing their rum rations, (B) excessive flogging, (C) depriving them of Sundays off work, or (D) half rations.

_____ The narrator (A) kills a Kanaka (Hawaiian) by mistake, (B) befriends a native of Hawaii who later saves his life, or (C) falls sick and nearly dies in Hawaii.

_____ The narrator (A) returns to Harvard and becomes a renowned lawyer and antislavery activist, (B) becomes a sea captain, or (C) resolves never to sail again.

_____ After the California Gold Rush of 1849, he (A) joins the Union army, (B) revisits British Columbia, (C) becomes a first mate on a ship, or (D) revisits California, seeing old friends and commenting on drastic changes.

Suggested Vocabulary Words

A. Before I end my explanations, it may be well to define a *day's work,* and to correct a mistake <u>prevalent</u> among landsmen about a sailor's life. (ch. 3)

B. But all these little <u>vexations</u> and labors would have been nothing. (ch. 14)

C. Each one knew that he must be a man, and show himself smart when at his duty, yet everyone was satisfied with the usage; and a <u>contented</u> crew, agreeing with one another, and finding no fault, was a contrast indeed with the small, hard-used, dissatisfied, grumbling, <u>desponding</u> crew of the Pilgrim. (ch. 23)

D. We hove them overboard with a good will; for there is nothing like being quit of the very last <u>appendages</u> and <u>remnants</u> of our evil fortune. (ch. 36)

E. I would not wish to have the power of the captain diminished an <u>iota</u>. . . . One would expect that the master who would abuse and impose upon a man under his power, would be the most <u>compliant</u> and <u>deferential</u> to his employers at home. (ch. 37)

Discussion Questions

A. The narrator begins as a Harvard boy, seasick and without sea legs, one who has never really done a hard day's work in his life. Yet through it all, he is able to survive, and he is a stronger and better man because of the many ordeals. That is one interpretation. What would be an alternative interpretation?

B. How reliable a narrator is this young, inexperienced, pampered Harvard College dropout?

C. Would the story be significantly different if the cruel Captain wrote the book?

D. The book has a strong journey motif. Explain.

E. Why does this book appeal to people who have never been to sea?

F. In your opinion, when is it appropriate to break the law?

Up from Slavery

Booker T. Washington

Up from Slavery is the story of the life and times of Booker T. Washington. He traces his deliverance from slavery to his position as director of the Tuskegee Institute. When criticized for limiting the educational horizons of African Americans by emphasizing agricultural subjects at his school, Washington declared that these are the true bases of black economic development. Although some contemporary African Americans condemned Washington as being too accommodating to white domination, Washington nonetheless became a force for good in all races of American society.

Objective Test

_____ Washington is born a slave in (A) Virginia, (B) North Carolina, (C) Alabama, or (D) Arkansas.

_____ Washington is greatly encouraged by descriptions fellow coal miners gave of a place called (A) the Tuskegee Institute, (B) Howard University, (C) Virginia Tech, or (D) the Hampton Institute.

_____ While taking corn to the mill, Washington is terrified that the corn would fall off his horse because (A) he would lose time, (B) the corn would be spoiled, (C) if he is late he would be beaten, or (D) he is so tired.

_____ Washington finds it difficult to work with Native Americans because (A) they hate African Americans, (B) they feel they are

139

superior to African Americans because they were never slaves, or (C) Washington does not personally like them.

_____ Washington opens the Tuskegee Institute (A) with a federal grant; (B) by invitation from a man in Tuskegee, Alabama; (C) with support from the University of Alabama; or (D) with no support.

_____ Tuskegee seems ideal for the school because (A) it is amid the bulk of the Negro population and secluded, with a five-mile branch line connecting it to the railroad; (B) it is in a beautiful place; or (C) it is in a region with a great climate for agriculture.

_____ Washington realizes early that he cannot (A) speak negatively about whites, (B) make enough money, or (C) duplicate education that he has seen in other parts of the country.

_____ When Washington begins to teach at Tuskegee, he sees (A) hungry and sad children; (B) a young man who has attended some high school, sitting in a one-room cabin, with grease on his clothing and filth around him, yet studying a French grammar; (C) young people staying away from church on Sunday morning.

_____ One of the greatest honors that Washington experiences is (A) to be given an honorary doctorate from Harvard University, (B) to see his grandchildren attend Tuskegee, (C) to be given an NAACP award, or (D) to return to his home in Virginia.

_____ While Washington is president of Tuskegee, the only U.S. president to visit there is (A) Grant, (B) Garfield, (C) McKinley, or (D) Wilson.

Suggested Vocabulary Words

A. I was awakened by my mother kneeling over her children and fervently praying that Lincoln and his armies might be successful, and that one day she and her children might be free. (ch. 1)

B. Finally the war closed, and the day of freedom came. It was a momentous and eventful day to all upon our plantation. (ch. 1)

C. He seemed to me to be the one young man in all the world who ought to be satisfied with his attainments. (ch. 2)

D. They were so much in earnest that only the ringing of the retiring-bell would make them stop studying. (ch. 6)

E. Mr. Campbell is a merchant and banker, and had had little experience in dealing with matters pertaining to education. (ch. 8)

F. The school was constantly growing in numbers, so much so that, after we had got the farm paid for, the cultivation of the land begun, and the old cabins which we had found on the place somewhat repaired, we turned our attention toward providing a large, substantial building. (ch. 9)

Discussion Questions

A. From the Armageddon of the Civil War rose this Moses, Booker T. Washington, who was born in 1856 or 1859 in Virginia, of a slave mother and a white father he never knew. But he gave no indication in his autobiography of the pain this parentage almost certainly caused him: "I do not even know his name. I have heard reports to the effect that he was a white man who lived on one of the nearby plantations. But I do not find especial fault with him. He was simply another unfortunate victim of the institution which the nation unhappily had engrafted upon it at that time." How could Washington apparently have no rancor in his heart toward his biological father?

B. After Emancipation, Washington went to the Hampton Normal Agricultural Institute in Virginia. When he arrived, he was allowed to work as the school's janitor in return for his board and part of his tuition. After graduating from Hampton, Washington was selected to head a new school at Tuskegee, Alabama, where he taught the virtues of hard work and sound morality as the best way for his race to advance. How was Washington able to overcome so many obstacles?

C. At the end of this autobiography Washington writes:

> Despite superficial and temporary signs which might lead one
> to entertain a contrary opinion, there was never a time when I
> felt more hopeful for the race than I do at the present. The great
> human law that in the end recognizes and rewards merit is ever-
> lasting and universal. The outside world does not know, neither
> can it appreciate, the struggle that is constantly going on in the
> hearts of both the Southern white people and their former slaves
> to free themselves from racial prejudice; and while both races
> are thus struggling they should have the sympathy, the support,
> and the forbearance of the rest of the world.

Yet, at the time, racism and prejudice were dominating the lives of millions of African-Americans. How could Washington write this?

D. Do you agree with critics who say that Washington was too passive in his relationship with white racism?

Utopia

Sir Thomas More

First published in 1516, Thomas More's *Utopia* is one of the most important examples of European Renaissance writing. Through the voice of the mysterious pilgrim Raphael Hythloday, More describes a pagan, communist city-state governed by reason. Addressing such issues as religious pluralism, women's rights, public education, and just war, *Utopia* remains a foundational text in philosophy and political theory.

Objective Test

_____ As an ambassador for England and King Henry VIII, More travels to (A) Barcelona, Spain; (B) Antwerp, the Netherlands; (C) New York, United States; or (D) Florence, Italy.

_____ More discusses philosophy with his friend (A) Peter Giles, (B) Henry VIII, (C) William Shakespeare, and (D) David Hume.

_____ Giles soon introduces More to (A) David Jones, (B) Descartes, (C) Raphael Hythloday, or (D) Morley Smith.

_____ Hythloday describes a mythological country called (A) Atlantis, (B) Cairo, (C) Timbuktu, or (D) Utopia.

_____ More laments that Utopia (A) is too warlike, (B) will probably never impact England, (C) is too large, or (D) is a poor country.

Suggested Vocabulary Words

A. Their council is concerning the <u>commonwealth</u>. If there be any <u>controversies</u> among the commoners, which be very few, they <u>despatch</u> and end them by-and-by. (book 2)

B. But either such as among themselves for <u>heinous</u> offences be punished with bondage, or else such as in the cities of other lands for great <u>trespasses</u> be condemned to death. (book 2)

C. But after they heard us speak of the name of Christ, of his doctrine, laws, miracles, and of the no less wonderful <u>constancy</u> of so many <u>martyrs</u>, whose blood willingly shed brought a great number of nations throughout all parts of the world into their sect; you will not believe with how glad minds, they agreed unto the same: whether it were by the secret <u>inspiration</u> of God, or else for that they thought it next unto that opinion, which among them is counted the chiefest. (book 2)

Discussion Questions

A. What form does More employ to write his philosophical treatise?

B. What is the status of women in Utopia?

C. Compare More's *Utopia* with Plato's *The Republic*.

D. Is Utopia a perfect society or a society full of perfect people?

Walden

Henry David Thoreau

 In 1845 the certifiable eccentric Henry David Thoreau leased some land owned by his friend and mentor, Ralph Waldo Emerson, on Walden Pond near Concord, Massachusetts, and lived in a cabin on it for two years, two months, and two days. While there, Thoreau wrote one of the most memorable, if egocentric, journals/novels in American literature –*Walden, or, Life in the Woods,* published in 1854.

Objective Test

_____ Thoreau spends two years (A) beside Walden Pond; (B) in Worcester, Massachusetts; or (C) on the Boston Commons.

_____ Local townspeople (A) admire his adventure, (B) help him out, (C) nearly kill him, or (D) think he is strange.

_____ The land on which he lives belongs to (A) Robert Louis Stevenson, (B) Franklin Pierce, (C) Nathaniel Hawthorne, or (D) Ralph Waldo Emerson.

_____ He stays (A) two years; (B) two years, two months, two days; (C) three years, three days; or (D) four months.

_____ Thoreau discovers that Walden Pond is (A) only a hundred feet deep, (B) bottomless, (C) salt water, or (D) full of trout.

Suggested Vocabulary Words

With a little more <u>deliberation</u> in the choice of their <u>pursuits</u>, all men would perhaps become <u>essentially</u> students and observers, for certainly their nature and destiny are interesting to all alike. In accumulating property for ourselves or our <u>posterity,</u> in founding a family or a state, or acquiring fame even, we are mortal; but in dealing with truth we are immortal, and need fear no change nor accident. The oldest Egyptian or Hindoo philosopher raised a corner of the veil from the statue of the divinity; and still the <u>trembling</u> robe remains raised, and I gaze upon as fresh a glory as he did, since it was I in him that was then so bold, and it is he in me that now reviews the vision. No dust has settled on that robe; no time has elapsed since that divinity was revealed. That time which we really improve, or which is improvable, is neither past, present, nor future.

My residence was more favorable, not only to thought, but to serious reading, than a university; and though I was beyond the range of the ordinary circulating library, I had more than ever come within the influence of those books which circulate round the world, whose sentences were first written on bark, and are now merely copied from time to time on to linen paper. Says the poet Mr Udd, "Being seated, to run through the region of the spiritual world; I have had this advantage in books. To be <u>intoxicated</u> by a single glass of wine; I have experienced this pleasure when I have drunk the liquor of the esoteric doctrines." I kept Homer's *Iliad* on my table through the summer, though I looked at his page only now and then. Incessant labor with my hands, at first, for I had my house to finish and my beans to hoe at the same time, made more study impossible. Yet I <u>sustained</u> myself by the prospect of such reading in future. I read one or two shallow books of travel in the intervals of my work, till that employment made me ashamed of myself, and I asked where it was then that I lived.

The student may read Homer or Aeschylus in the Greek without danger of <u>dissipation</u> or <u>luxuriousness,</u> for it implies that he in some measure <u>emulate</u> their heroes, and <u>consecrate</u> morning hours to their pages. The heroic books, even if printed in the character of our mother tongue, will always be in a language dead to degenerate times; and we must <u>laboriously</u> seek the meaning of each word and line, <u>conjecturing</u> a larger sense than common use permits out of what wisdom and valor and generosity we have. The modern cheap and fertile press, with all its translations, has done little to bring us nearer to the heroic writers of antiquity. They seem as solitary, and the letter in which they are printed as rare and curious, as ever. It is worth the expense of youthful days and costly hours, if you learn only some words of an ancient language, which are raised out of the trivialness of the street, to be perpetual suggestions and provocations. It is not in vain that the farmer remembers and repeats the few Latin words which he has heard. Men sometimes speak as if the study of the classics would at length make way for more modern and practical studies; but the adventurous student will always study classics, in whatever language they may be written and however ancient they may be. For what are the classics but the noblest recorded thoughts of man? They are the only oracles which are not decayed, and there are such answers to the most modern inquiry in them as Delphi and Dodona never gave. We might as well omit to study Nature because she is old. To read well, that is, to read true books in a true spirit, is a noble exercise, and one that will task the reader more than any exercise which the customs of the day esteem. It requires a training such as the athletes underwent, the steady intention almost of the whole life to this object. Books must be read as deliberately and reservedly as they were written. It is not enough even to be able to speak the language of that nation by which they are written, for there is a memorable interval between the spoken and the written language, the language heard and the language read. The one is commonly transitory, a sound, a tongue, a dialect merely, almost brutish, and we learn it unconsciously, like the brutes, of our mothers. The other is the maturity and experience of that; if that is our mother tongue, this is our father tongue, a reserved and select expression, too significant to be heard by the ear, which we must be born again in order to speak. The crowds of men who merely spoke the Greek and Latin tongues in the Middle Ages were not entitled by the accident of birth to read the works of genius written in those languages; for these were not written in that Greek or Latin which they knew, but in the select language of literature. They had not learned the nobler dialects of Greece and Rome, but the very materials on which they were written were waste paper to them, and they prized instead a cheap contemporary literature. But when the several nations of Europe had acquired distinct though rude written languages of their own, sufficient for the purposes of their rising literatures, then first learning revived, and scholars were enabled to discern from that remoteness the treasures of <u>antiquity</u>. What the Roman and Grecian multitude could not hear, after the lapse of ages a few scholars read, and a few scholars only are still reading it. (ch. 3)

Discussion Questions

A. The poet Ezra Pound said that Thoreau wrote *Walden* as the "first intellectual reaction to mere approach of industrialization: Thoreau tried to see how little he need bother about other humanity." Agree or disagree with this statement and explain your opinion.

B. Thoreau extols the working poor. Although he worked on his house and hoed his beans, as mentioned above, there is no evidence that he ever held a regular job with the working poor. Does this hurt his credibility?

C. State some of the aphorisms, truths, or generalizations that he is promoting in his book.

D. Compare the worldview of Thoreau with the worldview of his friend Emerson.

Watership Down

Richard Adams

Fleeing man and the certain destruction of their ancestral home, a band of rabbits encounters various trials and tribulations posed by predators and other hostile rabbits. They are searching for a rabbit Shangri-la, Watership Down. It is written in the same vein as Lewis Carroll's *Alice's Adventures in Wonderland* and J. R. R. Tolkien's *The Hobbit.*

Objective Test

_____ Fiver has a special gift of being (A) able to tell the future, (B) able to feel water under the ground, or (C) able to fly.

_____ Fiver tells everyone but is unable to convince the head rabbit (A) Hazel, (B) Rocky, or (C) Threarah.

_____ The warren finds a wonderful place to stay, but it is full of death because it is (A) a breeding ground for men to harvest rabbits, (B) over a volcano, or (C) full of diseased rabbits.

_____ Helping the rabbits is a wounded bird named (A) Robert, (B) Kehaar, or (C) Hazel.

_____ The warren has to fight to preserve (A) their leader, (B) Hazel, or (C) Watership Down.

Suggested Vocabulary Words

A. The rabbits became strange in many ways, different from other rabbits. They knew well enough what was happening. But even to themselves they <u>pretended</u> that all was well, for the food was good, they were protected, they had nothing to fear but the one fear; and that struck here and there, never enough at a time to drive them away.

B. "Did you see his body? No. Did anyone? No. Nothing could kill him. He made rabbits bigger than they've ever been—braver, more skillful, more <u>cunning</u>. I know we paid for it. Some gave their lives. It was worth it, to feel we were Efrafans. For the first time ever, rabbits didn't go <u>scurrying</u> away.

Discussion Questions

A. The search for home is a major theme of this novel. Discuss how Adams develops it.

B. What makes Hazel such a good leader?

C. Why do you think Adams chooses to tell his story by using rabbits?

D. How do humans fare in this novel?

White Fang

Jack London

 London presents a classic adventure novel detailing the savagery of life in the northern wilds. Its central character is a ferocious and magnificent creature, half dog, half wolf, through whose experiences we feel the harsh rhythms and patterns of wilderness life among animals and men.

Objective Test

_____ Bill and Henry are attacked by (A) wolves, (B) Native Americans, (C) grizzly bears, or (D) robbers.

_____ The protagonist is (A) Thornton, (B) White Fang, (C) Klondike Kelly, or (D) Theodore Roosevelt.

_____ White Fang is sold to (A) Marcus, (B) Thornton, (C) Seward, or (D) Beauty Smith.

_____ White Fang is saved by a man named (A) Thornton, (B) Scott, (C) Marcus, or (D) Beauty Smith.

_____ White Fang and Scott return to (A) South Dakota, (B) Minnesota, (C) California, or (D) Arizona.

Suggested Vocabulary Words

A. Dark spruce forest frowned on either side the frozen waterway. The trees had been stripped by a recent wind of their white covering of frost, and they seemed to lean towards each other, black and ominous, in the fading light. A vast silence reigned over the land. The land itself was a desolation, lifeless, without movement, so lone and cold that the spirit of it was not even that of sadness. There was a hint in it of laughter, but of a laughter more terrible than any sadness—a laughter that was <u>mirthless</u> as the smile of the <u>sphinx</u>, a laughter cold as the frost and partaking of the <u>grimness</u> of <u>infallibility</u>. It was the masterful and <u>incommunicable</u> wisdom of eternity laughing at the <u>futility</u> of life and the effort of life. (part 1, ch. 1)

B. Henry grunted with an <u>intonation</u> that was not all sympathy, and for a quarter of an hour they sat on in silence, Henry staring at the fire, and Bill at the circle of eyes that burned in the darkness just beyond the firelight. (part 1, ch. 2)

C. At such times, <u>confronted</u> by three sets of savage teeth, the young wolf stopped <u>precipitately</u>, throwing himself back on his <u>haunches</u>, with fore-legs stiff, mouth menacing, and mane bristling. This confusion in the front of the moving pack always caused confusion in the rear. The wolves behind <u>collided</u> with the young wolf and expressed their <u>displeasure</u> by <u>administering</u> sharp nips on his hind-legs and flanks. He was laying up trouble for himself, for lack of food and short tempers went together; but with the <u>boundless</u> faith of youth he <u>persisted</u> in repeating the <u>manoeuver</u> every little while, though it never succeeded in gaining anything for him but <u>discomfiture</u>. (part 2, ch. 1)

D. In San Quentin prison he had proved <u>incorrigible</u>. Punishment failed to break his spirit. He could die dumb-mad and fighting to the last, but he could not live and be beaten. The more fiercely he fought, the more <u>harshly</u> society handled him, and the only effect of harshness was to make him fiercer. (part 2, ch. 5)

Discussion Questions

A. Why is London subtly comparing the prisoner (part 2) with White Fang?

B. Why do the animals seem more compassionate than the human beings?

C. Why would pro-choice advocates admire London's worldview?

D. What part do women play in *White Fang*?

Wuthering Heights

Emily Brontë

 In the nineteenth-century, the passionate love between a stubborn high-society young lady and a poor adopted orphan boy brought up by her father causes disaster for them and many others. This book is one of the quintessential tragedies of Western literature . . . or is it?

Objective Test

_____ This entire novel is (A) a journal, (B) a narrative epic, (C) a flashback, or (D) a poem.

_____ The narrator is actually (A) the servant girl Nellie, (B) Heathcliff, (C) Catherine, or (D) Mary.

_____ Mr. Earnshaw prefers to (A) live in the city; (B) have Heathcliff as a son instead of his biological son, Hindley; or (C) see Catherine marry in society circles.

_____ Catherine marries (A) Heathcliff, (B) Edgar, (C) Hindley, or (D) Charles.

_____ Heathcliff runs away because Catherine (A) marries someone else, (B) dies, (C) also runs away, or (D) says some regrettable things that Heathcliff overhears.

Suggested Vocabulary Words

A. He was not insolent to his benefactor, he was simply insensible; though knowing perfectly the hold he had on his heart, and conscious he had only to speak and all the house would be obliged to bend to his wishes. (ch. 4)

B. To be sure, one might have doubted, after the wayward and impatient existence she had led, whether she merited a haven of peace at last. One might doubt in seasons of cold reflection; but not then, in the presence of her corpse. It asserted its own tranquillity, which seemed a pledge of equal quiet to its former inhabitant. (ch. 16).

C. Yesterday was bright, calm, and frosty. I went to the Heights as I proposed: my housekeeper entreated me to bear a little note from her to her young lady, and I did not refuse, for the worthy woman was not conscious of anything odd in her request. (ch. 31)

D. When Hareton was there, she generally paused in an interesting part, and left the book lying about: that she did repeatedly; but he was as obstinate as a mule, and, instead of snatching at her bait, in wet weather he took to smoking with Joseph; and they sat like automatons, one on each side of the fire. (ch. 32)

E. I uttered an ejaculation of discontent at seeing the dismal grate, and commenced shutting the casements, one after another, till I came to his. (ch. 34)

Discussion Questions

A. What do you think of this critic's comments?

Wuthering Heights, which has long been one of the most popular and highly regarded novels in English literature, seemed to hold little promise when it was published in 1847, selling very poorly and receiving only a few mixed reviews. Victorian readers found the book shocking and inappropriate in its depiction of passionate, ungoverned love and cruelty (despite the fact that the novel portrays no sex or bloodshed), and the work was virtually ignored. Even Emily Brontë's sister Charlotte—an author whose works contained similar motifs of Gothic love and desolate landscapes—remained ambivalent toward the unapologetic intensity of her sister's novel. In a preface to the book, which she wrote shortly after Emily Brontë's death, Charlotte Brontë stated, "Whether it is right or advisable to create beings like Heathcliff, I do not know. I scarcely think it is."

B. After Catherine offends Heathcliff, he leaves. Why? Is it to make himself worthy of her? To prepare for revenge?

C. Do you agree with critic Arnold Kettle in seeing Heathcliff as a hero?

> Heathcliff's revenge may involve a pathological condition of hatred, but it is not at bottom merely neurotic. It has a moral force. For what Heathcliff does is to use against his enemies with complete ruthlessness their own weapons, to turn on them (stripped of their romantic veils) their own standards, to beat them at their own game. The weapons he uses against the Earnshaws and Lintons are their own weapons of money and arranged marriages. He gets power over them by the classic methods of the ruling class, expropriation and property deals.

D. Does this novel have a happy or a sad ending?

Aids for the Teacher

Agamemnon

Aeschylus

Objective Test

__A__ *Agamemnon* begins with (A) a guard waiting for a signal announcing the fall of Troy to the Greek armies, (B) a recapitulation of the fall of Troy, or (C) the death of Aeneas.

__C__ A beacon flashes, and he joyfully runs to tell the news to (A) Hektor, (B) Apollinus, or (C) Queen Clytemnestra.

__A__ When he is gone, the Chorus—made up of (A) the old men of Argos, (B) widows of fallen soldiers, or (C) the gods—enters and tells the story of how the Trojan prince Paris stole Helen, the wife of the Greek king Menelaus, leading to ten years of war between Greece and Troy.

__B__ Then the Chorus recalls how—to obtain a favorable wind for the Greek fleet—(A) Clytemnestra's husband, Agamemnon (Menelaus's brother) sacrificed their son to the goddess Artemis; (B) Clytemnestra's husband, Agamemnon (Menelaus's brother), sacrificed their daughter to the goddess Artemis; or (C) Clytemnestra's husband, Agamemnon (Menelaus' brother), sacrificed their daughter to the god Zeus.

__A__ Clytemnestra (A) murders her husband, (B) throws a party to honor her husband, or (C) kills Paris.

Suggested Vocabulary Words

A. Thus upon mine unrestful couch I lie, Bathed with the dews of night, unvisited / By dreams—ah me!—for in the place of sleep / Stands Fear as my familiar, and repels / The soft repose that would mine eyelids seal. / And if at whiles, for the lost <u>balm</u> [soothing medicine] of sleep, I medicine my soul with melody / Of <u>trill</u> [tune] or song—anon to tears I turn, <u>Wailing</u> [crying] the woe that broods upon this home, / Not now by honour guided as of old. (lines 16–24)

B. And so he steeled his heart—ah, well-a-day—Aiding a war for one
false woman's sake, / His child to slay, / And with her spilt blood make
/ An offering, to speed the ships upon their way! / Lusting for war, the
bloody arbiters [deal makers] / Closed heart and ears, and would nor
hear nor heed / The girl-voice plead, *Pity me, Father!* nor her prayers,
Nor tender, virgin years. (lines 268–274)

C. Shamed, silent, unreproachful [without fault], stretching hands /
That find her not, and sees, yet will not see, That she is far away! / And
his sad fancy, yearning [fervently desiring] o'er the sea, Shall summon
[call forth] and recall / Her wraith, once more to queen it in his hall.
And sad with many memories, / The fair cold beauty of each sculptured
[beautifully formed] face—And all to hatefulness is turned their grace, /
Seen blankly by forlorn [sad] and hungering eyes! And when the night
is deep, Come visions, sweet and sad, and bearing pain (lines 486–498)

D. Lastly, whate'er be due to men or gods, / With joint debate
[rhetorical arguments/discussions], in public council held, We will
decide, and warily [suspiciously] contrive / That all which now is well
may so abide: / For that which haply needs the healer's art, That will we
medicine, discerning [knowing] well / If cautery or knife befit the time.
(Lines 980–984)

Discussion Questions

A. Is Clytemnestra's murder of her husband justified?
Answer: *Answers will vary.*

B. Although Shakespeare's tragedies employ some comic relief,
Greek tragedies are altogether tragic: every event leads the characters
toward imminent disaster. Discuss how Aeschylus accomplishes this.
Answer: *The oracles and chorus lyrics maintain a sense of imminent disaster.*

C. What function does Aegisthus's character have in the play?
Answer: *Any sympathy the audience may have toward Clytemnestra
is dissipated when it learns that she is unfaithful and manipulative. It
foreshadows the just revenge that will be inflicted on this despicable
pair in subsequent plays.*

And Then There Were None

Agatha Christie

Objective Test

__C__ When the guests arrive on the island, they are told (A) to go home, (B) that they will all be murdered, or (C) that the host will join them tomorrow.

__A__ That evening, as all the guests gather after an excellent dinner, they hear a recorded voice (A) accusing each of them of a specific murder committed in the past and never uncovered, (B) welcoming the guests to the house, or (C) asking them to help.

__C__ As they discuss what to do, (A) Vera dies, (B) Bob dies, or (C) Tony Marston dies.

__B__ The next morning (A) Vera is dead, (B) Mrs. Rogers is dead, or (C) General MacArthur is dead.

__C__ The murderer was (A) Tony, (B) Vera, or (C) the Judge.

Suggested Vocabulary Words

A. There was a silence—a comfortable <u>replete</u> [full] silence. Into that silence came The Voice. Without warning, inhuman, <u>penetrating</u> [strong; intrusive] . . . *"Ladies and gentlemen! Silence, please! . . .* You are charged with the following <u>indictments</u> [criminal charges]." (ch. 3)

B. But—<u>incongruous</u> [paradoxically out of order] as it may seem to some—I was <u>restrained</u> [hindered] and <u>hampered</u> [restricted] by my <u>innate</u> [internal] sense of justice. The innocent must not suffer. (Epilogue)

Discussion Questions

A. How does Christie build suspense?
Answer: *Foreshadowing and the setting.*

B. Do you agree with the Judge's decision to kill all these people?

Answer: *Answers will vary. Revenge is not a Christian response to an issue.*

C. How do the weaknesses of each character hasten their end?
Answer: *Aside from Wargrave, the last four characters left alive on the island are Armstrong, Blore, Lombard, and Vera. Wargrave is able to murder all four of them by exploiting their weaknesses.*

D. Did you guess who the murderer was before the novel ended?
Answer: *Answers will vary.*

Animal Farm

George Orwell

Objective Test

__B__ Old Major, a prize-winning boar, gathers the animals of the Manor Farm (A) to warn them of a great slaughter, (B) for a meeting in the big barn, or (C) to lead a revolt.

__A__ He tells them (A) about a dream he has had, (B) to prepare for winter, or (C) that he will die.

__B__ He tells the animals that they must (A) run away, (B) create a workers' paradise, or (C) kill all the rats.

__C__ He teaches them (A) to speak French, (B) to run fast, or (C) a song called "Beasts of England."

__A__ Ultimately the community-run government is taken over by (A) pigs who look more and more like the men they replaced, (B) horses who carry big whips, or (C) cows who try to bring consensus.

Suggested Vocabulary Words

A. The pigs had an even harder struggle to <u>counteract</u> [replace] the lies put about by Moses, the tame raven. Moses, who was Mr. Jones's special pet, was a spy and a tale-bearer, but he was also a clever talker. He claimed to know of the existence of a mysterious country called Sugarcandy Mountain, to which all animals went when they died. It was situated somewhere up in the sky, a little distance beyond the clouds, Moses said. In Sugarcandy Mountain it was Sunday seven days a week, clover was in season all the year round, and lump sugar and linseed cake grew on the hedges. The animals hated Moses because he told tales and did no work, but some of them believed in Sugarcandy Mountain, and the pigs had to argue very hard to <u>persuade</u> [convince] them that there was no such place. (ch. 2)

B. The animals were not badly off throughout that summer, in spite of the hardness of their work. If they had no more food than they had had in Jones's day, at least they did not have less. The <u>advantage</u> [benefit] of only having to feed themselves, and not having to support five <u>extravagant</u> [generous to excess] human beings as well, was so great that it would have taken a lot of failures to outweigh it. And in many ways the animal method of doing things was more <u>efficient</u> [productive by economy] and saved labour. Such jobs as weeding, for instance, could be done with a thoroughness impossible to human beings. And again, since no animal now stole, it was unnecessary to fence off pasture from <u>arable</u> [dry and fit for growing crops] land, which saved a lot of labour on the upkeep of hedges and gates. Nevertheless, as the summer wore on, various unforeseen shortages began to make themselves felt. (ch. 6)

C. At the beginning, when the laws of Animal Farm were first formulated, the retiring age had been fixed for horses and pigs at twelve, for cows at fourteen, for dogs at nine, for sheep at seven, and for hens and geese at five. Liberal old-age pensions had been agreed upon. As yet no animal had actually retired on pension, but of late the subject had been discussed more and more. Now that the small field beyond the orchard had been set aside for barley, it was rumoured that a corner of the large pasture was to be fenced off and turned into a grazing-ground for <u>superannuated</u> [disqualified for active duty by advanced age] animals. (ch. 9)

D. There was the same hearty cheering as before, and the mugs were emptied to the dregs. But as the animals outside gazed at the scene, it seemed to them that some strange thing was happening. What was it that had altered [changed] in the faces of the pigs? Clover's old dim eyes flitted from one face to another. Some of them had five chins, some had four, some had three. But what was it that seemed to be melting and changing? (ch. 10)

Discussion Questions

A. This book is a parody of what actual cultural/political revolution?
Answer: *Communist Revolution*

B. In what chapter does the plot turn in mood and meaning?
Answer: *Chapter 7.*

C. What style does Orwell employ in this book?
Answer: *Orwell's style, said one critic, has "relentless simplicity" and "pathetic doggedness" of the animals themselves. There is a tension between the sad story that this becomes and the simple way Orwell tells the story.*

D. To a Christian, when, if ever, is a revolution necessary?
Answer: *This is a very difficult question. In fact, rarely is a revolution necessary. However, if a government or nation asks the Christian to violate biblical truth in such extensive ways—as the Nazi government did—then at least nonviolent resistance or perhaps a revolution is necessary.*

E. How does Orwell use his narrative point of view to produce irony?
Answer: *Irony is a contradiction between what a statement seems to say and what it really means. Irony can also be a conflict between what characters expect to happen and what really happens. Orwell tells his story from the point of view of the slower, stupid animals, not from that of the clever pigs. Nor does he use a human, omniscient narrator.*

The Autobiography of Benjamin Franklin

Benjamin Franklin

Objective Test

__B__ Franklin was the first American (A) to express openly his discontent with England, (B) to be considered an equal to European scientists, or (C) to send a telegraph message to England.

__A__ Franklin was (A) the youngest son of seventeen children, (B) the oldest of four children, or (C) an only child.

__C__ Franklin did not enter the ministry because (A) he did not feel called, (B) he preferred to be a lawyer, or (C) after considering the paltry salary that ministers received, his father made him work at his shop.

__A__ At age twelve Franklin (A) was apprenticed to his brother James, (B) traveled to Georgia, or (C) invented the Franklin Stove.

__B__ Franklin founded (A) the *Philadelphia Enquirer*, (B) the *Pennsylvania Gazette*, or (C) the Spectator Society.

__A__ Franklin practiced (A) twelve virtues, (B) seven virtues, or (C) thirteen virtues.

__C__ Franklin was fluent in (A) Italian, German, and English; (B) Spanish, French, and English; or (C) French, Spanish, Italian, and English.

__A__ While postmaster of Philadelphia, Franklin (A) reorganized the fire department, (B) founded a hospital, or (C) experimented with electricity.

__B__ In 1732 he published (A) his memoirs, (B) *Poor Richard's Almanac*, or (C) a book of verse.

Suggested Vocabulary Words

A. Having emerged from the poverty and obscurity [anonymity] in

165

which I was born and bred, to a state of affluence [prosperity] and some degree of reputation in the world, and having gone so far through life with a considerable share of felicity [great happiness], the conducing [contributing] means I made use of, which with the blessing of God so well succeeded, my posterity [descendants] may like to know, as they may find some of them suitable to their own situations, and therefore fit to be imitated. (part 1)

B. It was written in 1675, in the home-spun verse of that time and people, and addressed to those then concerned in the government there. It was in favor of liberty of conscience, and in behalf of the Baptists, Quakers, and other sectaries that had been under persecution, ascribing the Indian wars, and other distresses that had befallen the country, to that persecution, as so many judgments of God to punish so heinous [terrible] an offense, and exhorting [strongly urging] a repeal of those uncharitable [unjust; ungenerous] laws. (part 1)

C. At his table he liked to have, as often as he could, some sensible friend or neighbor to converse with, and always took care to start some ingenious [original] or useful topic for discourse [conversation], which might tend to improve the minds of his children. (part 1)

D. I continu'd this method some few years, but gradually left it, retaining only the habit of expressing myself in terms of modest diffidence [shyness]. (part 2)

E. In his house I lay that night, and the next morning reach'd Burlington, but had the mortification [humiliation; shame] to find that the regular boats were gone a little before my coming, and no other expected to go before Tuesday, this being Saturday; wherefore I returned to an old woman in the town, of whom I had bought gingerbread to eat on the water, and ask'd her advice. (part 2)

F. My ideas at that time were, that the sect should be begun and spread at first among young and single men only; that each person to be initiated should not only declare his assent to such creed, but should have exercised himself with the thirteen weeks' examination and practice of the virtues as in the before-mention'd model; that the existence

of such a society should he kept a secret, till it was become considerable, to prevent solicitations [entreaties, allurements] for the admission
of improper persons, but that the members should each of them search
among his acquaintance for ingenuous [natural; genuine], well-disposed
youths, to whom, with prudent [wise] caution, the scheme should be
gradually communicated these proverbs, which contained the wisdom of
many ages and nations, I assembled and form'd into a connected discourse prefix'd to the *Almanack* of 1757, as the harangue [angry dia-
tribe] of a wise old man to the people attending an auction. (part 3)

G. In 1751, Dr. Thomas Bond, a particular friend of mine, conceived
the idea of establishing a hospital in Philadelphia (a very beneficent
[beneficial; advantageous] design, which has been ascrib'd to me, but
was originally his), for the reception and cure of poor sick persons,
whether inhabitants of the province or strangers. He was zealous [enthu-
siastic] and active in endeavoring to procure [obtain] subscriptions for
it, but the proposal being a novelty [new thing] in America, and at first
not well understood, he met with but small success. (part 4)

Discussion Questions

A. Based on this quote, and other passages, describe Franklin's faith
journey:

> Before I enter upon my public appearance in business, it may be
> well to let you know the then state of my mind with regard to
> my principles and morals, that you may see how far those influ-
> enc'd the future events of my life. My parents had early given
> me religious impressions, and brought me through my child-
> hood piously in the Dissenting way. But I was scarce fifteen,
> when, after doubting by turns of several points, as I found them
> disputed in the different books I read, I began to doubt of
> Revelation itself. Some books against Deism fell into my hands;
> they were said to be the substance of sermons preached at
> Boyle's Lectures. It happened that they wrought an effect on me
> quite contrary to what was intended by them; for the arguments
> of the Deists, which were quoted to be refuted, appeared to me
> much stronger than the refutations; in short, I soon became a
> thorough Deist. My arguments perverted some others, particu-

larly Collins and Ralph; but, each of them having afterwards wrong'd me greatly without the least compunction, and recollecting Keith's conduct towards me (who was another freethinker), and my own towards Vernon and Miss Read, which at times gave me great trouble, I began to suspect that this doctrine, tho' it might be true, was not very useful.

Answer: *While Franklin was not an active church member, nor does he ever indicate that he was a Christian believer, he nonetheless exhibited strong moral fiber. By his own admission he was a Deist (someone who does not believe that God is active in human affairs). Of course, this book only discusses Franklin's life until 1752. There is evidence that later he became far more religious. Let's hope so.*

B. Discuss Franklin's quest for moral perfection.
Answer: *Franklin approaches morality like everything else: he designs a discipline and sticks to it. Morality is a sort of "law" to him. He studies and practices it the same way he self-teaches himself other knowledge.*

C. Who was General Braddock, and what advice did he receive from Franklin?
Answer: *General Braddock was British and led a force to capture the French Fort Duquesne (now Pittsburgh) at the beginning of the French and Indian War (1758). He was unsuccessful partly because he did not accept Franklin's sagacious advice about Native Americans.*

D. What writing style does Franklin employ?
Answer: *Franklin writes in a simple style for his age, even though what he says is profound.*

E. Is the *Autobiography* a rags-to-riches story or a self-serving, egotistical story of a man's self-absorption?
Answer: *Answers will vary.*

Brave New World

Aldous Huxley

Objective Test

__B__ The Bokanovsky and Podsnap Processes (A) do not work, (B) allow the Hatchery to produce thousands of nearly identical human embryos, (C) are a new project, or (D) produce identical sheep.

__A__ Alpha, Beta, Gamma, Delta, and Epsilon refer to (A) classes of people, (B) college fraternities, (C) new weapons, or (D) the Director's pets.

__D__ Lenina Crowne, an employee at the factory, describes (A) how the embryos are used to create new specimens, (B) how to make stronger horses, (C) how she aborts unborn infants, or (D) how she vaccinates embryos destined for tropical climates.

__A__ Hypnopaedic is (A) a way to teach young people, (B) the end of the world, (C) a fear of water, or (D) a nonsense world to describe human psychology.

__D__ The new order is called (A) the Universe, (B) the Brave New World, (C) the New Order, or (D) the World-State Society.

Suggested Vocabulary Words

A. The Director opened a door. They were in a large bare room, very bright and sunny; for the whole of the southern wall was a single window. Half a dozen nurses, trousered [wearing pants] and jacketed in the regulation white viscose-linen [clear; like rayon] uniform, their hair aseptically [extremely clean] hidden under white caps, were engaged in setting out bowls of roses in a long row across the floor. Big bowls, packed tight with blossom. Thousands of petals, ripe-blown and silkily smooth, like the cheeks of innumerable [a large number] little cherubs, but of cherubs, in that bright light, not exclusively pink and Aryan, but also luminously [light] Chinese, also Mexican, also apoplectic [debilitative, about to have a stroke] with too much blowing of celestial [relating to the stars; heavenly] trumpets, also pale as death, pale with the posthumous [after-death] whiteness of marble. (ch. 2)

B. An almost naked Indian was very slowly climbing down the ladder from the first-floor terrace of a neighboring house—rung after rung, with the tremulous [extreme] caution of extreme old age. His face was profoundly [deeply; thoroughly] wrinkled and black, like a mask of obsidian [black]. The toothless mouth had fallen in. At the corners of the lips, and on each side of the chin, a few long bristles gleamed almost white against the dark skin. The long unbraided hair hung down in grey wisps [small strands] round his face. His body was bent and emaciated [very thin] to the bone, almost fleshless. Very slowly he came down, pausing at each rung before he ventured another step. (ch. 7)

C. Lenina alone said nothing. Pale, her blue eyes clouded with an unwonted [unusual] melancholy [sadness], she sat in a corner, cut off from those who surrounded her by an emotion which they did not share. She had come to the party filled with a strange feeling of anxious exultation [jubilant]. "In a few minutes," she had said to herself, as she entered the room, "I shall be seeing him, talking to him, telling him" (for she had come with her mind made up) "that I like him—more than anybody I've ever known. And then perhaps he'll say . . ." (ch. 12)

D. When morning came, he felt he had earned the right to inhabit the lighthouse; yet, even though there still was glass in most of the windows, even though the view from the platform was so fine. For the very reason why he had chosen the lighthouse had become almost instantly a reason for going somewhere else. He had decided to live there because the view was so beautiful, because, from his vantage point, he seemed to be looking out on to the incarnation of a divine being. But who was he to be pampered [spoiled] with the daily and hourly sight of loveliness? Who was he to be living in the visible presence of God? All he deserved to live in was some filthy sty, some blind hole in the ground. Stiff and still aching after his long night of pain, but for that very reason inwardly reassured, he climbed up to the platform of his tower, he looked out over the bright sunrise world which he had regained the right to inhabit. On the north the view was bounded by the long chalk ridge of the Hog's Back, from behind whose eastern extremity rose the towers of the seven skyscrapers which constituted Guildford. Seeing them, the Savage made a grimace [frown]; but he was to become reconciled [made peace] to them in course of time; for at night they twinkled gaily with geometrical constellations [stars], or else, flood-lighted, pointed their luminous [full of light] fingers (with a gesture whose significance nobody in England but the Savage now understood) solemnly towards the plumbless mysteries of heaven. (ch. 18)

Discussion Questions

A. What narrative point of view does Aldous Huxley employ? Why?

Answer: *Third-person omniscient. He is in the story but uses one narrator-participant to interpret the story. He allows the narrator to see inside everyone's mind.*

B. This novel is about the creation of a utopia. Explain.

Answer: *The Whole World Society is supposed to be a perfect society.*

C. The Controller has a meeting with John, the Savage, in the climactic confrontation of the book. John laments that the world has paid a high price for happiness by giving up art and science. The Controller adds religion to this list and says, "God isn't compatible with machinery and scientific medicine and universal happiness." What does the Controller mean?

Answer: *He is putting "God" in the same category as the aesthetics, John sees God as a nameless abstraction—a view quite popular among Transcendentalists and Romantics.*

D. Agree or disagree with this analysis by a critic: "For Huxley, it is plain, there is no need to travel into the future to find the brave new world; it already exists, only too palpably, in the American Joy City, where the declaration of dependence begins and ends with the single-minded pursuit of happiness."

Answer: *This critic argues that Huxley is really talking about the modern world, not the future world. Science fiction writer Kurt Vonnegut Jr. once remarked: "I don't write science fiction. I write non-fiction that is so true that it is strange and appears to be science fic-*

tion." Huxley wrote the same sort of thing.

E. Scholar Peter Bowering concludes:

> In the World-State man has been enslaved by science, or as the hypnopaedic platitude puts it, "Science is everything." But, while everything owes its origin to science, science itself has been paradoxically relegated to the limbo of the past along with culture, religion, and every other worthwhile object of human endeavor. It is ironic that science, which has given the stablest equilibrium in history, should itself be regarded as a potential menace, and that all scientific progress should have been frozen since the establishment of the World-State.

This is called postmodernism. Define *postmodernism.*

Answer: *Postmodernism is inherently suspicious of science, celebrates the subjective, and calls for a radical reappraisal of modern assumptions.*

The Brothers Karamazov

Fyodor Dostoyevsky

Objective Test

__B__ Karamazov has (A) three sons, (B) four sons, or (C) six sons.

__B__ Father and son quarrel over (A) an estate, (B) money and a woman, (C) the cause of the Russian Revolution.

__C__ One of Karamazov's sons loves to (A) farm, (B) shoot pool, (C) discuss philosophy.

__B__ Ivan really loves (A) Maria, (B) Katerina, or (C) Grushenka.

__B__ The character who represents the religious impulse of nineteenth century Russia is (A) Karamazov, (B) Alyosha, or (C) Ivan.

Suggested Vocabulary Words

A. At the time of Yefim Petrovitch's death, Alyosha had two more years to complete at the <u>provincial</u> [country; unsophisticated] gymnasium. The <u>inconsolable</u> [unable to be comforted] widow went almost immediately after his death for a long visit to Italy with her whole family, which consisted only of women and girls. (part 1, book 1, ch. 4)

B. As he hastened out of the hermitage <u>precincts</u> [districts] to reach the monastery in time to serve at the Father Superior's dinner, he felt a sudden <u>pang</u> [pain] at his heart, and stopped short. He seemed to hear again Father Zossima's words, foretelling his approaching end. What he had foretold so exactly must <u>infallibly</u> [without fail] come to pass. Alyosha believed that <u>implicitly</u> [with no evidence]. But how could he go? (part 1, book 2, ch. 7)

C. "Quite so, quite so," cried Ivan, with <u>peculiar</u> [unique] eagerness, obviously <u>annoyed</u> [irritated] at being interrupted, "in anyone else this moment would be only due to yesterday's impression and would be only a moment. But with Katerina Ivanovna's character, that moment will last all her life. What for anyone else would be only a promise is for her an everlasting burdensome, grim perhaps, but <u>unflagging</u> [untiring] duty. And she will be <u>sustained</u> [supported; nourished] by the feeling of this duty being fulfilled. Your life, Katerina Ivanovna, will henceforth be spent in painful <u>brooding</u> [contemplating] over your own feelings, your own heroism, and your own suffering; but in the end that suffering will be softened and will pass into sweet <u>contemplation</u> [deep thought] of the fulfillment of a bold and proud design. Yes, proud it certainly is, and desperate in any case, but a triumph for you. And the consciousness of it will at last be a source of complete satisfaction and will make you resigned to everything else." (part 2, book 4, ch. 5)

D. "After a month of hopeless love and moral <u>degradation</u> [humiliation], during which he betrayed his <u>betrothed</u> [fiancée] and <u>appropriated</u> [took] money entrusted to his honour, the prisoner was driven almost to frenzy, almost to madness by continual jealousy—and of whom? His father! And the worst of it was that the crazy old man was alluring and <u>enticing</u> [tempting; attracting] the object of his affection by means of that very three thousand roubles, which the son looked upon as his own property, part of his inheritance from his mother, of which his father was cheating him. Yes, I admit it was hard to bear! It might well drive a man to madness. It was not the money, but the fact that this money was used with such revolting cynicism to ruin his happiness!" (part 3, book 12, ch. 7)

Discussion Questions

A. Why do you think that novels celebrating Christian values were being written in Russia in the nineteenth century, when no such novels were being written in America?

Answer: *A worldview called Naturalism—arguing that God was not intimately involved in human life—was dominating the arts during the nineteenth century in England and America.*

B. Why does Dostoyevsky tease the reader with Dimitri's innocence or guilt?

Answer: *Dimitri is a key figure in the novel. His innocence will give the reader hope; his guilt dooms us all. He is the irredeemable man—or not. In fact, his innocence gives us all hope that God can change even the most obstinate heart.*

C. While *The Brothers Karamazov* is not a religious text, it has at its core the theme of redemption. Explain.

Answer: *All the characters are dynamic and changing. They are on a quest for meaning. Some find that meaning in Christ; others find that meaning in money and sex. But all are seeking redemption. The only genuine redemption, of course, is redemption by the blood of Christ, the Lamb of God. This is Dostoyevsky's indirect statement.*

D. Why would some critics argue that this is the greatest novel ever written?

Answer: *It has so many layers of meanings. It has such richness. It has eternal value. One could read it five or six times and still find new meaning in the text.*

The Chosen

Chaim Potok

Objective Test

_A_ Reuven Malter is (A) the narrator, (B) antagonist, (C) a foil, or (D) a Gentile.

_B_ He is the son of David Malter, (A) a Hasidic Jew, (B) a dedicated scholar and humanitarian, (C) an Israeli army general, or (D) a converted Christian.

_C_ Danny Saunders, the other protagonist, is (A) a brilliant Hasid with a love of baseball, (B) a rabbi, (C) a brilliant Hasid with a photographic memory and a passion for psychoanalysis, or (D) a Zionist.

_B_ Danny is the son of Reb Saunders, (A) an Israeli army general, (B) the respected head of a great Hasidic dynasty, (C) the author of a famous book written on the Torah, or (D) a psychology professor.

_D_ Danny ultimately (A) is killed by a freak accident, (B) converts to Christianity, (C) becomes a Hasidic leader, or (D) enters Columbia University.

Suggested Vocabulary Words

A. I had spent five days in a hospital and the world around seemed sharpened [made sharp] now and pulsing [moving with purpose] with life. (ch. 5)

B. A span of life is nothing. But the man who lives that span [period of time], he is something. (ch. 13)

C. It makes us aware of how frail [weak] and tiny we are and of how much we must depend upon the Master of the Universe. (ch. 18)

D. We shook hands and I watched him walk quickly away, tall, lean, bent <u>forward</u> [pushing ahead] with eagerness and hungry for the future, his metal capped shoes tapping against the sidewalk. (last chapter)

Discussion Questions

A. Should Danny have become a psychotherapist even though it violated his father's wishes?

Answer: *Answers will vary.*

B. Do you like the ending of the book?

Answer: *Answers will vary.*

C. If you were making a movie of this book, who would you want to play Danny? Reuven?

Answer: *Answers will vary.*

D. Potok is a master storyteller. In some ways "what he does not write" is important as "what he does write." Explain.

Answer: *Potok skillfully flatters his readers by trusting them to pick up subtle signals between Reuven and Danny. He shows more than tells the reader how these two young men grow to be such close friends.*

E. What role do women have in this novel?

Answer: *Very little. They are there to develop the characters.*

F. Why does Potok tell the story from Reuven's rather than Danny's point of view?

Answer: *One suspects that Potok can identify with Reuven more than Danny. Reuven also is a more modern interpreter.*

The Civil War

Shelby Foote

Objective Test: True or False

__F__ Jefferson Davis welcomed the Civil War.

__F__ Abraham Lincoln was elected in 1860 by a landslide vote.

__T__ Initially Abraham Lincoln, while favoring the prohibition of slavery in new territories, opposed the abolition of slavery in the present states.

__T__ Robert E. Lee was offered the command of all Union forces.

__F__ Stonewall Jackson performed admirably in the Seven Days Campaign.

__F__ The South won the Battle of Shiloh.

__T__ Lee's greatest tactical victory was the Battle of Chancellorsville.

__F__ J. E. B. Stuart was the brilliant Union commander of cavalry.

__F__ One reason the South lost Gettysburg was that the North had a new, secret weapon.

__T__ New Orleans was captured by the North before Vicksburg.

__T__ Lincoln was pleased and irritated by General Meade's victory at Gettysburg. On one hand, the South was soundly defeated. On the other hand, Meade neglected to pursue and to destroy Lee's army.

__T__ General Banks lost the Red River campaign.

__F__ General Albert Sidney Johnston saved Petersburg.

__T__ Hood led an ill-fated expedition to capture Nashville.

__F__ The most brilliant cavalry officer of the War, Nathan Bedford Forrest, was a West Point graduate.

Suggested Vocabulary Words

A. Perhaps by now McClellan had learned to abide the tantrums [fits of bad temper] and exasperations [irritations] of his former friend and sympathizer. (vol. 1)

B. McClellan was quite aware of the danger of straddling [going on both sides of] what he called "the confounded [frustrating] Chickahominy." (vol. 1)

C. In addition to retaining the services of Seward and Chase, both excellent men at their respective [particular] posts, he had managed to turn aside the wrath [intense anger] of the Jacobins [extreme political radicals] without increasing their bitterness toward himself or incurring [bringing upon himself] their open hatred. . . . Paradoxically [the opposite of expected], because of the way he had done it . . . (vol. 2)

D. Stuart had accepted the gambit [sacrifices to gain advantage; maneuver]. . . . (vol. 3)

E. Poor as the plan was in the first place, mainly because of its necessary surrender of the initiative [making the first move] to the enemy, it was rendered even poorer—in fact inoperative [dysfunctional; not working]—by the speed in which Sherman moved through the supposedly impenetrable [impassable] swamps. (vol. 3)

Discussion Questions

A. As you read this book, did you feel that Shelby Foote, a native of Memphis, Tennessee, was prejudiced in favor of the Confederacy? Defend your answer.
Answer: *Answers will vary, but that is not this reader's impression.*

B. What were the causes of the American Civil War?
Answer: *Foote would say that the South was afraid that if slavery expansion was halted, it would doom their culture. That was old news. However, by 1860 the American political system could no longer solve this problem, and war became inevitable.*

C. Why was the loss of Vicksburg, Mississippi, such a grievous blow to the Confederacy?
Answer: *The Western Confederacy, with all its resources, was cut off from the Eastern Confederacy.*

D. Do you believe that Forrest ordered, or even condoned, the massacre of Black troops at Fort Pillow? Defend your answer.

Answer: *Foote makes a strong case that Forrest was not aware of the massacre and did not condone it.*

E. Even though McClellan had access to Lee's strategic plan, he still managed merely to stop, not destroy, Lee as he advanced northward. Why?

Answer: *McClellan was too cautious, and Lee was a great general.*

F. What sort of man was Stonewall Jackson?

Answer: *Jackson was a paradox: a sincerely pious Presbyterian and a cold-blooded killer. He was without a doubt the best general under Robert E. Lee's command.*

G. What do you think would have happened if the South had won the Battle of Gettysburg?

Answer: *Probably not much. The South, according to Foote, never had the resources to win the Civil War.*

The Count of Monte Cristo

Alexandre Dumas

Objective Test

__B__ At the age of (A) eighteen, (B) nineteen, (C) twenty-one, or (D) twenty-four, Edmond Dantès has the perfect life.

__A__ He is about to become the captain of a ship, and (A) he is engaged to a beautiful woman, (B) he has inherited a fortune, (C) he has won the lottery, or (D) he is appointed a magistrate.

__C__ Two people resent his success, however. The treasurer of his ship, Danglers, and (A) Pierre, (B) Marcus, (C) Fernand, or (D) Jacques.

__B__ Caderousse is (A) Dantès's good friend, (B) angry that Dantès is so much better off than he is, (C) the jailer, or (D) sick.

__D__ Dantès is accused of (A) larceny, (B) murder, (C) grand theft, or (D) treason.

__D__ The Deputy Public Prosecutor, Villefort, sees through the plot to frame Dantès and is prepared to set him free. At the last moment, though, Dantès jeopardizes his freedom by revealing the name of the man to whom he is supposed to deliver Napoleon's letter. He is (A) Villefort's brother, (B) Villefort's father-in-law, (C) Villefort's uncle, or (D) Villefort's father.

__A__ While in prison Dantès is tutored by (A) an Italian priest, (B) Leonardo da Vinci, (C) an imprisoned professor, or (D) a death-row inmate.

__C__ Before he dies, The priest tells Dantès about a (A) treasure map, (B) secret code, (C) treasure in Monte Cristo, or (D) new cure for cancer.

__B__ Dantès collects the fortune and (A) retires happily, (B) ruins his enemies, (C) invests in the stock market, or (D) closes the prison.

__A__ Dantès falls in love with (A) Haydee, (B) Mary, (C) Susan, or (D) Evangeline.

Suggested Vocabulary Words

A. Now, in spite of the mobility [changeability] of his countenance [face], the command of which, like a finished actor, he had carefully studied before the glass, it was by no means easy for him to assume an air of judicial [legal] severity [seriousness]. Except the recollection of the line of politics his father had adopted, and which might interfere [impede], unless he acted with the greatest prudence [cautious wisdom], with his own career, Gerard de Villefort was as happy as a man could be. (ch. 7)

B. "Then," answered the elder prisoner, "the will of God be done!" and as the old man slowly pronounced [declared] those words, an air of profound [deep] resignation [surrender; acceptance] spread itself over his careworn [grieving; anguished] countenance. Dantès gazed on the man who could thus philosophically [thoughtfully and theoretically] resign hopes so long and ardently [fervently] nourished [maintained] with an <u>astonishment</u> [extreme excitement] <u>mingled</u> [mixed] with <u>admiration</u> [astonished approbation]. (ch. 16)

C. He had a very clear idea of the men with whom his lot had been cast. . . . It spared him <u>interpreters</u> [people who explain], persons always <u>troublesome</u> [causing problems] and frequently <u>indiscreet</u> [imprudent], gave him great <u>facilities</u> [aptitudes] of communication, either with the vessels he met at sea, with the small boats sailing along the coast, or with the people without name, country, or occupation, who are always seen on the <u>quays</u> [landing places; docks] of seaports, and who live by hidden and mysterious means which we must suppose to be a direct gift of providence, as they have no visible means of support. It is fair to assume that Dantès was on board a smuggler. (ch. 22)

D. It would be difficult to describe the state of <u>stupor</u> [a state of supreme, debilitative disbelief] in which Villefort left the Palais. Every <u>pulse</u> [heartbeat] beat with <u>feverish</u> [extreme] excitement, every nerve was <u>strained</u> [under stress], every vein swollen, and every part of his body seemed to suffer distinctly from the rest, thus multiplying his agony a thousand-fold. He made his way along the <u>corridors</u> [passageways] through force of habit; he threw <u>aside</u> [away] his <u>magisterial</u> [official; ceremonial] robe, not out of <u>deference</u> [respect] to <u>etiquette</u> [polite custom], but because it was an <u>unbearable</u> [too much to carry] burden, a <u>veritable</u> [genuine; true] garb of Nessus, <u>insatiate</u> [unable to be satisfied] in torture. Having <u>staggered</u> [walked in uncoordinated style] as far as the Rue Dauphine, he perceived his carriage, awoke his sleeping coachman by opening the door himself, threw himself on the cushions, and pointed towards the Faubourg Saint-Honoré; the carriage drove on. The weight of his fallen fortunes seemed suddenly to crush him; he could not foresee the <u>consequences</u> [outcome; results]; he could not contemplate the future with the <u>indifference</u> [without regard] of the hardened criminal who merely faces a <u>contingency</u> [unforeseen result] already familiar. God was still in his heart. "God," he <u>murmured</u> [spoke in complaint], not knowing what he said,—"God—God!" Behind the event that had <u>overwhelmed</u> [deeply upset] him he saw the hand of God. The carriage rolled rapidly onward. Villefort, while turning restlessly on the cushions, felt something press against him. He put out his hand to remove the object; it was a fan which Madame de Villefort had left in the carriage; this fan awakened a <u>recollection</u> [remembrance] which darted through his mind like lightning. He thought of his wife. (ch. 111)

Discussion Questions

A. If you can, watch several movie versions of this book and compare them with the book itself.

Answer: *Answers will vary.*

B. In what way, metaphorically, does Dantès die in prison?

Answer: *His relationship with the priest gave him new strength, direction, and skills necessary for his next journey. He was "reborn" as a new man.*

C. Discuss how Valentine de Villefort and Haydee function as foils.

Answer: *They develop the protagonist. Villefort shows the ruthlessness and unforgivingness that is so much a part of Dantes's character. Haydee shows his compassionate, loving side—the latter superseding the former by the end of the novel.*

D. What does the Bible say about unforgivingness and revenge?

Answer: *God does not forgive someone who does not forgive another. God also reserves to himself the right to administer vengeance.*

E. Contrast Dantès and Heathcliff (in *Wuthering Heights*). Contrast them both to Jean Valjean in *Les Misérables*.

Answer: *Dantès and Heathcliff both revenge wrongs done to them. However, Heathcliff is destroyed; Dantès is not. Valjean, on the other hand, is the recipient of forgiveness and shares the same with others, forgiving them.*

The Crucible

Arthur Miller

Objective Test

_A_ In the Puritan New England town of Salem, Massachusetts, a group of girls (A) dance in the forest with a black slave named Tituba, (B) run away with a slave named Tituba, or (C) skip school and hang around Rev. Parris's house.

_C_ A crowd gathers in the Parris home while rumors are filling the town, rumors of (A) a new outbreak of cholera, (B) the British invasion, or (C) witchcraft.

_B_ Miller implies that the girls are pretending there are witches to (A) cause excitement, (B) deflect attention from themselves, or (C) make some money.

_C_ John Proctor refuses to participate in this activity and calls their bluff. He is (A) reprimanded, (B) dunked, or (C) hanged.

_A_ Abigail loves (A) Proctor, (B) Rev. Parris, or (C) Ishmael.

Suggested Vocabulary Words

A. I look for John Proctor that took me from my sleep and put knowledge in my heart! I never knew what pretense [false presentation] Salem was, I never knew the lying lessons I was taught by all these Christian women and their covenanted [husbands by agreement before God] men! And now you bid me tear the light out of my eyes? I will not, I cannot! You loved me, John Proctor, and whatever sin it is, you love me yet!

B. You must understand, sir, that a person is either with this court or he must be counted against it, there be no road between. This is a sharp time, now, a precise [exact] time—we live no longer in the dusky afternoon when evil mixed itself with good and befuddled [confused] the world. Now, by God's grace, the shining sun is up, and them that fear not light will surely praise it.

Discussion Questions

A. Discuss the McCarthy trials of the 1950s.

Answer: *Joseph McCarthy pursued a similar witch hunt against Communists in 1950s America, playing on people's fears and ruining innocent people by false accusations. One should remember that there actually were a few witches in Salem and communists in 1950s America. Though one may and should argue that the punishments were too severe and too extensive, there were some enemies in the camp.*

B. Is John Proctor a realistic character? Does he seem more a product of the 1950s than a character living in the seventeenth century?

Answer: *He is clearly a product of Arthur Miller's century. Proctor's mannerisms and self-reflection are part of the twentieth century, not the seventeenth.*

C. Why doesn't Proctor pretend to be guilty so that he can live?

Answer: *He partly feels that he should be punished for being unfaithful to his wife. On the other hand, he does not wish to give the evil court any satisfaction.*

D. Would you forgive John Proctor if you were Elizabeth Proctor?
Answer: *Answers will vary.*

E. What is Abigail's motivation?
Answer: *One supposes that if Abigail cannot have John Proctor, then no one can.*

F. Later, after the play was written, Arthur Miller said: "In my play, Danforth seems about to conceive of the truth, and surely there is a disposition in him at least to listen to arguments that go counter to the line of the prosecution. There is no such swerving in the record, and I think now, almost four years after writing it, that I was wrong in mitigating the evil of this man and the judges he represents. Instead, I would perfect his evil to its utmost and make an open issue, a thematic consideration of it, in the play." Do you agree with Miller? Say why or why not.

Answer: *Answers will vary. However, this reader does not agree. Miller betrays his own ignorance and prejudices by supposing that the court had any motivation other than the good of the community.*

Daisy Miller

Henry James

Objective Test

__D__ Daisy, her mother, and brother Randolph are (A) traveling in Asia, (B) visiting Chicago, (C) fishing in Mexico, or (D) visiting Europe.

__B__ Winterbourne, who lives in Geneva, is (A) related to Daisy, (B) attracted to her charm but repelled by her straightforward manner, (C) returning home with Daisy, or (D) instantly in love with Daisy.

__A__ Daisy falls in love with (A) Giovanelli, (B) Winterbourne, (C) Maurice, or (D) Peter.

__B__ Winterbourne finds Daisy and Giovanni at (A) the park, (B) in the Colosseum, (C) at home, or (D) in the theater.

__C__ Daisy (A) marries Giovanni (B) marries Winterbourne (C) dies or (D) returns home.

Suggested Vocabulary Words

A. I hardly know whether it was the <u>analogies</u> [similar in meaning] or the differences that were <u>uppermost</u> [at the front] in the mind of a young American, who, two or three years ago, sat in the garden of the "Trois Couronnes," looking about him, rather idly, at some of the graceful objects I have mentioned. It was a beautiful summer morning, and in whatever fashion the young American looked at things, they must have seemed to him charming. He had come from Geneva the day before by the little steamer, to see his aunt, who was staying at the hotel—Geneva having been for a long time his place of residence. But his aunt had a headache—his aunt had almost always a headache—and now she was shut up in her room, smelling camphor, so that he was at liberty to wander about. He was some seven-and-twenty years of age; when his friends spoke of him, they usually said that he was at Geneva "studying." When his enemies spoke of him, they said—but, after all, he had

no enemies; he was an extremely amiable [likeable] fellow, and univer-
sally [by everyone] liked. What I should say is, simply, that when certain persons spoke of him they affirmed that the reason of his spending
so much time at Geneva was that he was extremely devoted to a lady
who lived there—a foreign lady—a person older than himself. Very few
Americans—indeed, I think none—had ever seen this lady, about whom
there were some singular [unique] stories. But Winterbourne had an old
attachment [emotional pull; preference; inclination] for the little metrop-
olis [urban center] of Calvinism [theology in the track of Calvin]; he
had been put to school there as a boy, and he had afterward gone to college there—circumstances which had led to his forming a great many
youthful friendships. Many of these he had kept, and they were a source
of great satisfaction to him. (part 1)

B. Daisy evidently had a natural talent for performing introductions;
she mentioned the name of each of her companions to the other. She
strolled alone with one of them on each side of her; Mr. Giovanelli, who
spoke English very cleverly—Winterbourne afterward learned that he
had practiced the idiom upon a great many American heiresses [women
who inherit]—addressed her a great deal of very polite nonsense; he
was extremely urbane [polite and polished in manner], and the young
American, who said nothing, reflected upon that profundity [deep mean-
ing] of Italian cleverness which enables people to appear more gracious
in proportion [in degree] as they are more acutely disappointed.
Giovanelli, of course, had counted upon something more intimate; he
had not bargained for a party of three. But he kept his temper in a manner which suggested far-stretching intentions. Winterbourne flattered
[thought highly of] himself that he had taken his measure. "He is not a
gentleman," said the young American; "he is only a clever imitation of
one. He is a music master, or a penny-a-liner, or a third-rate artist.
Damn his good looks!" Mr. Giovanelli had certainly a very pretty face;
but Winterbourne felt a superior indignation at his own lovely fellow
countrywoman's not knowing the difference between a spurious [false;
fake] gentleman and a real one. Giovanelli chattered and jested and
made himself wonderfully agreeable. It was true that, if he was an imitation, the imitation was brilliant. "Nevertheless," Winterbourne said to
himself, "a nice girl ought to know!" And then he came back to the
question whether this was, in fact, a nice girl. Would a nice girl, even

allowing for her being a little American flirt, make a <u>rendezvous</u> [meeting] with a presumably low-lived foreigner? The rendezvous in this case, indeed, had been in broad daylight and in the most crowded corner of Rome, but was it not impossible to regard the choice of these circumstances as a proof of extreme cynicism? Singular though it may seem, Winterbourne was <u>vexed</u> [irritated] that the young girl, in joining her <u>amoroso</u> [lover], should not appear more impatient of his own company, and he was vexed because of his <u>inclination</u> [attraction]. It was impossible to regard her as a perfectly well-conducted young lady; she was wanting in a certain indispensable delicacy. It would therefore simplify matters greatly to be able to treat her as the object of one of those <u>sentiments</u> [feelings] which are called by romancers "lawless passions." That she should seem to wish to get rid of him would help him to think more lightly of her, and to be able to think more lightly of her would make her much less <u>perplexing</u> [difficult to understand]. But Daisy, on this occasion, continued to present herself as an <u>inscrutable</u> [not to be understood and replicated] combination of <u>audacity</u> [outward boldness] and innocence. (part 2)

Discussion Questions

A. How credible a person is Daisy?

Answer: *Daisy is not credible to this reader. She is neither an Anna Karenina (*Anna Karenina, *by Leo Tolstoy) nor an Emma Woodhouse (*Emma, *by Jane Austen). She is an archetype more than a person. In this reader's opinion, she is not developed well.*

B. Is the ending satisfactory?

Answer: *It seems incredible that Daisy would die so suddenly.*

C. If Daisy Miller is representing America in Europe, as some critics suggest, what is James saying?

Answer: *America is naive and ostentatious but not able to compete with the urbane, sophisticated Europe.*

D. Would you assign this book to a high school class?

Answer: *Answers will vary.*

David Copperfield

Charles Dickens

Objective Test

__C__ David Copperfield (A) is born in a workhouse, (B) is abused by his stepfather, or (C) enjoys his early childhood with his mother and their kindly servant, Peggotty.

__C__ But when his mother marries the cruel Mr. Murdstone, he is (A) forced to work in a factory, (B) sent to live with an aunt, or (C) sent away to Salem House, a run-down London boarding school where the boys are beaten by Mr. Creakle.

__A__ David's mother dies, and David is (A) forced to go to work at Murdstone's wine warehouse, (B) David returns home to live, or (C) is disowned.

__B__ Who adopts David? (A) Mr. Murdstone, (B) Miss Trotwood, or (C) Old Peggotty.

__A__ Uriah Heep is (A) an evil law clerk, (B) a robber, or (C) a friend to David.

Suggested Vocabulary Words

A. And yet my thoughts were idle [unimportant; empty]; not intent on the calamity that weighed upon my heart, but idly loitering [standing with no purpose] near it. I thought of our house shut up and hushed. I thought of the little baby, who, Mrs. Creakle said, had been pining [grieving] away for some time, and who, they believed, would die too. I thought of my father's grave in the churchyard, by our house, and of my mother lying there beneath the tree I knew so well. I stood upon a chair when I was left alone, and looked into the glass to see how red my eyes were, and how sorrowful my face. I considered, after some hours were gone, if my tears were really hard to flow now, as they seemed to be, what, in connection with my loss, it would affect me most to think of when I drew near home—for I was going home to the funeral. I am sensible of having felt that a dignity [respect; honor] attached to me among the rest of the boys, and that I was important in my <u>affliction</u> [stress]. (ch. 9)

B. While I advanced in friendship and <u>intimacy</u> [closeness; friendship] with Mr. Dick, I did not go backward in the favour of his <u>staunch</u> [steadfast] friend, my aunt. She took so kindly to me, that, in the course of a few weeks, she shortened my adopted name of Trotwood into Trot; and even encouraged me to hope, that if I went on as I had begun, I might take equal rank in her <u>affections</u> [attraction; caring interest] with my sister Betsey Trotwood. (ch. 15)

C. He was a little light-haired gentleman, with <u>undeniable</u> [without a doubt] boots, and the stiffest of white cravats and shirt-collars. He was buttoned up, mighty trim and tight, and must have taken a great deal of pains with his whiskers, which were accurately curled. His gold watch-chain was so <u>massive</u> [huge], that a fancy came across me, that he ought to have a sinewy golden arm, to draw it out with, like those which are put up over the goldbeaters' shops. He was got up with such care, and was so stiff, that he could hardly bend himself; being obliged, when he glanced at some papers on his desk, after sitting down in his chair, to move his whole body, from the bottom of his spine, like Punch. (ch. 23)

D. It feel as if it were not for me to record, even though this manuscript is intended for no eyes but mine, how hard I worked at that <u>tremendous</u> [massive] short-hand, and all improvement <u>appertaining</u> [relating] to it, in my sense of responsibility to Dora and her aunts. I will only add, to what I have already written of my perseverance at this time of my life, and of a patient and continuous energy which then began to be matured within me, and which I know to be the strong part of my character, if it have any strength at all, that there, on looking back, I find the source of my success. I have been very fortunate in worldly matters; many men have worked much harder, and not succeeded half so well; but I never could have done what I have done, without the habits of <u>punctuality</u> [on time], order, and <u>diligence</u> [industriousness], without the determination to concentrate myself on one object at a time, no matter how quickly its successor should come upon its heels, which I then formed. (ch. 42)

Discussion Questions

A. What was the narrative point of view? Why did Dickens choose this narrative technique?

Answer: *First-person narration, which allows the reader to grow close to the protagonist. Dickens feels that he needs an interpreter who is part of the action.*

B. Dickens is a masterful descriptive writer. Using the following description from chapter 23, discuss the way Dickens describes characters. "He was a little light-haired gentleman, with undeniable boots, and the stiffest of white cravats and shirt-collars. He was buttoned up, mighty trim and tight, and must have taken a great deal of pains with his whiskers, which were accurately curled. His gold watch-chain was so massive, that a fancy came across me, that he ought to have a sinewy golden arm, to draw it out with, like those which are put up over the goldbeaters' shops. He was got up with such care, and was so stiff, that he could hardly bend himself; being obliged, when he glanced at some papers on his desk, after sitting down in his chair, to move his whole body, from the bottom of his spine, like Punch."

Answer: *His use of descriptive adjectives and metaphors is legendary. Dickens brings the person alive by these descriptions and subsequent narration. He does not hesitate to pontificate on the very heart of the person described.*

C. G. K. Chesterton said, "[Dickens's] books are full of baffled villains stalking out or cowardly bullies kicked downstairs. But the villains and the cowards are such delightful people that the reader always hopes the villain will put his head through a side window and make a last remark; or that the bully will say one more thing, even from the bottom of the stairs." What does Chesterton mean? Do you agree?

Answer: *Dickens's characters are so alive and real that the reader enjoys having them around—even if they are evil.*

Don Quixote

Miguel de Cervantes

Objective Test

__B__ At one point Don Quixote frees some prisoners. They respond by (A) thanking him, (B) attacking him, (C) giving him a prize, or (D) ignoring him.

__A__ The name of Don Quixote's squire is (A) Sancho, (B) Pere, (C) Jacques, or (D) Maurice.

__B__ Sancho seeks to learn more from his master than he is able to learn. What does he really want to learn? (A) Don Quixote's middle name, (B) how to be heroic knight, (C) how to ride a horse with eloquence, or (D) the source of Don Quixote's income.

__D__ Dulcinea is really (A) a princess, (B) a prostitute, (C) a neighbor, or (D) an ordinary local girl who was not remotely interested in Don Quixote.

__C__ Windmills, to Don Quixote, are (A) dragons, (B) ships, (C) giants, or (D) opposing knights.

Suggested Vocabulary Words

A. You must know, then, that the above-named gentleman whenever he was at leisure (which was mostly all the year round) gave himself up to reading books of <u>chivalry</u> [valor] with such <u>ardor</u> [enthusiasm] and <u>avidity</u> [affinity] that he almost entirely neglected the pursuit of his field-sports, and even the management of his property; and to such a pitch did his eagerness and <u>infatuation</u> [foolish and extravagant love] go that he sold many an acre of land to buy books of chivalry to read, and brought home as many of them as he could get. (part 1, ch. 1)

B. He approved highly of the giant Morgante, because, although of the giant breed which is always <u>arrogant</u> [extremely self-centered] and ill-conditioned, he alone was <u>affable</u> [friendly] and well-bred. (part 1, ch. 1)

C. Thus setting out, our new-fledged adventurer paced along, talking to himself and saying, "Who knows but that in time to come, when the veracious [honest; truthful] history of my famous deeds is made known, the sage who writes it, when he has to set forth my first sally in the early morning, will do it after this fashion? 'Scarce had the rubicund [red-complexed] Apollo spread o'er the face of the broad spacious earth the golden threads of his bright hair, scarce had the little birds of painted plumage attuned their notes to hail with dulcet [agreeable] and mellifluous [richly flowing] harmony the coming of the rosy Dawn, that, deserting the soft couch of her jealous spouse, was appearing to mortals at the gates and balconies of the Manchegan horizon, when the renowned knight Don Quixote of La Mancha, quitting the lazy down, mounted his celebrated steed Rocinante and began to traverse the ancient and famous Campo de Montiel;'" which in fact he was actually traversing. "Happy the age, happy the time," he continued, "in which shall be made known my deeds of fame, worthy to be moulded in brass, carved in marble, limned in pictures, for a memorial for ever. And thou, O sage magician, whoever thou art, to whom it shall fall to be the chronicler of this wondrous history, forget not, I entreat thee, my good Rocinante, the constant companion of my ways and wanderings." Presently he broke out again, as if he were love-stricken in earnest, "O Princess Dulcinea, lady of this captive heart, a grievous wrong hast thou done me to drive me forth with scorn, and with inexorable [relentless] obduracy [stubbornness] banish me from the presence of thy beauty. O lady, deign to hold in remembrance this heart, thy vassal, that thus in anguish pines for love of thee." (part 1, ch. 2)

D. Seeing what was going on, Don Quixote said in an angry voice, "Discourteous knight, it ill becomes you to assail [attack] one who cannot defend himself; mount your steed and take your lance" (for there was a lance leaning against the oak to which the mare was tied), "and I will make you know that you are behaving as a coward." The farmer, seeing before him this figure in full armor brandishing [flaunting; waving] a lance over his head, gave himself up for dead, and made answer meekly, "Sir Knight, this youth that I am chastising is my servant, employed by me to watch a flock of sheep that I have hard by, and he is so careless that I lose one every day, and when I punish him for his carelessness and knavery [mischievously evil] he says I do it out of niggardliness [stinginess], to escape paying him the wages I owe him, and before God, and on my soul, he lies." (part 1, ch. 4)

E. Such was the end of the Ingenious Gentleman of La Mancha, whose village Cide Hamete would not indicate precisely, in order to leave all the towns and villages of La Mancha to contend among themselves for the right to adopt him and claim him as a son, as the seven cities of Greece contended for Homer. The lamentations [expressions of grief] of Sancho and the niece and housekeeper are omitted here, as well as the new epitaphs [brief positive statements] upon his tomb. (part 2, ch. 74)

Discussion Questions

A. In what way is Don Quixote a parody of the struggle between Renaissance thought and medieval thought?

Answer: *Cervantes is making fun of the old guard, the old Spanish knights who retained archaic worldviews in the midst of Renaissance revivals. They are old knights fighting metaphorical windmills.*

B. Examine Cervantes's life and discuss how much personal disappointment colored the sarcasm that *Don Quixote* exhibited.

Answer: *Cervantes, a Spanish nobleman, nonetheless had a very hard and disappointing life. A prisoner in North Africa, he returned home to be unjustly imprisoned again. He used his sarcastic pen to attack the hypocrisy he found around him. Dante did the same thing in his masterpiece* The Divine Comedy.

C. *Don Quixote* generated new interest in 1960s America. Why?

Answer: *The notion that this highly individualistic, highly self-centered era was "charging windmills" made Cervantes's book very popular.*

D. Respond to the following criticism by Vladimir Nabokov:

> Both parts of *Don Quixote* form a veritable encyclopedia of cruelty. From that viewpoint it is one of the most bitter and barbarous books ever penned. And its cruelty is artistic. The extraordinary commentators who talk through their academic

caps or birettas of the humorous and humane mellowly Christian atmosphere of the book, or a happy world where "all is sweetened by the humanities of love and good fellowship," and particularly those who talk of a certain "kindly duchess" who "entertains the Don" in the second Part—these gushing experts have probably been reading some other book or are looking through some rosy gauze at the brutal world of Cervantes' novel.

Answer: *Answers will vary. This reader does not agree with Nabokov. Nabokov suggests that Cervantes was more vitriolic than sarcastic in tone. This reader does not see that in the book.*

E. Critic Joseph Wood Krutch argued that *Don Quixote* strove "for that synthesis of the comedy and tragedy of life which we recognize as the distinguishing mark of the modern novel." Agree or disagree.

Answer: *When one compares this novel to early English novels such as* Robinson Crusoe, *it appears more modern in tone.*

F. In what ways, if any, was Don Quixote a Christlike figure?

Answer: *Some scholars say he is Christlike because he is trying to save the helpless; yet, I don't see it. The Christ I know was not attacking windmills. He went after the real enemy and won!*

G. Several years ago, the story of *Don Quixote* was adapted as the musical play *Man of La Mancha.* In this version, at Quixote's deathbed, Sancho promises to continue Don Quixote's mission. Do you think Cervantes would have been pleased with this ending?

Answer: *No. Through Don Quixote, Cervantes tells Sancho to give up the quest.*

Emma

Jane Austen

Objective Test

_B_ Emma is persuaded that (A) she will someday be rich, (B) that she will never marry, or (C) that she will die in childbirth.

_A_ Emma then embarks on a series of (A) matchmaking plans, (B) trips, or (C) jobs.

_C_ Emma is trying to place her friend Harriet with Mr. Elton, but it does not work out because (A) Harriet is too poor, (B) Mr. Elton is terminally ill, or (C) Mr. Elton really likes Emma and feels that Harriet is below him socially.

_A_ Emma has a very close friend who speaks frankly with her. His name is (A) Mr. Knightley, (B) Mr. Martin, or (C) Mr. Elton.

_C_ Ultimately Emma marries (A) Mr. Churchill, (B) Mr. Martin, or (C) Mr. Knightley.

Suggested Vocabulary Words

A. Harriet Smith's <u>intimacy</u> [closeness] at Hartfield was soon a settled thing. Quick and decided in her ways, Emma lost no time in inviting, encouraging, and telling her to come very often; and as their acquaintance increased, so did their satisfaction in each other. As a walking companion, Emma had very early foreseen how useful she might find her. In that respect Mrs. Weston's loss had been important. Her father never went beyond the shrubbery, where two divisions of the ground <u>sufficed</u> [satisfied] him for his long walk, or his short, as the year varied; and since Mrs. Weston's marriage her exercise had been too much confined. (vol. 1, ch. 4)

B. In short, she sat, during the first visit, looking at Jane Fairfax with twofold <u>complacency</u> [satisfaction]; the sense of pleasure and the sense of rendering justice, and was determining that she would dislike her no longer. When she took in her history, indeed, her situation, as

well as her beauty; when she considered what all this elegance was destined to, what she was going to sink from, how she was going to live, it
seemed impossible to feel any thing but compassion and respect; especially, if to every well-known particular entitling her to interest, were
added the highly probable circumstance of an attachment to Mr. Dixon,
which she had so naturally started to herself. In that case, nothing could
be more pitiable [lamentable] or more honourable than the sacrifices she
had resolved on. Emma was very willing now to acquit her of having
seduced Mr. Dixon's actions from his wife, or of any thing mischievous
[harmful] which her imagination had suggested at first. If it were love,
it might be simple, single, successless love on her side alone. She might
have been unconsciously sucking in the sad poison, while a sharer of his
conversation with her friend; and from the best, the purest of motives,
might now be denying herself this visit to Ireland, and resolving to
divide herself effectually from him and his connections by soon beginning her career of laborious [boring; tedious] duty. (vol. 2, ch. 2)

  C. As long as Mr. Knightley remained with them, Emma's fever
continued; but when he was gone, she began to be a little tranquillized
[made quiet] and subdued [overcome]—and in the course of the sleepless night, which was the tax for such an evening, she found one or two
such very serious points to consider, as made her feel, that even her
happiness must have some alloy. Her father—and Harriet. She could not
be alone without feeling the full weight of their separate claims; and
how to guard the comfort of both to the utmost, was the question. With
respect to her father, it was a question soon answered. She hardly knew
yet what Mr. Knightley would ask; but a very short parley [talk] with
her own heart produced the most solemn resolution of never quitting her
father.—She even wept over the idea of it, as a sin of thought. While he
lived, it must be only an engagement; but she flattered [thought well of]
herself, that if divested [lost ownership] of the danger of drawing her
away, it might become an increase of comfort to him.—How to do her
best by Harriet, was of more difficult decision;—how to spare her from
any unnecessary pain; how to make her any possible atonement; how to
appear least her enemy?—On these subjects, her perplexity and distress
were very great—and her mind had to pass again and again through
every bitter reproach and sorrowful regret that had ever surrounded it.—
She could only resolve at last, that she would still avoid a meeting with

her, and communicate all that need be told by letter; that it would be inexpressibly desirable to have her removed just now for a time from Highbury, and—indulging in one scheme more—nearly resolve, that it might be practicable to get an invitation for her to Brunswick Square.— Isabella had been pleased with Harriet; and a few weeks spent in London must give her some amusement.—She did not think it in Harriet's nature to escape being benefited by novelty and variety, by the streets, the shops, and the children.—At any rate, it would be a proof of attention and kindness in herself, from whom every thing was due; a separation for the present; an <u>averting</u> [removal] of the evil day, when they must all be together again. (book 3, ch. 14)

Discussion Questions

A. Compare Emma to other protagonists in Jane Austen's novels.

Answer: *Emma is clearly more developed and complicated a character than any of Austen's protagonists.*

B. Where is the climax in the novel?

Answer: *The climax is when Emma realizes that she loves her good friend Mr. Knightly and they decide to marry.*

C. What is the purpose of so many parlor scenes?

Answer: *Austen uses these scenes to develop her characters in depth.*

D. Most critics think that *Emma* is superior to other works by Austen because she develops her characters better. What do you think?

Answer: *This reader agrees.*

E. Do you feel that Emma is a nineteenth-century feminist?

Answer: *No, she readily accepts her role; however, she also is not afraid to appear intelligent in the company of men.*

F. Pretend that you are casting the roles of this novel for a dramatic version. Who would you choose to play the major roles?

Answer: *Answers will vary.*

The Fairie Queen

Edmund Spenser

Objective Test

_A_ *The Faerie Queene* is (A) an allegory, (B) a massive prose work, or (C) originally written in Latin.

_C_ As the poet examines the two virtues—holiness and chastity—in books 1 and 3, he follows the journeys of two knights, (A) Pilgrim and Christian, (B) Richard and David, or (C) Redcrosse and Britomart.

_A_ In a magic mirror, Britomart sees (A) her future husband, (B) her death, or (C) her salvation.

_B_ Spenser reveres (A) King Philip, (B) Queen Elizabeth, or (C) Joan of Arc.

_C_ He attacks (A) Protestantism, (B) the French, or (C) Roman Catholicism.

Suggested Vocabulary Words

A. Scarsely had *Phoebus* in the <u>glooming</u> [becoming pale with dawn] East / Yet harnessed his firie-footed teeme, / Ne reard aboue the earth his flaming creast, / When the last deadly smoke aloft did steeme, / That signe of last outbreathed life did seeme, / Vnto the watchman on the castle wall; / Who thereby dead that <u>balefull</u> [baleful; evil] Beast did deeme, / And to his Lord and Ladie lowd gan call, / To tell, how he had seene the Dragons fatall fall. (book 1, canto 12)

B. For all so soone, as *Guyon* thence was gon / Vpon his voyage with his trustie guide, / That wicked band of <u>villeins</u> [villains; bad people] fresh begon / That castle to assaile on euery side, / And lay strong siege about it far and wide. / So huge and <u>infinite</u> [without end] their numbers were, / That all the land they vnder them did hide; / So fowle and <u>vgly</u> [ugly], that exceeding feare / Their visages imprest, when they approched neare. (book 2, canto 11)

C. Who backe returning, told as he had seene, / That they were doughtie knights of <u>dreaded</u> [disliked] name; / And those two Ladies, their two loues vnseene; / And therefore wisht them without blot or blame, / To let them passe at will, for dread of shame. / But *Blandamour* full of <u>vainglorious</u> [prideful] spright, / And rather stird by his discordfull Dame, / Vpon them gladly would haue prov'd his might, / But that he yet was sore of his late lucklesse fight. (book 4, canto 3)

Discussion Questions

A. Contrast this long narrative poem with Virgil's *Aeneid*.

Answer: *Both are long, nationalistic poems extolling the virtues of a monarch (Elizabeth I for Spenser; Emperor Augustus for Virgil).*

B. Define courtly love and discuss how Spenser uses it in his epic poem.

Answer: *Courtly love celebrates the chivalry of King Arthur's court. To Spenser, courtly love is much inferior to agape, Christian love.*

C. Give evidence that Spenser dislikes the Roman Catholic Church.

Answer: *It is the dragon at the end of book 1. One would expect the Englishman Spenser, whose nation was at war with Roman Catholic Spain, to intensely dislike Roman Catholicism.*

D. Suppose you are retained by a famous publishing company to decide whether or not *The Fairie Queen* should be republished in contemporary setting and English. What would you advise? Does it have any present relevance?

Answer: *Answers will vary.*

Giants in the Earth

O. E. Rølvaag

Objective Test

__B__ Per Hansa and his family (A) move to California to pan for gold, (B) get lost, or (C) are attacked by Native Americans.

__A__ With other Norwegian immigrant families, they (A) establish a small settlement along Spring Creek, (B) reach the Oregon Territory, or (C) turn back.

__C__ They live in a (A) log cabin, (B) teepee, or (C) sod house.

__A__ Per Hansa's wife, Beret, (A) is homesick for Norway, (B) is killed by Native Americans, or (C) dies in childbirth.

__B__ Per (A) strikes it rich in gold, (B) dies in a blizzard, or (C) leaves Beret.

Suggested Vocabulary Words

A. It bent resiliently [with strength and purpose] under the trampling [deliberately walking] feet; it did not break, but it complained aloud every time—for nothing like this had ever happened to it before. (book 1, ch. 1)

B. How could human beings continue to live here while that magic ring encompassed [surrounded] them? And those who were strong enough to break through were only being enticed [drawn] still farther to their destruction. (book 2, ch. 3)

C. For you and me, life out here is nothing; but there may be others so constructed [built; created] that they don't fit into this life at all; and yet they are finer and better souls than either one of us. (book 1, ch. 4)

Discussion Questions

A. How well does the author develop his characters?
Answer: *Characterization is one of the great strengths of this novel.*

B. Does Beret's religious conversion seem realistic to you?
Answer: *Not to this reader. I found it to be exaggerated and strange, more of a psychological than a spiritual event.*

C. Did you like the ending? How would you change it?
Answer: *Answers will vary.*

D. Does Per love Beret?
Answer: *Answers will vary, but this reader feels that he does.*

The Grapes of Wrath

John Steinbeck

Objective Test

__C__ Tom Joad has recently (A) left the army, (B) been fired from a job, or (C) been released from prison.

__A__ Jim is (A) a former preacher, (B) a rich landowner, (C) another dust-bowl farmer, or (D) Tom's brother.

__D__ To find work the whole family travels to (A) Texas, (B) South America, (C) Chicago, or (D) California.

__C__ As they travel across country, older members of the family (A) return to Oklahoma, (B) stop and homestead, (C) die, or (D) join the army.

__B__ When they reach California, they (A) find work, (B) find fewer jobs than they had heard, (C) return home, or (D) take a boat to New York City.

Suggested Vocabulary Words

A. But we've been here for generations [grandparents, parents, children, and so on; progeny]. Besides, where'll we go? (ch. 5)

B. Fella like that bust the holiness [pertaining to holy; sacred]. But when they're all workin' together, not one fella for another fella, but one fella kind of <u>harnessed</u> [connected; pulling together] to the whole shebang—that's right, that's holy. (ch. 8)

C. "We're Joads. We don't look up to nobody. Grampa's grampa, he fit in the <u>Revolution</u> [violent upheaval; the American Revolutionary War]. We was farm people till the debt. And then—them people. They done somepin to us. (ch. 22)

Discussion Questions

A. Does the novel end in hope or hopelessness?
Answer: *This is really open to debate.*

B. What is Jim Casey's role?
Answer: *Like the priest in Dostoyevsky's* The Brothers Karamazov, *this ex-preacher is Steinbeck's voice about metaphysical reality. He is a secular priest, to be sure, whining for meaning and hope in Steinbeck's Naturalistic universe, which is basically devoid of hope.*

C. Do you think the vulgar language was necessary to the theme, plot, or tone of the story?
Answer: *This reader does not think it was necessary.*

D. How would the novel be different if a California grower wrote the novel?
Answer: *Answers will vary.*

The Great Gatsby

F. Scott Fitzgerald

Objective Test

__B__ The narrator in this book is (A) Jay Gatsby, (B) Nick Carraway, (C) Tom Buchanan, or (D) Daisy Buchanan.

__A__ Nick's neighbor is (A) Jay Gatsby, (B) Nick Carraway, (C) Tom Buchanan, or (D) Daisy Buchanan.

__D__ Nick's cousin is (A) Jay Gatsby, (B) Nick Carraway, (C) Tom Buchanan, or (D) Daisy Buchanan.

__A__ The book is primarily about the life of (A) Jay Gatsby, (B) Nick Carraway, (C) Tom Buchanan, or (D) Daisy Buchanan.

__A__ Nick meets Jordan Baker at (A) a Gatsby party, (B) the shore, (C) the opera, (D) Yale.

__B__ Gatsby tells Jordan (A) he has a terminal disease, (B) he knew Daisy in Louisville in 1917 and is deeply in love with her, (C) Tom is no good, or (D) how to play the stock market.

__A__ Nick brings Gatsby and Daisy together by (A) inviting them both to tea, (B) passing notes back and forth, (C) making a video of Daisy, or (D) staying out of everything.

__C__ Tom is bothered because (A) Daisy is spending too much money, (B) Jay is richer than he, (C) Daisy obviously likes Gatsby, or (D) Nick is interfering.

__A__ While driving Gatsby's car, Tom accidentally kills (A) his mistress, (B) his best pet, (C) Jay, or (D) Daisy.

__C__ At the end of the novel (A) Gatsby and Daisy get married, (B) Tom dies, (C) Gatsby is killed, or (D) Nick and Daisy marry.

Suggested Vocabulary Words

A. In my younger and more <u>vulnerable</u> [needful; open] years my father gave me some advice that I've been turning over in my mind ever since. (ch. 1)

B. There was the boom of a bass drum, and the voice of the orchestra leader rang out suddenly above the echolalia [repeating what is said by others] of the garden. (ch. 3)

C. "We've met before," muttered [spoken offhandedly and softly] Gatsby. His eyes glanced momentarily [quickly; briefly] at me, and his lips parted with an abortive [failed] attempt at a laugh. Luckily the clock took this moment to tilt dangerously at the pressure of his head, whereupon he turned and caught it with trembling fingers, and set it back in place. Then he sat down, rigidly [stiffly], his elbow on the arm of the sofa and his chin in his hand. (ch. 5)

D. It was a random [unplanned] shot, and yet the reporter's instinct was right. Gatsby's notoriety [high reputation], spread about by the hundreds who had accepted his hospitality and so become authorities on his past, had increased all summer until he fell just short of being news. Contemporary legends such as the "underground pipe-line to Canada." attached themselves to him, and there was one persistent [repeated for a long time] story that he didn't live in a house at all, but in a boat that looked like a house and was moved secretly up and down the Long Island shore. Just why these inventions were a source of satisfaction to James Gatz of North Dakota, isn't easy to say. (ch. 6)

E. After a little while Mr. Gatz opened the door and came out, his mouth ajar, his face flushed slightly, his eyes leaking isolated [alone] and unpunctual [untimely] tears. He had reached an age where death no longer has the quality of ghastly [awful] surprise, and when he looked around him now for the first time and saw the height and splendor of the hall and the great rooms opening out from it into other rooms, his grief began to be mixed with an awed pride. I helped him to a bedroom up-stairs; while he took off his coat and vest I told him that all arrangements had been deferred [put off] until he came. (ch. 9)

Discussion Questions

A. If you were producing this book as a movie, which actor would you have play Gatsby? Tom? Daisy? Nick? Why?

Answer: *Answers will vary.*

B. The characters all represent 1920 American "types." Discuss the type represented by each main character: Jay, Nick, Daisy, Tom, and Jordan.

Answer: *Jay Gatsby represents the naive, honest person who is ill-prepared to survive in the ruthless materialism of the 1920s. Nick Carraway portrays the clever, Ivy League interpreter of reality. Daisy Buchanan stands for the weak-willed, shallow person captured by materialism. Tom Buchanan represents the cynical, dishonest, ruthless, immoral American. Jordan portrays the dishonest, self-serving feminist.*

C. Why does Fitzgerald wait until chapter 4 to begin the plot?
Answer: *The development of the characters takes this long.*

D. In what way is this novel autobiographical?
Answer: *Fitzgerald's wife, Zelda, is amazingly like Daisy.*

E. Discuss how Fitzgerald uses symbolism in this novel.
Answer: *There are many examples. Critic Daniel J. Schneider suggests that the white Daisy embodies the vision that Gatsby (who, like Lord Jim, usually wears white suits) seeks to embrace—but which Nick, who discovers the corrupt admixture of dream and reality, rejects in rejecting Jordan. Except in Gatsby's extravagant imagination, the white does not exist purely: it is invariably stained by the money, the yellow. Daisy is the white flower with the golden center. In her virginal beauty she "dressed in white and had a little white roadster," and thus Nick realizes that she is "high in a white palace the king's daughter, the golden girl." "Her voice is like money"; she carries a "little gold pencil"; when she visits Gatsby, there are "two rows of brass buttons on her dress."*

Hard Times

Charles Dickens

Objective Test

__B__ Thomas Gradgrind, is (A) a wealthy philanthropist who lives in Liverpool, England, (B) a wealthy, retired merchant in the industrial city of Coketown, England, or (C) a banker in London, England.

__A__ He felt strongly that (A) government should have a hands-off policy, (B) government should help the poor, or (C) poor people are inevitable.

__B__ Ultimately, in his view, self-interest would (A) corrupt the country, (B) take care of the most people with the least effort, or (C) be unchristian.

__C__ Gradgrind realizes the liability of his worldview because of (A) the situation of his workers, (B) the example of America, or (C) the problems his daughter faces.

__A__ Gradgrind (A) gives up his philosophy of facts and devotes his political power to helping the poor, (B) joins a union, or (C) fires his workers.

Suggested Vocabulary Words

A. "I trust, sir," rejoined Mrs. Sparsit, with decent <u>resignation</u> [quiet submission], "it is not necessary that you should do anything of that kind. I hope I have learnt how to <u>accommodate</u> [cause to participate] myself to the changes of life. If I have acquired an interest in hearing of your <u>instructive</u> [giving knowledge or information] experiences, and can scarcely hear enough of them, I claim no merit for that, since I believe it is a general sentiment." (book 1, ch. 7)

B. Herein, too, the sense of even thinking unselfishly aided him. Before he had so much as closed Mr. Bounderby's door, he had reflected that at least his being obliged to go away was good for her, as it would save her from the chance of being brought into question for not withdrawing from him. Though it would cost him a hard <u>pang</u> [pain] to leave her, and though he could think of no similar place in which his <u>condemnation</u> [negative feelings] would not pursue him, perhaps it was almost a relief to be forced away from the <u>endurance</u> [steadfastness] of the last four days, even to unknown difficulties and distresses. (book 2, ch. 6)

C. Every night, Sissy went to Rachael's lodging, and sat with her in her small neat room. All day, Rachael toiled as such people must toil, whatever their anxieties. The smoke-serpents were <u>indifferent</u> [uninterested; uncaring] who was lost or found, who turned out bad or good; the melancholy mad elephants, like the Hard Fact men, abated nothing of their set routine, whatever happened. Day and night again, day and night again. The <u>monotony</u> [consistent repetition] was unbroken. Even Stephen Blackpool's disappearance was falling into the general way, and becoming as monotonous a wonder as any piece of machinery in Coketown. (book 3, ch. 5)

D. Here was Mr. Gradgrind on the same day, and in the same hour, sitting thoughtful in his own room. How much of <u>futurity</u> [the future] did he see? Did he see himself, a white-haired <u>decrepit</u> [ancient; broken] man, bending his hitherto inflexible theories to appointed circumstances; making his facts and figures <u>subservient</u> [as servants] to Faith, Hope, and Charity; and no longer trying to grind that Heavenly trio in his dusty little mills? Did he catch sight of himself, therefore much despised by his late political associates? Did he see them, in the era of its being quite settled that the national dustmen have only to do with one another, and owe no duty to an <u>abstraction</u> [opposite to concrete; theory] called a People, "taunting the honourable gentleman" with this and with that and with what not, five nights a-week, until the small hours of the morning? Probably he had that much <u>foreknowledge</u> [knowing ahead of time], knowing his men. (book 3, ch. 9)

Discussion Questions
A. Compare this novel to Upton Sinclair's *The Jungle*.
Answer: *Both are trying to make a social statement.*

B. What form and structure does Dickens employ in this novel?

Answer: *Hard Times is divided into three sections, or books, and each book is divided into three separate chapters. The structure of the book takes its shape from the titles of the books, all of which are drawn from farming images with biblical connotations.*

C. Discuss two themes in *Hard Times*.

Answer: *Exploitation of the working class and the effects of the industrial revolution.*

D. What is the point of view in this novel? Why does Dickens choose to write *Hard Times* this way?

Answer: *Third-person omniscient allows Dickens to give insights into the plot development and character motivation. In a novel so complicated and full of so many subplots, this is critical.*

E. Who is the protagonist?

Answer: *That could be debated, but this reader would argue that Thomas Gradgrind is the protagonist.*

The House of the Seven Gables

Nathaniel Hawthorne

Objective Test

__B__ In the late 1600s, a local farmer named Matthew Maule builds a house on prime land near a generous spring, but the land is coveted by (A) Cotton Mather, (B) Colonel Pyncheon, or (C) Uncle Venner.

__A__ Maule is hanged for (A) witchcraft, (B) robbery, (C) murder, or (D) treason.

__C__ Pyncheon is behind Maule's conviction. Maule curses the

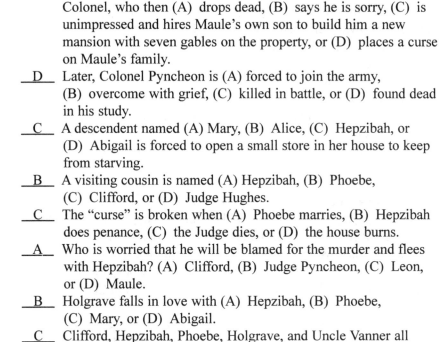

Colonel, who then (A) drops dead, (B) says he is sorry, (C) is unimpressed and hires Maule's own son to build him a new mansion with seven gables on the property, or (D) places a curse on Maule's family.

__D__ Later, Colonel Pyncheon is (A) forced to join the army, (B) overcome with grief, (C) killed in battle, or (D) found dead in his study.

__C__ A descendent named (A) Mary, (B) Alice, (C) Hepzibah, or (D) Abigail is forced to open a small store in her house to keep from starving.

__B__ A visiting cousin is named (A) Hepzibah, (B) Phoebe, (C) Clifford, or (D) Judge Hughes.

__C__ The "curse" is broken when (A) Phoebe marries, (B) Hepzibah does penance, (C) the Judge dies, or (D) the house burns.

__A__ Who is worried that he will be blamed for the murder and flees with Hepzibah? (A) Clifford, (B) Judge Pyncheon, (C) Leon, or (D) Maule.

__B__ Holgrave falls in love with (A) Hepzibah, (B) Phoebe, (C) Mary, or (D) Abigail.

__C__ Clifford, Hepzibah, Phoebe, Holgrave, and Uncle Vanner all (A) live in Seven Gables, (B) move to Boston, or (C) move to the country estate.

Suggested Vocabulary Words

A. The aspect [component; quality] of the venerable [ancient and honored] mansion has always affected me like a human countenance, bearing the traces not merely of outward storm and sunshine, but expressive also, of the long lapse [stoppage] of mortal life, and accompanying vicissitudes [changes] that have passed within. Were these to be worthily recounted, they would form a narrative of no small interest and instruction, and possessing, moreover, a certain remarkable unity, which might almost seem the result of artistic arrangement. But the story would include a chain of events extending over the better part of two centuries, and, written out with reasonable amplitude [fullness], would fill a bigger folio [document; oversized] volume, or a longer series of duodecimos [large sheet from which twelve pages can be cut], than could prudently [wisely] be appropriated [attached] to the annals [story; records] of all New England during a similar period. (ch. 1)

B. In proof of the authenticity [genuineness] of this legendary [famous] renown, Hepzibah could have exhibited the shell of a great egg, which an ostrich need hardly have been ashamed of. Be that as it might, the hens were now scarcely larger than pigeons, and had a queer, rusty, withered [wrinkled] aspect, and a gouty [impaired; diseased] kind of movement, and a sleepy and melancholy [sad] tone throughout all the variations [divergent characters] of their clucking and cackling. It was evident that the race had degenerated [deteriorated], like many a noble race besides, in consequence of too strict a watchfulness to keep it pure. (ch. 6)

C. By this time the sun had gone down, and was tinting the clouds towards the zenith [high point] with those bright hues [shades of colors] which are not seen there until some time after sunset, and when the horizon has quite lost its richer brilliancy. The moon, too, which had long been climbing overhead, and unobtrusively [inconspicuously; modestly] melting its disk into the azure [blue],—like an ambitious [aspiring] demagogue [charismatic leader who uses prejudice to rule], who hides his aspiring [ascending] purpose by assuming the prevalent [dominant] hue of popular sentiment,—now began to shine out, broad and oval, in its middle pathway. These silvery beams were already powerful enough to change the character of the lingering [remaining] daylight. (ch. 14)

D. The artist looked paler than ordinary; there was a thoughtful and severe contraction [thickening; wrinkling] of his forehead, tracing a deep, vertical line between the eyebrows. His smile, however, was full of genuine warmth, and had in it a joy, by far the most vivid [forceful; colorful] expression that Phoebe had ever witnessed, shining out of the New England reserve [shyness] with which Holgrave habitually masked whatever lay near his heart. It was the look wherewith a man, brooding alone over some fearful object, in a dreary forest or illimitable [measureless] desert, would recognize the familiar aspect of his dearest friend, bringing up all the peaceful ideas that belong to home, and the gentle current of every-day affairs. And yet, as he felt the necessity of responding to her look of inquiry, the smile disappeared. (ch. 20)

Discussion Questions

A. What is the role of "fate" in this novel?

Answer: *It has a ubiquitous presence in the novel. One wonders how much the "curse" is related to "fate" or to evil, bad choices.*

B. Who is the protagonist? Supply your reasoning.

Answer: *I would argue for Phoebe. Reasons will vary.*

C. Is the hypnotism in this novel crucial to Hawthorne's purposes, or is it merely a distraction?

Answer: *It adds to the moody, dreary tone but generally is not essential to the action.*

D. Compare Phoebe in *The House of the Seven Gables* with Hester Prynne in *The Scarlet Letter*.

Answer: *Both are strong, moral female characters.*

E. Discuss the mood of this novel and how Hawthorne creates it.

Answer: *The dreary mansion is described in minute detail. The weather is dreary; the people wear dreary clothes.*

Intruder in the Dust

William Faulkner

Objective Test: True or False

__F__ When a twelve-year-old white boy, Chick Mallison, falls through the ice and is rescued by old Lucas Beauchamp, Lucas is insulted by Chick's racist comments.

__T__ In turn, Chick resents being indebted to a black man.

__T__ Four years later Lucas is arrested for murdering Vinson Gowrie and is taken to jail, where a crowd of Vinson's friends are expected to lynch Lucas.

_F_ He tells Chick to get Chick's grandfather, Gavin Stevens, to defend him.

_T_ Aided by the young black Aleck Sander and the seventy-year-old spinster Eunice Habersham, Chick digs up Vinson's grave.

_F_ They find the body of Vinson.

_T_ They convince Gavin and the sheriff to reopen the grave, but the bodies of both Vinson and Montgomery are found in nearby quicksand.

_T_ Back in town, Lucas explains that Crawford Gowrie murdered the two men.

_F_ Crawford is arrested and then commits suicide in jail, but Lucas is lynched anyhow.

_T_ Determined to accept no charity from a white, he pays Gavin a two-dollar fee in coins and demands a receipt. He becomes "tyrant over the whole county's white conscience."

Suggested Vocabulary Words

A. [They] whetted [sharpened on a stone] knives or already moved about the pens; . . . [the hogs were] not quite startled [excited; moving suddenly], not alarmed but just alerted as though sensing already even though only dimly their rich and immanent [inherent] destiny.

B. By nightfall the whole land would be hung with their spectral [ghostly] intact [entire] tallow-colored carcasses [dead bodies] immobilized [held motionless] by the heels in attitudes of frantic [desperately excited] running as though full tilt [at high speed] at the center of the earth.

C. It took but one glance to see . . . [that] they had an affinity [attraction to] and rapport [harmonious relation; accord] with rabbits.

D. He knew the true reason was that he could no more imagine himself contradicting [negating; saying no to] the man striding [moving with long steps] on ahead of him.

E. . . . but a savage gash half gully and half road mounting a hill with an air solitary [alone] independent and intractable [stubborn].

Discussion Questions

A. The idea that a black man standing over a dead white man must be guilty of murder is an important moment in the novel. Why?

Answer: *That one scene captures a theme of the novel: racism. The notion that an African American is guilty by virtue of the fact that he is standing over a dead white man, without trial, is a metaphor for this setting.*

B. In Faulkner's writing, the mentality of the Southern man becomes startlingly clear. At one point Chick's Uncle Gavin Stevens, a lawyer, explains that blacks and whites in the South were all assigned roles and expected to play the part:

> That's why we must resist the North: not just to preserve our-selves nor even the two of us as one to remain one nation because that will be the inescapable by-product of what we will preserve: which is the very thing that three generations ago we lost a bloody war in our own back yards so that it remain intact: the postulate that Sambo is a human being living in a free coun-try and hence must be free. That's what we are really defending: the privilege of setting him free ourselves.

Respond to this theory.

Answer: *This serious yet comical picture of race relations is insightful.*

C. Faulkner ends the novel with the business of paying the bill as Lucas settles his debt, so that he is not indebted to any man. A movie made a few years after the book, ended by Uncle John calling Lucas "the conscience of the town," to which Chick corrected him and called him "the conscience of us all." Which ending do you like better?

Answer: *Answers will vary. This reader likes the book ending because it is not sentimental.*

D. Why is Chick so humiliated to be helped by Lucas?

Answer: *In Chick's mind, to owe a favor to an African American is to imply that he is equal to you—which in fact he was, but Chick was struggling with that fact.*

The Invisible Man

H. G. Wells

Objective Test

__B__ In the first scene in the book the invisible man arrives (A) home from a long journey, (B) at Mrs. Hall's boarding house, (C) at a scientific convention, or (D) hot and tired.

__A__ Mr. Henfrey suspects that the invisible man is (A) wanted by the police, (B) burned in an accident, (C) friendly, or (D) sick.

__C__ How does Wells let the reader know that the invisible man has broken into the parsonage? (A) The invisible man tells the pastor, (B) the reader just knows, or (C) both the pastor and his wife know someone is in the room whom they cannot see.

__A__ The invisible man is forced to rob his father. This has tragic consequences because (A) it is not his father's money and his father commits suicide, (B) the invisible man is caught, (C) the old man has no more money, or (D) the invisible man uses the money to buy drugs.

__C__ The invisible man (A) escapes to Algiers, (B) moves to another English town, (C) is killed by Kemp and others, or (D) literally disappears.

Suggested Vocabulary Words

A. And with that much introduction, that and a ready <u>acquiescence</u> [submission] to terms and a couple of sovereigns flung upon the table, he took up his quarters in the inn. (ch. 1)

B. "You don't say so!" said Hall, who was a man of sluggish <u>apprehension</u> [understanding]. (ch. 2)

C. The first to appear was the <u>proprietor</u> [owner] of the Cocoanut Shy, a <u>burly</u> [rough] man in a blue jersey. (ch. 12)

D. His meditation [reflective thought] became profound [deep, serious]. (ch. 18)

E. He laughed, and put his hand to the locked door. "Barred out of my own bedroom, by a flagrant [conspicuously offensive] absurdity [something ridiculous]!" he said. (ch. 18)

F. "Is there such a thing as an invisible animal? In the sea, yes. Thousands! millions! All the larvae, all the little nauplii and tornarias, all the microscopic things, the jelly-fish. In the sea there are more things invisible than visible! I never thought of that before. And in the ponds too. All those little pond-life things,—specks of colourless translucent [clear] jelly! But in air? No! (ch. 18)

G. Oliver, my professor, was a scientific bounder [a person of unsociable behavior], a journalist by instinct, a thief of ideas,—he was always prying! And you know the knavish [dishonest] system of the scientific world. I simply would not publish, and let him share my credit. I went on working, I got nearer and nearer making my formula into an experiment, a reality. . . . Kemp gave a cry of incredulous [unbelievable] amazement. (ch. 19)

H. What I want, Kemp, is a goal-keeper, a helper, and a hiding-place, an arrangement whereby I can sleep and eat and rest in peace, and unsuspected. I must have a confederate [ally, accomplice]. With a confederate, with food and rest—a thousand things are possible. (ch. 24)

I. Mr. Heelas stood up, exclaiming vaguely and vehemently [passionately] at all these wonderful things. (ch. 28)

Discussion Questions

A. One critic who dislikes the book said, "There's one obvious reason for the novel's lack of potency: it is a victim of its own success. The invisible man's story has become embedded in our culture and offers no surprises." Respond to this critic.

Answer: *While it is true that later authors and movie producers have enhanced the story, this book remains the genuine product. Therefore, I think that the critic is ungenerous.*

B. *The Invisible Man* has a distinctly antiscience message. What is it?

Answer: *Wells recognizes the limits of science: the Invisible Man is unable to return to visibility. His mental brilliance ultimately, in fact, creates a science that kills him. In effect, he is playing "God." This theme asks the reader to be careful not to put unlimited faith in science.*

C. This novel is full of suspense. Give an example.

Answer: *In the first chapter Mrs. Hall is busy doing ordinary things, such as preparing a meal, while she ascertains the nature of this strange visitor. The juxtaposition of ordinary events and the extraordinary person present creates much tension and suspense.*

D. Explain how Wells uses Kemp as a foil (someone or something that acts as a contrast for another).

Answer: *Since Wells is using objective, omniscient narration, he needs to tell the story through a character. He heeds, furthermore, an intelligent interpreter who is also moral. Kemp fits the bill.*

F. What narrative technique does Wells employ? Why?

Answer: *Wells rarely allows the reader to see into the mind of a character (unless that character is speaking to himself). This technique is called third-person narration. Wells tells the story objectively from several different viewpoints.*

G. Compare the Invisible Man to Hyde (in Robert Louis Stevenson's *Dr. Jekyll and Mr. Hyde*).

Answer: *Stevenson is clearly a Theistic author; Wells is more a Naturalistic author. Both authors create scientific creatures who get out of hand (as Mary Shelley does in her book* Frankenstein*).*

H. In the movie *League of Extraordinary Gentlemen* (2003), the protagonist gathered a group of superhumans to save the world from a nefarious villain named the Fantom. He gathered heroes/villains from literature to help him. The invisible man (from this book) was counted among this number. What does it say about our culture that we have to use villains to save us from other villains?

Answer: *In postmodern America, there is much confusion about what is right and what is wrong. Thus, a pragmatic murderer, if he acts in a good cause, is supposedly able to make a change for the good of the cause. In the allegedly consequenceless postmodern age, intentions and feelings are paramount.*

Jane Eyre

Charlotte Brontë

Objective Test

__A__ How does Jane relate to the Reeds? (A) She will not be bullied, (B) she is intimidated, (C) she is disrespectful, or (D) she is neutral.

__C__ During her interview at Thornfield, Jane is curious when she (A) hears a dog bark, (B) sees a wild woman, (C) hears loud laughter, or (D) sees no children.

__D__ Jane saves Rochester's life by (A) giving him a home remedy, (B) keeping him from falling out of his window, (C) speaking up as he walks into a glass door, or (D) putting out a fire.

__C__ Eventually Rochester asks Jane to marry him. The wedding is disrupted when someone protests (A) that Rochester has not obtained a license, (B) that Jane is not of the right social class, (C) that Rochester is already married, or (D) that the priest is not credentialed.

__A__ Rochester claims that he married his insane wife because (A) his father misled him, (B) he really loved her, (C) she had a lot of money, or (D) he was too tired of dating.

__B__ Ultimately Jane marries Rochester when he is a broken man because she (A) feels sorry for him, (B) loves him, (C) needs a home, or (D) is tired of being a governess.

Suggested Vocabulary Words

A. "What do you want?" I asked, with awkward <u>diffidence</u> [shyness]. (ch. 2)

B. John had not much affection for his mother and sisters, and an <u>antipathy</u> [hatred] to me. (ch. 2)

C. This will be thought cool language by persons who entertain solemn doctrines about the angelic nature of children, and the duty of those charged with their education to conceive for them an <u>idolatrous</u> [excessive] devotion: but I am not writing to flatter parental <u>egotism</u> [self-centeredness], to echo cant, or prop up humbug; I am merely telling the truth. I felt a <u>conscientious</u> [sensitively careful] <u>solicitude</u> [concern] for Adele's welfare and progress, and a quiet liking for her little self: just as I cherished towards Mrs. Fairfax a thankfulness for her kindness, and a pleasure in her society <u>proportionate</u> [in proper relationship] to the tranquil regard she had for me, and the moderation of her mind and character. (ch. 12)

D. I rose up suddenly, terror-struck at the <u>solitude</u> [silence] which so ruthless a judge haunted,—at the silence which so awful a voice filled. My head swam as I stood erect. I perceived that I was sickening from excitement and <u>inanition</u> [exhaustion]; neither meat nor drink had passed my lips that day, for I had taken no breakfast. (ch. 22)

E. This was said with a careless, abstracted <u>indifference</u> [lack of concern], which showed that my solicitude was, at least in his opinion, wholly <u>superfluous</u> [unnecessary]. (ch. 23)

F. He replied not: he seemed serious—<u>abstracted</u> [absent-minded]; he sighed; he half-opened his lips as if to speak: he closed them again. I felt a little embarrassed. Perhaps I had too rashly over-leaped <u>conventionalities</u> [accepted custom or practice]; and he, like St. John, saw impropriety in my inconsiderateness. I had indeed made my proposal from the idea that he wished and would ask me to be his wife: an expectation, not the less certain because unexpressed, had <u>buoyed</u> [raised my spirits] me up, that he would claim me at once as his own. But no hint to that effect escaping him and his <u>countenance</u> [facial expressions] becoming more overcast, I suddenly remembered that I might have been all wrong, and was perhaps playing the fool unwittingly; and I began gently to withdraw myself from his arms—but he eagerly snatched me closer.

Discussion Questions

A. Jane was an entirely new character in the reticent Victorian Age. Why did the public find her so appealing?

Answer: *Victorian England was hungry for literary characters with whom they could identify. Jane Eyre was what the doctor ordered. She seemed like one of them.*

B. Was Jane a social revolutionary?

Answer: *No, Jane merely wished to be left alone. She wanted to live her life unencumbered by the superficialities that pompous British society demanded. This made her all the more appealing.*

C. Why did Brontë choose first-person narration to tell her story?

Answer: *This allowed the reader to identify with her.*

D. How does Brontë use the weather to mirror Jane's moods?

Answer: *The icy cold, moonlit night creates an aura of suspense surrounding Jane's first impression of Mr. Rochester. Also, just before dark, Jane was watching a brilliant red. Red is associated with strong feelings.*

E. Compare Charlotte Brontë's parlor scenes with those found in Jane Austen's novels.

Answer: *Brontë obviously did not have as much experience in British highbrow society as Austen. Brontë's parlor scenes were awkward and stilted compared with Austen's.*

F. A critic wrote, "Not one of the main incidents on which its action turns is but incredible. It is incredible that Rochester should hide a mad wife on the top floor of Thornfield Hall, and hide her so imperfectly that she constantly gets loose and roams yelling about the house, without any of his numerous servants and guests suspecting anything: it is incredible that Mrs. Reed, a conventional if disagreeable woman, should conspire to cheat Jane out of a fortune because she had been rude to her as a child of ten: it is supremely incredible that when Jane Eyre collapses on an unknown doorstep after her flight from Rochester it should be on the doorstep of her only surviving amiable relations." Respond to this critic.

Answer: *These things are all true but entirely appropriate for Victorian novels. Compare this novel to the masterpiece* Middlemarch, *by George Eliot. Coincidence played a part in both novels and was not only tolerated by the Victorian audience, but also appreciated.*

Julius Caesar

William Shakespeare

Objective Test

__B__ The play begins with (A) the assassination of Julius Caesar, (B) Caesar's triumphant ride into Rome, (C) the battle between Antony and Brutus, or (D) the invasion of the Goths (Germans).

__A__ Brutus and his friends fear (A) that Caesar will create a dictatorship, (B) that Caesar will let the masses rule, (C) that the Senate will take over, or (D) that Mark Antony will replace Caesar as emperor.

__C__ Caesar's wife Calpurnia (A) is delighted to join her husband on the throne, (B) stays in Capri, (C) begs Caesar not to go to the senate, or (D) goes with him to the senate.

__C__ After Caesar is assassinated, a civil war results between (A) Octavius and Brutus against Cassius and Antony, (B) Antony and Brutus against Cassius and Octavius, (C) Brutus and Cassius against Octavius and Antony, or (D) Claudius against Antony.

__B__ At the end of the play Brutus (A) dies in battle, (B) commits suicide, (C) wins a great victory, or (D) flees to Egypt.

Suggested Vocabulary Words

A. You are dull, Casca, and those sparks of life / that should be in a Roman you do want, / or else you use not. You look pale and gaze / and put on fear and cast yourself in wonder / to see the strange <u>impatience</u> [lacking ability to wait] of the heavens. / But if you would consider the true cause / why all these fires, why all these <u>gliding</u> [moving smoothly] ghosts, / why birds and beasts from quality and kind, / why old men, fools, and children calculate, / why all these things change from their <u>ordinance</u> [command; order], / their natures, and preformed faculties / to monstrous quality, why, you shall find / that heaven hath <u>infused</u> [filled completely] them with these spirits / to make them instruments of fear and warning / unto some monstrous state. / Now could I, Casca, name to thee a man / most like this <u>dreadful</u> [awful] night, / that thunders, lightens, opens graves, and roars / as doth the lion in the Capitol, / a man no mightier than thyself or me / in personal action, yet <u>prodigious</u> [huge] grown / and fearful, as these strange <u>eruptions</u> [explosions; things breaking out] are. (act 1, scene 3)

B. Romans, countrymen, and lovers! Hear me for my / cause, and be silent, that you may hear. Believe me / for mine honor, and have respect to mine honor, that / you may believe. <u>Censure</u> [rebuke] me in your wisdom, and / awake your senses, that you may the better judge. / If there be any in this assembly, any dear friend of / Caesar's, to him I say that Brutus' love to Caesar / was no less than his. If then that friend demand / why Brutus rose against Caesar, this is my answer: / —Not that I loved Caesar less, but that I loved / Rome more. Had you rather Caesar were living and / die all slaves, than that Caesar were dead to live / all freemen? As Caesar loved me, I weep for him; / as he was fortunate, I rejoice at it; as he was / <u>valiant</u> [brave], I honor him; but as he was <u>ambitious</u> [self-aggrandizing], I / slew him. There is tears for his love, joy for his / fortune, honor for his valor, and death for his / ambition. Who is here so base that would be a / bondman? If any, speak, for him have I offended. / Who is here so rude that would not be a Roman? If / any, speak, for him have I offended. Who is here so / vile that will not love his country? If any, speak, / for him have I offended. I pause for a reply. (act 3, scene 2)

C. Thou hast described / a hot friend cooling. Ever note, Lucilius, / when love begins to sicken and decay / it useth an enforced ceremony. / There are no tricks in plain and simple faith; / but hollow men, like horses hot at hand, / make gallant show and promise of their mettle [capabilities]; / but when they should endure the bloody spur, / they fall their crests and like deceitful jades [disreputable people] / sink in the trial. Comes his army on? (act 4, scene 2)

D. This was the noblest Roman of them all. / All the conspirators [plotters], save only he, / did that they did in envy of great Caesar; / he only, in a general honest thought / and common good to all, made one of them. / His life was gentle, and the elements / so mix'd in him that Nature might stand up / and say to all the world, "This was a man!" (act 5, scene 5)

Discussion Questions

A. React to Brutus's words "Not that I loved Caesar less, but that I loved Rome more" (act 3, scene 2).

Answer: *Was Brutus a noble man? Antony at the end of the play says, "This was the noblest Roman of them all: / All the conspirators, save only he, / did that they did in envy of great Caesar; / he only, in a general honest thought / and common good to all, made one of them. / His life was gentle, and the elements / so mix'd in him that Nature might stand up / and say to all the world, 'This was a man!'" If one agrees with Antony, Brutus was not so bad. If one does not, then he was a self-serving murderer.*

B. How does Shakespeare use prophecies and omens to build suspense?

Answer: *Among others, Shakespeare uses the dreams of Calpurnia and the prophecies if the soothsayers to warn Julius Caesar of his imminent doom. This form of foreshadowing obviously builds suspense.*

C. How does this play reflect on Elizabethan English politics?

Answer: *Shakespeare lived during the reign of Queen Elizabeth, who was a leader of early British nationalism and had no heir like Julius Caesar. Nevertheless, she was not assassinated. Apparently Shakespeare greatly admired her.*

D. Who is the protagonist?
Answer: *Most argue that Brutus is the protagonist; others argue Julius Caesar is the main character.*

E. If you were casting this play, which contemporary actors would you cast as Julius Caesar? Mark Antony? Brutus? Calpurnia?
Answer: *Answers will vary.*

The Jungle

Upton Sinclair

Objective Test

__D__ Jurgis Rudkus and Ona Lukoszaite have recently immigrated to Chicago from (A) Russia, (B) Poland, (C) Romania, or (D) Lithuania.

__A__ They hold their wedding feast in an area of Chicago known as (A) Packingtown, (B) Cedar Grove, (C) Oak Park, or (D) Shelbyville.

__B__ After the reception, Jurgis and Ona discover that they (A) have over $100 in gifts, (B) owe more than $100, (C) receive an anonymous gift of $100, or (D) must give the best man $100.

__C__ Jurgis (A) decides to go home, (B) borrows money, (C) vows that he will simply work harder to make more money, or (D) kills the owner of the bar.

__B__ Jurgis works in a (A) cotton mill, (B) meatpacking facility, (C) steel mill, or (D) bar.

__A__ Jurgis's wife gives birth to a healthy boy, whom she and Jurgis name Antanas, after Jurgis's late father, but (A) she is forced to return to work only seven days later, (B) the baby dies, (C) the baby needs special medicine, or (D) Jurgis loses his job.

__C__ After being injured and then fired from his job, Jurgis (A) joins the church, (B) regrets coming to America, (C) starts to drink alcohol, or (D) falls and dies.

__A__ Jurgis's wife, Ona, (A) dies in childbirth, (B) leaves him, (C) marries someone else, or (D) joins the church.

__B__ Eventually Jurgis (A) dies in despair, (B) lives on the street, (C) gets a job in another meatpacking plant, or (D) returns home.

__A__ At the end of the novel, Jurgis (A) joins a political party, (B) leaves his wife, (C) marries again, or (D) returns home.

Suggested Vocabulary Words

A. Their good luck, they felt, had given them the right to think about a home; and sitting out on the doorstep that summer evening, they held consultation [discussion; meeting] about it, and Jurgis took occasion to broach [bring up] a weighty subject. Passing down the avenue to work that morning he had seen two boys leaving an advertisement from house to house; and seeing that there were pictures upon it, Jurgis had asked for one, and had rolled it up and tucked it into his shirt. (ch. 4)

B. Such were the cruel terms upon which their life was possible, that they might never have nor expect a single instant's respite [rest] from worry, a single instant in which they were not haunted by the thought of money. (ch. 10)

C. The other asked him what had led him to safebreaking—to Jurgis a wild and appalling [awful] occupation to think about. (ch. 17)

D. "Ask the woman," said the farmer, nodding over his shoulder. The "woman" was more tractable [able to be persuaded], and for a dime Jurgis secured two thick sandwiches and a piece of pie and two apples. (ch. 22)

E. Jeweled images are made of him, sensual [gratifying the senses] priests burn incense to him, and modern pirates of industry bring their dollars, wrung from the toil of helpless women and children, and build temples to him, and sit in cushioned seats and listen to his teachings expounded [explained] by doctors of dusty divinity." (ch. 31)

Discussion Questions

A. Compare the immigrant protagonist in this novel with Antonia in *My Antonia*, by Willa Cather.

Answer: *They are exactly opposite. The immigrants in Cather's novel are fulfilled, happy, successful people, well-pleased with their decision to immigrate to America.*

B. How accurate is Sinclair's image of late-nineteenth-century industrial America?

Answer: *It is a caricature and yet fairly accurate.*

C. Marija, Ona's cousin, is one of the most striking characters in the novel. She is the character we think will most likely succeed. Her sad ending, then, becomes a metaphor for one theme of this novel. Explain.

Answer: *Marija, arguably the strongest character in the novel, deteriorates rapidly, as does every other character in the novel.*

D. Did Sinclair go too far in his description of the meatpacking plant? Judging from other reports, do you think he exaggerated? Would the owners of the meatpacking facility write a different version of the story?

Answer: *He did exaggerate, but his description was substantially correct. The owners would obviously have a much different view.*

E. Jurgis is the protagonist. In literature, he is a typical figure who gains wisdom through hard times. At the end he is converted to socialism. Does Sinclair adequately develop this character?

Answer: *Yes, Jurgis is developed well.*

F. Scholar Van Wyck Brooks writes, "The conversion of Jurgis to socialism, at the end of the book, was really impossible after his soul had been 'murdered,' as one was told, and the story of his life was quite unreal when, after the death of his wife and his child, he became a hobo, a scab, and a crook. He was as unreal, in fact, as his friend Duane, the fancy man, or the young millionaire who invites him to his house in Chicago, a figure of pure melodrama in which Sinclair reverted to his early pulp-writing. Sinclair's characters, as a rule, were puppets." Is Jurgis's conversion credible?

Answer: *No, I think that this is the great weakness of this novel.*

G. Write a brief report on the socialist movement in American history.

Answer: *Socialism never took root in America as it did in Europe, but it was a popular political force in the late-nineteenth and early-twentieth century.*

H. Does Sinclair's obvious prejudice toward a political viewpoint damage the artistic components of this novel? How?

Answer: *The ending is contrived and foreign to the form and purpose of this novel.*

Kidnapped

Robert Louis Stevenson

Objective Test

__C__ David is a young man from (A) England, (B) Wales, (C) Scotland, or (D) Boston.

__A__ He is (A) an orphan, (B) adopted by a rich sea captain, (C) on board a ship, or (D) the King's son.

__C__ In fact, David (A) is dying of cancer, (B) has no funds at all, (C) has a wealthy uncle, or (D) is forced to work in a factory.

__D__ David is kidnapped on the ship (A) *Robert E. Lee,* (B) *Testament,* (C) *Comedy of Errors,* or (D) Covenant.

__B__ After much adventure David (A) is shipwrecked in New Guinea, (B) becomes a very wealthy young man, (C) hides a treasure in Cuba, or (D) returns to France.

Suggested Vocabulary Words

A. There was now no doubt about my uncle's enmity [hatred]; there was no doubt I carried my life in my hand, and he would leave no stone unturned that he might compass [accomplish] my destruction. But I was young and spirited, and like most lads that have been country-bred, I had a great opinion of my shrewdness [cleverness]. I had come to his door no better than a beggar and little more than a child; he had met me with treachery [evil betrayal] and violence; it would be a fine consummation [completion] to take the upper hand, and drive him like a herd of sheep. (ch. 5)

B. He was smallish in stature [size], but well set and as nimble [agile] as a goat; his face was of a good open expression, but sunburnt very dark, and heavily freckled and pitted with the small-pox; his eyes were unusually light and had a kind of dancing madness in them, that was both engaging [outgoing] and alarming; and when he took off his great-coat, he laid a pair of fine silver-mounted pistols on the table, and I saw that he was belted with a great sword. His manners, besides, were elegant [refined], and he pledged the captain handsomely. Altogether I thought of him, at the first sight, that here was a man I would rather call my friend than my enemy. (ch. 9)

C. Doubtless it was a great relief to walk disencumbered [unengaged]; and perhaps without that relief, and the consequent [resulting] sense of liberty and lightness, I could not have walked at all. I was but new risen from a bed of sickness; and there was nothing in the state of our affairs to hearten [call] me for much exertion [physical effort]; traveling, as we did, over the most dismal deserts in Scotland, under a cloudy heaven, and with divided hearts among the travelers. (ch. 24)

D. The soldiers let us be; although once a party of two companies and some dragoons went by in the bottom of the valley, where I could see them through the window as I lay in bed. What was much more astonishing [greatly surprising], no magistrate [judicial official] came near me, and there was no question put of whence [from where] I came or whither I was going; and in that time of excitement, I was as free of all inquiry [questions] as though I had lain in a desert. Yet my presence was known before I left to all the people in Balquhidder and the adjacent [next to] parts; many coming about the house on visits and these (after the custom of the country) spreading the news among their neighbours. The bills, too, had now been printed. There was one pinned near the foot of my bed, where I could read my own not very <u>flattering</u> [complimentary] portrait and, in larger characters, the amount of the blood money that had been set upon my life. (ch. 25)

Discussion Questions

A. Compare this novel to other novels by Stevenson. Which one do you like the best? Why?
Answer: *Answers will vary.*

B. Does David handle Ebenezer fairly?
Answer: *Fairly, yes; generously, yes; justly, no. David was incredibly forgiving to this scoundrel!*

C. What relationship exists between David and Alan?
Answer: *Alan is a very effective foil. While David develops throughout the novel, Alan basically stays the same but is an effective tool for Stevenson to develop David.*

D. Alan has the "Long John Silver" role in *Kidnapped*. Explain.
Answer: *Both Long John and Alan are unscrupulous characters whose main function is to develop the protagonist.*

The Last of the Mohicans

James Fenimore Cooper

Objective Test

__B__ This book occurs during (A) the American Revolution, (B) the French and Indian War, or (C) the War of 1812.

__A__ Alice and Cora set out from Fort Edward to visit their (A) father, (B) brother, (C) cousin, or (D) uncle.

__C__   Major Duncan Heyward escorts them through the dangerous forest, as guided by an Indian named Magua. Soon David Gamut joins them. Traveling cautiously, the group encounters (A) Davy Crockett, (B) Daniel Boone, (C) Natty Bumppo, or (D) George Washington.

__B__   Natty Bumppo calls himself (A) Bear Claw, (B) Hawkeye, (C) Bobcat Bob, or (D) Cougar Charlie.

__C__   Chingachgook and Uncas, Chingachgook's son, are the only surviving members of the (A) Leni-Lenape tribe, (B) Delaware tribe, (C) Mohican tribe, or (D) Sioux tribe.

__A__   Hawkeye says that Magua, a Huron, is (A) leading them in the wrong direction, (B) doing okay, (C) a spy for the British, or (D) sick.

__B__   Hawkeye and the Mohicans lead the group to safety in a cave, but Huron allies of Magua attack early the next morning and capture (A) Hawkeye and the Mohicans; (B) Alice, Cora, Heyward, and Gamut; (C) no one, or (D) David Gamut.

__C__   Hawkeye shoots (A) Heywood, (B) Gamut, (C) Magua, or (D) Cora.

__C__   Cora has romantic feelings toward (A) Gamut, (B) Magua, (C) Uncas, or (D) Natty.

__A__   Cora and Uncas both (A) die, (B) are married, (C) leave the territory, or (D) join the French.

__D__   Uncas's death is especially sad because (A) he was so young, (B) he loved Cora, (C) he was a great shot, or (D) he was the last of the Mohicans.

Suggested Vocabulary Words

A. In a moment of such painful doubt, Duncan did not hesitate to look around him, without <u>consulting</u> [considering] that protection from the rocks which just before had been so necessary to his safety. Every effort, however, to detect the least evidence of the approach of their hidden enemies was as fruitless as the <u>inquiry</u> [questions about] after his late companions. The wooded banks of the river seemed again deserted by everything possessing animal life. The uproar which had so lately echoed through the vaults of the forest was gone, leaving the rush of the waters to swell and sink on the currents of the air, in the <u>unmingled</u> [untainted] sweetness of nature. A fish-hawk, which, secure on the topmost branches of a dead pine, had been a distant <u>spectator</u> [observer] of the fray, now swooped from his high and ragged perch, and soared, in wide sweeps, above his prey; while a jay, whose noisy voice had been stilled by the hoarser cries of the savages, ventured again to open his discordant throat, as though once more in <u>undisturbed</u> [untouched] possession of his wild domains. Duncan caught from these natural accompaniments of the solitary scene a glimmering of hope; and he began to rally his <u>faculties</u> [abilities; powers] to renewed exertions, with something like a <u>reviving</u> [renewed] confidence of success. (ch. 9)

B. "If you judge of Indian <u>cunning</u> [clever] by the rules you find in books, or by white <u>sagacity</u> [wisdom], they will lead you <u>astray</u> [off course], if not to your death," returned Hawkeye, examining the signs of the place with that <u>acuteness</u> [sharpness] which distinguished him. "If I may be permitted to speak in this matter, it will be to say, that we have but two things to choose between: the one is, to return, and give up all thoughts of following the Hurons." (ch. 20)

C. The <u>impatience</u> [unwillingness to wait] of the savages who <u>lingered</u> [remained] about the prison of Uncas, as has been seen, had overcome their <u>dread</u> [fear] of the <u>conjurer's</u> [magician's] breath. They stole cautiously, and with beating hearts, to a crevice, through which the faint light of the fire was glimmering. For several minutes they mistook the form of David for that of the prisoner; but the very accident which Hawkeye had foreseen occurred. Tired of keeping the <u>extremities</u> [legs and arms] of his long person so near together, the singer gradually suffered the lower limbs to extend themselves, until one of his misshapen feet actually came in contact with and shoved aside the embers of the fire. At first the Hurons believed the Delaware had been thus deformed by witchcraft. But when David, unconscious of being observed, turned his head, and exposed his simple, mild countenance, in place of the haughty lineaments of their prisoner, it would have exceeded the <u>credulity</u> [belief] of even a native to have doubted any longer. They rushed together into the lodge, and, laying their hands, with but little ceremony, on their captive, immediately detected the <u>imposition</u> [deception]. They [then] arose the cry first heard by the fugitives. It was succeeded by the most frantic and angry <u>demonstrations</u> [examples; threatening gestures] of vengeance. David, however, firm in his determination to cover the retreat of his friends, was compelled to believe that his own final hour had come. Deprived of his book and his pipe, he was <u>fain</u> [inclined; willing] to trust to a memory that rarely failed him on such subjects; and breaking forth in a loud and impassioned strain, he endeavored to smooth his passage into the other world by singing the opening verse of a funeral anthem. The Indians were seasonably reminded of his <u>infirmity</u> [sickness; weakness], and, rushing into the open air, they aroused the village in the manner described. (ch. 27)

D. Chingachgook was a <u>solitary</u> [only] <u>exception</u> [exclusion] to the interest <u>manifested</u> [shown] by the native part of the audience. His look never changed throughout the whole of the scene, nor did a muscle move in his <u>rigid</u> [stiff] countenance, even at the wildest or the most <u>pathetic</u> [pathos; sadly suffering] parts of the <u>lamentation</u> [grief]. The cold and senseless remains of his son was all to him, and every other sense but that of sight seemed frozen, in order that his eyes might take their final gaze at those <u>lineaments</u> [outline of a body] he had so long loved, and which were now about to be closed forever from his view. (ch. 33)

Discussion Questions

A. How does Cooper treat the Native Americans in his book?

Answer: *For the most part, they are "noble savages." Cooper wrote in a Romantic worldview style, which posited that nature and everything in nature and like nature was the penultimate good thing.*

B. How does Cooper create Hawkeye as a hero?

Answer: *Intrepid in warfare, noble in peacetime, Hawkeye is the noble uncivilized man who is "naturally" good—untainted by civilization.*

C. What is Heyward's role?

Answer: *He represents well-intentioned but easily corrupted weak-willed civilized man. He is the opposite of Hawkeye.*

D. How accurate is Cooper's description of the French and Indian War?

Answer: *Fairly accurate. There was a French siege of Fort Henry, and the Hurons were allies of the French.*

Little Women

Louisa May Alcott

Objective Test

__C__ The novel begins during the (A) summer, (B) fall, (C) winter, or (D) spring.

__A__ The girls decide that they will buy presents for (A) their mother, (B) their dad, (C) the poor, or (D) injured soldiers.

__A__ Mr. March, the girls' father, is serving as a (A) Union private, (A) Union chaplain, or (B) Confederate General.

__D__ That year, the Marches form the Pickwick Club, in which they (A) take canned goods to the poor, (B) sew socks for soldiers, (C) take poor children to the park, or (D) write a family newspaper.

__A__ Beth (A) dies, (B) marries Laurie, (C) goes to college, or (D) joins the nursing corps.

Suggested Vocabulary Words

A. Amy rebelled <u>outright</u> [openly; directly], and <u>passionately</u> [with deep feeling] declared that she had rather have the fever than go to Aunt March. Meg reasoned, pleaded, and commanded, all in vain. Amy protested that she would not go, and Meg left her in <u>despair</u> [hopelessness] to ask Hannah what should be done. Before she came back, Laurie walked into the parlor to find Amy sobbing, with her head in the sofa cushions. She told her story, expecting to be <u>consoled</u> [comforted], but Laurie only put his hands in his pockets and walked about the room, whistling softly, as he knit his brows in deep thought. Presently he sat down beside her, and said, in his most <u>wheedlesome</u> [pleading; irritating] tone, "Now be a sensible little woman, and do as they say. No, don't cry, but hear what a jolly plan I've got. You go to Aunt March's, and I'll come and take you out every day, driving or walking, and we'll have capital times. Won't that be better than <u>moping</u> [whining in despair] here?" (ch. 17)

B. Jo's face was a study next day, for the secret rather weighed upon her, and she found it hard not to look <u>mysterious</u> [unusual; secretive] and important. Meg observed it, but did not trouble herself to make inquiries, for she had learned that the best way to manage Jo was by the law of <u>contraries</u> [contradictions], so she felt sure of being told everything if she did not ask. She was rather surprised, therefore, when the silence remained unbroken, and Jo assumed a <u>patronizing</u> [condescending] air, which decidedly aggravated Meg, who in turn assumed an air of dignified reserve and devoted herself to her mother. This left Jo to her own devices, for Mrs. March had taken her place as nurse, and <u>bade</u> [ordered; urged] her rest, exercise, and amuse herself after her long <u>confinement</u> [kept indoors]. Amy being gone, Laurie was her only refuge, and much as she enjoyed his society, she rather dreaded him just then, for he was an <u>incorrigible</u> [obstinate; persistant] tease, and she feared he would <u>coax</u> [persuade] the secret from her. (ch. 21)

C. There were to be no <u>ceremonious</u> [ritual; formal] performances, everything was to be as natural and homelike as possible, so when Aunt March arrived, she was <u>scandalized</u> [offended] to see the bride come running to welcome and lead her in, to find the bridegroom fastening up a garland that had fallen down, and to catch a glimpse of the <u>paternal</u> [fatherly] minister marching upstairs with a <u>grave</u> [serious] countenance and a wine bottle under each arm. (ch. 25)

D. "You look like the <u>effigy</u> [death image] of a young knight asleep on his tomb," she said, carefully tracing the well-cut <u>profile</u> [outline of figure] defined against the dark stone. (ch. 39)

E. Yes, Jo was a very happy woman there, in spite of hard work, much anxiety, and a <u>perpetual</u> [ongoing] racket. She enjoyed it <u>heartily</u> [with enthusiasm] and found the applause of her boys more satisfying than any praise of the world, for now she told no stories except to her flock of enthusiastic believers and admirers. As the years went on, two little lads of her own came to increase her happiness—Rob, named for Grandpa, and Teddy, a happy-go-lucky baby, who seemed to have <u>inherited</u> [obtained from birth; in the genes] his papa's sunshiny temper as well as his mother's lively spirit. How they ever grew up alive in that whirlpool of boys was a mystery to their grandma and aunts, but they flourished [prospered] like dandelions in spring, and their rough nurses loved and served them well. (ch. 47)

Discussion Questions

A. Some critics find the young girls to be archetypes, one-dimensional, and static. What do you think?
Answer: *Except for Jo, this reader might agree.*

B. Why does Alcott call her book *Little Women*?
Answer: *In America at this time, young ladies were considered to be smaller versions of their mothers and sisters. There was no concept of a "young girl" or a "teenager." These young ladies were considered to be younger versions of their older mothers and siblings.*

C. Contrast these young women with contemporary young women.
Answer: *Answers will vary.*

D. How important is the setting to this novel?
Answer: *The Civil War adds tension and focus to the book.*

Madame Bovary

Gustave Flaubert

Objective Test

__B__ Charles Bovary is (A) a spoiled rich boy, (B) unable to fit in at his new school, (C) injured in a nasty fall, or (D) called to be a pastor.

__A__ Bovary is (A) a mediocre and ordinary doctor, (B) a promising surgeon, (C) an important pastor, or (D) an unemployed bricklayer.

__C__ Bovary marries (A) Mary, (B) Susan, (C) Emma, or (D) Margaret.

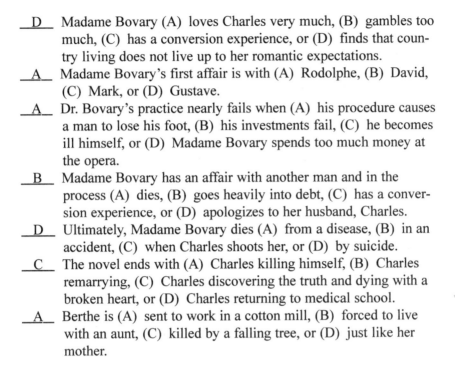

_D_   Madame Bovary (A) loves Charles very much, (B) gambles too much, (C) has a conversion experience, or (D) finds that country living does not live up to her romantic expectations.

_A_   Madame Bovary's first affair is with (A) Rodolphe, (B) David, (C) Mark, or (D) Gustave.

_A_   Dr. Bovary's practice nearly fails when (A) his procedure causes a man to lose his foot, (B) his investments fail, (C) he becomes ill himself, or (D) Madame Bovary spends too much money at the opera.

_B_   Madame Bovary has an affair with another man and in the process (A) dies, (B) goes heavily into debt, (C) has a conversion experience, or (D) apologizes to her husband, Charles.

_D_   Ultimately, Madame Bovary dies (A) from a disease, (B) in an accident, (C) when Charles shoots her, or (D) by suicide.

_C_   The novel ends with (A) Charles killing himself, (B) Charles remarrying, (C) Charles discovering the truth and dying with a broken heart, or (D) Charles returning to medical school.

_A_   Berthe is (A) sent to work in a cotton mill, (B) forced to live with an aunt, (C) killed by a falling tree, or (D) just like her mother.

Suggested Vocabulary Words

A. And she detested her <u>instinctively</u> [spontaneously]. At first she solaced herself by <u>allusions</u> [references] that Charles did not understand, then by casual observations that he let pass for fear of a storm, finally by open <u>apostrophes</u> [expressions] to which he knew not what to answer. (part 1, ch. 2)

B. Emma's heart beat rather faster when, her partner holding her by the tips of the fingers, she took her place in a line with the dancers, and waited for the first note to start. But her emotion soon <u>vanished</u> [disappeared], and, <u>swaying</u> [rocking back and forth] to the rhythm of the orchestra, she glided forward with slight movements of the neck. A smile rose to her lips at certain delicate phrases of the violin, that sometimes played alone while the other instruments were silent; one could hear the clear clink of the <u>louis d'or</u> [French gold coins] that were being thrown down upon the card tables in the next room; then all struck again, the cornet-a-piston uttered its <u>sonorous</u> [sounding impressive] note, feet marked time, skirts swelled and rustled [moved with small sounds and energy], hands touched and parted; the same eyes falling before you met yours again. (part 1, ch. 8)

C. "Do you think that to be an agriculturist it is necessary to have tilled the earth or fattened fowls oneself? It is necessary rather to know the composition of the substances in question—the geological strata, the atmospheric actions, the quality of the soil, the minerals, the waters, the density [mass per unit volume] of the different bodies, their capillarity [ability to conduct liquids], and what not. And one must be master of all the principles of hygiene in order to direct, criticize the construction of buildings, the feeding of animals, the diet of domestics. And, moreover, Madame Lefrançois, one must know botany, be able to distinguish [see the difference] between plants, you understand, which are the wholesome and those that are deleterious, which are unproductive and which nutritive [building up life], if it is well to pull them up here and re-sow them there, to propagate [multiply; cause to flourish] some, destroy others; in brief, one must keep pace with science by means of pamphlets and public papers, be always on the alert to find out improvements." (part 2, ch. 8)

D. And fixing her eyes upon an embossed carabine [carbine; rifle], that shone against its panoply [a magnificent array], "But when one is so poor one doesn't have silver on the butt of one's gun. (part 3, ch. 8)

E. The other went on talking agriculture, cattle, pasturage, filling out with banal [trite] phrases all the gaps where an allusion [hint; implied reference] might slip in. Charles was not listening to him; Rodolphe noticed it, and he followed the succession [sequence; series] of memories that crossed his face. This gradually grew redder; the nostrils throbbed [moved rapidly; pulsed] fast, the lips quivered. There was at last a moment when Charles, full of a somber [serious] fury, fixed his eyes on Rodolphe, who, in something of fear, stopped talking. But soon the same look of weary lassitude [flexibility] came back to his face. (part 3, ch. 11)

Discussion Questions

A. How did you like the ending? Would you change it?

Answer: *Answers will vary.*

B. Compare Madame Bovary with Don Quixote.

Answers: *Both fail in their desire to obtain or create a Romantic world. Quixote, however, dies a natural death.*

C. Critic Mark Tunnell expresses sympathy for Madame Bovary:

> We cannot help noticing that Flaubert displayed a marked reluctance to give due weight to what was valid and genuine in Emma. She was not, as Henry James alleged, a woman who was "naturally depraved." She possessed a number of solid virtues which were deliberately played down by the novelist. It was after all to her credit that she possessed too much sensibility to fit comfortably into the appalling provincial society of Yonville-l'Abbaye and it was her misfortune that she was not big enough to find a way out of the dilemma. We cannot withhold our approval from her attempts to improve her mind or from the pride that she took in her personal appearance and in the running of her house.

Do you agree?

Answer: *While I can be sympathetic with Bovary, I cannot excuse her unfaithfulness to her husband, ungodly lifestyle, and decisions.*

D. Contrast the worldview clashes that occur between Madame Bovary and her husband.

Answer: *Charles Bovary, while he is no paradigm of virtue, does advance a moral, faithful, Theistic worldview that is directly opposed to Emma's self-centered, misguided sort of Romanticism.*

Middlemarch

George Eliot

Objective Test

__A__ Both and Rosamond and Lydgate think of courtship and marriage (A) in terms of ideals taken directly from conventional story-books, (B) from a marriage manual, or (C) from the Bible.

__C__ Dorothea's husband (A) leaves her, (B) is a millionaire, or (C) dies.

__B__ Mary refuses to marry Fred if he (A) becomes a doctor, (B) becomes a pastor, or (C) continues to work at night.

__C__ Dorothea has a passion for (A) Chinese checkers, (B) the poor, or (C) medical reform.

__A__ *Middlemarch* (A) refuses to present a typical Victorian marriage, (B) tries to advance women's liberation, or (C) has very unhealthy women.

Suggested Vocabulary Words

A. Dorothea by this time had looked deep into the ungauged [unmeasured] reservoir of Mr. Casaubon's mind, seeing reflected there in vague labyrinthine [intricate] extension [enlargement in scope] every quality she herself brought; had opened much of her own experience to him, and had understood from him the scope of his great work, also of attractively labyrinthine extent. For he had been as instructive as Milton's "affable [likeable; at ease in conversation] archangel [chief angel];" and with something of the archangelic manner he told her how he had undertaken to show (what indeed had been attempted before, but not with that thoroughness [completeness], justice of comparison, and effectiveness of arrangement at which Mr. Casaubon aimed) that all the mythical systems or erratic mythical fragments in the world were corruptions of a tradition originally revealed. Having once mastered the true position and taken a firm footing there, the vast field of mythical constructions became intelligible, nay, luminous [bright] with the reflected light of correspondences." (ch. 3)

B. "What do you think of that for a fine bit of <u>antithesis</u> [contrasting ideas]?" said the German, searching in his friend's face for responding admiration, but going on volubly without waiting for any other answer. "There lies antique beauty, not <u>corpse-like</u> [deathlike] even in death, but arrested in the complete contentment of its sensuous perfection: and here stands beauty in its breathing life, with the consciousness of Christian centuries in its bosom. But she should be dressed as a nun; I think she looks almost what you call a Quaker; I would dress her as a nun in my picture. However, she is married; I saw her wedding-ring on that wonderful left hand, otherwise I should have thought the <u>sallow</u> [greyish colored] <u>Geistlicher</u> [clergyman] was her father. I saw him parting from her a good while ago, and just now I found her in that <u>magnificent</u> [great; extraordinary] pose. Only think! he is perhaps rich, and would like to have her portrait taken. Ah! it is no use looking after her—there she goes! Let us follow her home!" (ch. 19)

C. "I am aware of that. The only course is to try by all means, direct and indirect, to <u>moderate</u> [lessen intensity or extremeness] and vary his occupations. With a happy <u>concurrence</u> [cooperation] of circumstances, there is, as I said, no immediate danger from that <u>affection</u> [disease] of the heart, which I believe to have been the cause of his late attack." (ch. 30)

D. "Close the book now, my dear. We will resume our work to-morrow. I have <u>deferred</u> [delayed] it too long, and would gladly see it completed. But you observe that the principle on which my selection is made, is to give adequate, and not <u>disproportionate</u> [out of proportion; unsuitable] illustration to each of the theses <u>enumerated</u> [numbered; listed] in my introduction, as at present sketched. You have perceived that distinctly, Dorothea?" (ch. 48)

Discussion Questions

A. Most critics feel that this novel is vastly superior to other Victorian novels (e.g., *Wuthering Heights*). Do you agree? Why? What makes this novel superior?

Answer: *The characters defy convention. They are unique, well-developed, complicated, and strong—but never predictable. Eliot, no doubt, was a genius.*

B. Why were so many British Victorian novels written by women?
Answer: *For one thing, women were better at handling the typical subjects at that time. Furthermore, Britain was one of the few nineteenth-century countries consciously educating its women.*

C. What actor would you cast for Dorothea?
Answer: *Answers will vary.*

Les Misérables

Victor Hugo

Objective Test

__B__ In 1815, Charles-François-Bienvenu Myriel, Bishop of Digne, is (A) 65 years old, (B) 75 years old, (C) 45 years old, or (D) 55 years old.

__A__ Jean Valjean was imprisoned for (A) stealing bread, (B) murder, (C) assaulting the Bishop, or (D) tax evasion.

__A__ Inspector Javert is obsessed with capturing Valjean because (A) he feels responsible for his original escape, (B) Valjean hurt Javert's sister, or (C) there is a big reward on Valjean's head.

__C__ Valjean takes care of Cosette because (A) she is his granddaughter, (B) she is a handicapped neighbor, (C) he promised Cosette's mom that he would take care of her, or (D) he needs to pretend to be a father.

__B__ Cosette falls in love with (A) Jacques, (B) Marius, or (C) André.

Suggested Vocabulary Words

A. Although this detail has no connection whatever with the real substance of what we are about to relate, it will not be <u>superfluous</u> [unnecessary], if merely for the sake of exactness in all points, to mention here the various <u>rumors</u> [unsubstantiated comments] and remarks which had been in circulation about him from the very moment when he arrived in the diocese. (vol. 1, ch. 1)

B. Whether this penalty, complicated by successive <u>aggravations</u> [provocations] for attempts at escape, had not ended in becoming a sort of <u>outrage</u> [intense anger] <u>perpetrated</u> [caused] by the stronger upon the feebler, a crime of society against the individual, a crime which was being committed afresh every day, a crime which had lasted nineteen years. (vol. 1, ch. 7)

C. This 1815 was a sort of <u>lugubrious</u> [mournful] April, . . . a <u>recrudescence</u> [renewal] of divine right. (vol. 2, ch. 8)

D. And, on abandoning society, he had <u>immured</u> [imprisoned] himself in his habits. The principal one, and that which was <u>invariable</u> [constant], was to keep his door absolutely closed during the day, and never to receive any one whatever except in the evening. (vol. 3, ch. 7)

E. The <u>vicissitudes</u> [changes; mutability] of flight . . . The New Building, which was the most cracked and <u>decrepit</u> [ancient; run-down] thing to be seen anywhere in the world, was the weak point in the prison. (vol. 4, ch. 3)

F. These <u>felicities</u> [happinesses] are the true ones. (vol. 5, ch. 2)

Discussion Questions

A. Here is Hugo's description of Jean Valjean's imprisonment: "Jean Valjean had entered the galleys sobbing and shuddering; he emerged impassive. He had entered in despair; he emerged gloomy." Do you think Jean Valjean is unjustly imprisoned?

Answer: *His conviction for a crime was just, but his imprisonment term was excessive.*

B. Is there a time when violating the law might be necessary? Is Valjean's crime morally acceptable?

Answer: *Christians should always obey God's law. If God's law violates human law, then he should disobey human authorities. During*

*World War II Dietrich Bonhoeffer, for example, decided that he had no
choice but to violate German laws that violated the Word of God.
Valjean's crime is not morally acceptable. Stealing is stealing.*

C. Why does the Bishop overlook Jean Valjean's crime?
Answer: *The Bishop, who is only present at the beginning of the
novel, takes an opportunity to be Christlike to poor, angry Valjean.*

D. In what way does the Bishop represent Christ?
Answer: *He is forgiving and is willing to suffer for the sake of a
soul.*

E. How does Jean Valjean repay the Bishop?
Answer: *By acting Christlike to others.*

F. Discuss how Inspector Javert develops as a character?
Answer: *Javert is one of the most interesting characters in Western
literature (rivaled only by the police inspector in* Crime and
Punishment*). Javert is changed from a cold, angry, unforgiving person
to a converted soul. It is ironical that Javert assumes Valjean's earlier
role, which Valjean manifests at the beginning of the novel. Javert
shows how hatred and unforgivingness capture those who harbor such
attitudes and perpetrate hateful deeds.*

G. Why does Hugo have Javert commit suicide? Is he reconciled
with Jean Valjean?
Answer: *Javert understands Valjean, and I suppose that they are
reconciled. In any event, Javert sacrifices himself for Valjean and in
that sense becomes Christlike.*

H. What is Cosette's role in this novel?
Answer: *Cosette is the classic foil, whose role is to develop the protagonist, Jean Valjean.*

Moby Dick

Herman Melville

Objective Test

<u>D</u> The narrator is (A) Melville, (B) Ahab, (C) Queequeg, or (D) Ishmael.

<u>A</u> Before the *Pequod* sails, Ishmael stops at (A) a chapel, (B) a market, (C) home, or (D) the post office.

<u>B</u> Queequeg is (A) the name of Ahab's dog, (B) a Native who is also a master harpooner, (C) second in command, or (D) a New Bedford native.

<u>C</u> During the quest thunder destroys the compass. Ahab decides to (A) return home, (B) follow the tides, (C) build another compass, or (D) use his own instincts.

<u>D</u> Ahab dies when he (A) is attached to his own line, (B) is eaten by Moby Dick, or (C) falls to the deck of the ship.

Suggested Vocabulary Words

A. What do you see?—Posted like silent <u>sentinels</u> [guards] all around the town, stand thousands upon thousands of mortal men fixed in ocean <u>reveries</u> [daydreams]. (ch. 1)

B. Should you ever be athirst in the great American desert, try this experiment, if your caravan happen to be supplied with a <u>metaphysical</u> [dealing with the supernatural] professor. (ch. 1)

C. Affected by the <u>solemnity</u> [seriousness] of the scene, there was a <u>wondering</u> [feeling surprise] gaze of <u>incredulous</u> [disbelieving] curiosity in his <u>countenance</u> [facial expression]. (ch. 7)

D. In behalf of the dignity of whaling, I would <u>fain</u> [willingly] advance <u>naught</u> [nothing] but <u>substantiated</u> [supported] facts. But after <u>embattling</u> [preparing to do battle with] his facts, an <u>advocate</u> [one who

243

pleads the cause of another] who should wholly suppress [subdue] a not unreasonable surmise, which might tell eloquently [with fluent expression] upon his cause—such an advocate, would he not be blame-worthy? (ch. 25)

E. Now, with the subordinate [subservient] phantoms [ghosts], what wonder remained soon waned [dwindled] away; for in a whaler wonders soon wane. (ch. 50)

F. "Yes, I may as well," said the surgeon, coolly. "I was about observing, sir, before Captain Boomer's facetious [joking] interruption, that spite of my best and severest endeavors [efforts], the wound kept getting worse and worse; the truth was, sir, it was as ugly gaping [opening wide] wound as surgeon ever saw; more than two feet and several inches long. (ch. 100)

G. It was a clear steel-blue day. The firmaments [expanses] of air and sea were hardly separable in that all-pervading azure; only, the pensive [thoughtful] air was transparently pure and soft, with a woman's look, and the robust [vigorous; strong] and man-like sea heaved with long, strong, lingering [tarrying] swells, as Samson's chest in his sleep. (ch. 132)

H. While Daggoo and Queequeg were stopping the strained [stressed] planks; and as the whale swimming out from them, turned, and showed one entire flank as he shot by them again; at that moment a quick cry went up. Lashed round and round to the fish's back; pinioned [tied against] in the turns upon turns in which, during the past night, the whale had reeled the involutions [entangling] of the lines around him, the half torn body of the Parsee was seen; his sable [dark; gloomy] raiment frayed to shreds; his distended [extended; protruding] eyes turned full upon old Ahab. (ch. 135)

Discussion Questions

A. The critic Alfred Kazin writes:

> Ahab . . . is a hero; we cannot insist enough on that. Melville
> believed in the heroic and he specifically wanted to cast his

Moby Dick 245

hero on American lines—someone noble by nature, not by birth, who would have "not the dignity of kings and robes, but that abounding dignity which has no robed investiture." Ahab sinned against man and God, and like his namesake in the Old Testament, becomes "a wicked king." But Ahab is not just a fanatic who leads the whole crew to their destruction; he is a hero of thought who is trying, by terrible force, to reassert man's place in nature. And it is the struggle that Ahab incarnates that makes him so magnificent a voice, thundering in Shakespearean rhetoric, storming at the gates of the inhuman, awful world. Ahab is trying to give man, in one awful, final assertion that his will does mean something, a feeling of relatedness with his world.

Do you agree that Ahab is a "hero?"
Answer: *Yes, but in my opinion he is more an antihero than a hero.*

B. The critic Richard B. Sewall describes Ahab:

As Ahab in his whaleboat watches the Pequod founder under the attack of the whale, he realizes that all is lost. He faces his "lonely death on lonely life," denied even "the last fond pride of meanest shipwrecked captains," the privilege of going down with his ship. But here, at the nadir of his fortunes, he sees that in his greatest suffering lies his greatest glory. He dies spitting hate at the whale, but he does not die cynically or in bitterness. The whale conquers—but is "unconquering." The "god bullied hull" goes down "death glorious." What Ahab feels is not joy or serenity or goodness at the heart of things. But with his sense of elation, even triumph, at having persevered to the end, there is also a note of reconciliation: "Oh now I feel my topmost greatness lies in my topmost grief." This is not reconciliation with the whale, or with the malice in the universe, but it is a reconciliation of Ahab with Ahab. Whatever justice, order, or equivalence there is, he has found not in the universe but in himself. . . . In finally coming to terms with existence (though too late), he is tragic man; to the extent that he transcends it, finds "greatness" in suffering, he is a tragic hero.

Paraphrase Sewall and agree or disagree with him.

Answer: *Sewall suggests that Ahab has some sort of existential experience where he discovers himself, so to speak. I would say that this is a modern interpretation of a mid-nineteenth-century novel, where most people do not think of themselves as much as today. The concept of an "identity crisis" was a 1960s phenomenon, not an 1850s phenomenon. I doubt Ahab had an identity crisis, as Sewall implies.*

C. Some scholars argue that *Moby Dick* is a transitional novel from the Romanticism of Emerson to the Naturalism of a Stephen Crane. They argue that Ahab is the budding Naturalist who sees the subjective universe come unglued. In one scene Ahab watches a dying whale turn to face the sun. Ahab identifies with the great beast he's slain, for both are fire-worshipers. Both are in a futile struggle with "God." What do you think?

Answer: *Answers will vary, but I agree with this statement. Contrast Ahab with Hawthorne's Hester Prynne in* The Scarlet Letter. *Prynne is a principled Theist in a Romantic world. Ahab is clearly a man in transition in his worldviews.*

D. The harpooner, Queequeg, a classic foil, is a pagan who rejects Christianity. Obviously, Melville admires this creature. At the Spouter-Inn, Ishmael at first is terrified to be near Queequeg, but he soon concludes that Queequeg is more noble than most of Ishmael's Christian friends. "We cannibals must help these Christians," Queequeg says after he rescues from drowning the very man who had been rude to him moments before. What is Melville trying to say to his reader by creating a character like Queequeg?

Answer: *Melville obviously thinks that Christianity is a lightweight worldview and does not deserve any particular respect above any other faith.*

E. On one level Moby Dick is a stupid animal. On the other hand, he seems to represent so much more. He appears to be ubiquitous, alternately evil and then good. What do you think?

Answer: *Moby Dick is all those things: he is both a physical whale and a representative of many other things.*

F. If you were the editor of *Moby Dick*, would you keep the lengthy sections on whaling? Do they make the novel more or less effective?
Answer: *Answers will vary.*

My Antonia

Willa Cather

Objective Test

__B__ The story line of this novel is that Jim Burden, a successful lawyer, (A) talks about his mother, Antonia; (B) remembers growing up in Nebraska; or (C) returns unexpectedly to his Nebraska home.

__A__ Burden first arrives in Nebraska at the age of (A) 10, (B) 12, (C) 14, or (D) 16.

__C__ He makes the trip west to live with his grandparents because (A) he has always wanted to see the West, (B) his parents have left him, or (C) he is an orphan.

__A__ On the train going out west, Jim meets (A) a Bohemian immigrant family traveling in the same direction, (B) Wild Bill Cody, (C) Billy the Kid, or (D) his uncle.

__D__ Jim makes friends with (A) Barbara, (B) Nellie, (C) David, or (D) Antonia.

__C__ Antonia's mother (A) dies of cancer, (B) returns to her native land, (C) commits suicide, or (D) dies of pneumonia.

__A__ Jim attends (A) Harvard, (B) the University of Chicago, (C) Yale, or (D) Stanford.

__B__ Antonia (A) dies, (B) has a child out of wedlock, (C) returns to Bohemia, or (D) visits Jim.

__B__ Jim returns home in twenty years to find (A) his home destroyed, (B) Antonia happily married, or (C) his grandparents dead.

__A__ Antonia (A) stays in Nebraska but remembers Jim, (B) leaves with Jim, or (C) dies suddenly.

Suggested Vocabulary Words

A. As for Jim, no disappointments have been severe enough to chill his naturally romantic and ardent [with warmth; enthusiastic] disposition [state of mind]. (introduction)

B. Magnified [emphasized; enlarged] across the distance by the horizontal light, it stood out against the sun, was exactly contained within the circle of the disk; the handles, the tongue, the share—black against the molten [liquified; melted; glowing] red. (book 2, ch. 14)

C. She lent herself to immemorial [timeless] human attitudes which we recognize by instinct as universal and true. I had not been mistaken. She was a battered [physically damaged] woman now, not a lovely girl; but she still had that something which fires the imagination, could still stop one's breath for a moment by a look or gesture [physical movement] that somehow revealed the meaning in common things. (book 5, ch. 1)

Discussion Questions

A. Who is the protagonist?
Answer: *There is some debate. This reader feels that Jim is the protagonist. Others argue that Antonia is the protagonist.*

B. What is Jim's relationship with Antonia?
Answer: *She is a good friend. She also draws him back to his nostalgic past.*

C. Does Willa Cather, a woman, effectively present the perspective of Jim, a man?
Answer: *Answers will vary.*

D. In this novel is Cather agitating for social change?
Answer: *Cather is merely giving a glimpse of the nineteenth-century immigrant experience.*

Old Indian Legends

Zitkala-¨Sa

Objective Test

__C__ What kills the unwary ducks? (A) Hunger, (B) anger, (C) curiosity, or (D) lightning.

__A__ Iktomi calls his god (A) Grandfather, (B) God, (C) Lord, or (D) King.

__D__ The moral of the story "The Badgers and the Bear" is that (A) one should work hard and save for winter, (B) one should take care of oneself first, or (D) if one returns evil for good, evil will also soon come to that evildoer.

__C__ The avenger is (A) a lion, (B) a spirit, (C) a warrior, or (D) a demon.

__B__ Patkasa is easily tricked but gets the last laugh on (A) Dancing Wolf, (B) Iktomi, (C) Sharp Arrow, or (D) Running Brook.

Suggested Vocabulary Words

A. Iktomi is a wily [sly] fellow. (legend 1)

B. His black nose was dry and parched [arid; scorched; shriveled]. (legend 6)

C. Wordless, like a bashful [shy] Indian maid, the avenger [one bringing revenge, judgment] ate in silence the food set before him on the ground in front of his crossed shins. (legend 8)

D. Patkasa was always ready to believe the words of scheming [crafty] people and to do the little favors any one asked of him. However, on this occasion, he did not answer "Yes, my friend." He realized that Iktomi's flattering [excessively praising] tongue had made him foolish. (legend 9)

Discussion Questions

A. Do you agree with this statement by the author, Zitkala-ˈSa? "The old legends of America belong quite as much to the blue-eyed little patriot as to the black-haired aborigine. And when they are grown tall like the wise grown-ups may they not lack interest in a further study of Indian folklore, a study which so strongly suggests our near kinship with the rest of humanity and points a steady finger toward the great brotherhood of mankind, and by which one is so forcibly impressed with the possible earnestness of life as seen through the teepee door!"

Answer: *The author suggests that universal truths are to be found in Native American stories.*

B. Moral fables with animals as characters are quite effective. Why?

Answer: *Fables allow the author to communicate profound truth while using disarming animals. The reader naturally identifies with common animals.*

C. Some Native Americans claim that the God of their fathers is the same God as the Judeo-Christian God of the European-Americans. Do you agree?

Answer: *The animalistic, existential Native American gods exemplify some characteristics similar to our God, but generally they are different, part of creation rather than the Creator.*

D. Native Americans have been sorely wronged by European Americans. They were betrayed and slaughtered by settlers, lynching gangs, and regiments from the ruling authorities. Today, some Christians are calling for a massive repentance on the part of European-Americans. Do you think it is advisable for contemporary people to confess the sins of their fathers and mothers and to offer some sort of restitution?

Answer: *Answers will vary.*

Oliver Twist

Charles Dickens

Objective Test

__C__ Oliver Twist is born in (A) a run-down hospital, (B) a tenement, (C) a workhouse, or (D) Ireland.

__A__ His mother is (A) found on the street and dies just after Oliver's birth, (B) an unknown relative of Queen Victoria, (C) sick with the flu, or (D) confused and lonely.

__B__ After several adventures, Oliver works for (A) Appleby, (B) Fagin, (C) Nancy, or (D) Jack.

__D__ While bungling a burglary, Oliver is captured by (A) Nancy, (B) Fagin, (C) Dick, or (D) Mr. Brownlow.

__D__ Mr. Brownlow is surprised about (A) Oliver's resemblance to his deceased son, (B) how young Oliver is, (C) how strong Oliver is, or (D) Oliver's resemblance to a daughter.

__B__ Bill Sikes and Nancy (A) send Oliver some food, (B) kidnap Oliver and take him back to Fagin, or (C) go to the police.

__A__ It is revealed that (A) Oliver's mother left behind a gold locket when she died, (B) Oliver is very rich, or (C) that Oliver has a rare disease.

__B__ Monks is (A) a rich man, (B) Oliver's half brother, or (C) a good friend to Oliver.

__D__ Rose is actually (A) Fagin's mother, (B) Fagin's sister, (C) Fagin's wife, or (D) Oliver's aunt.

__A__ Oliver (A) inherits a fortune, (B) dies suddenly, or (C) decides to live with Fagin.

Suggested Vocabulary Words

A. In great families, when an advantageous place cannot be obtained, either in possession, <u>reversion</u> [throwback; returning], remainder, or <u>expectancy</u> [anticipation], for the young man who is growing up, it is a very general custom to send him to sea. The board, in imitation of so wise and salutary [appealing; positive] an example, took counsel together on the expediency [necessity; fitness] of shipping off Oliver Twist, in some small trading vessel bound to a good unhealthy port. This suggested itself as the very best thing that could possibly be done with him: the probability being, that the skipper would flog him to death, in a playful mood, some day after dinner, or would knock his brains out with an iron bar; both pastimes being, as is pretty generally known, very favourite and common recreations among gentleman of that class. The more the case presented itself to the board, in this point of view, the more manifold [many; varied] the advantages of the step appeared; so, they came to the conclusion that the only way of providing for Oliver effectually, was to send him to sea without delay. (ch. 4)

B. It is the custom on the stage, in all good murderous melodramas [sentimental stories], to present the tragic and the comic scenes, in as regular alternation, as the layers of red and white in a side of streaky bacon. The hero sinks upon his straw bed, weighed down by fetters [bindings] and misfortunes; in the next scene, his faithful but unconscious squire regales [entertains] the audience with a comic song. We behold, with throbbing [moving; thumping] bosoms, the heroine in the grasp of a proud and ruthless baron: her virtue and her life alike in danger, drawing forth her dagger to preserve the one at the cost of the other; and just as our expectations are wrought up to the highest pitch, a whistle is heard, and we are straightway transported to the great hall of the castle; where a grey-headed seneschal [steward in charge of an estate] sings a funny chorus with a funnier body of vassals [subjects; feudal tenants], who are free of all sorts of places, from church vaults to palaces, and roam about in company, carolling perpetually [without ceasing]. (ch. 17)

C. "By mine," replied Mr. Brownlow. 'Those persons are indemnified [redeemed; with losses paid] by me. If you complain of being deprived of your liberty—you had power and opportunity to retrieve it as you came along, but you deemed it advisable to remain quiet—I say again, throw yourself for protection on the law. I will appeal to the law too; but when you have gone too far to recede, do not sue to me for leniency [tolerant, magnanimous actions], when the power will have passed into other hands; and do not say I plunged you down the gulf into which you rushed, yourself." (ch. 49)

D. I would <u>fain</u> [willingly] linger yet with a few of those among whom I have so long moved, and share their happiness by endeavouring to depict it. (ch. 53)

Discussion Questions

A. How does Dickens develop his most memorable villains, Fagin and the Artful Dodger?

Answer: *With much descriptive language. Fagin is devious, manipulative, and just plain evil: there appears to be no good in him. The Dodger, on the other hand, has a few redeeming qualities: at least he appears to be more the participant in evil than the instigator of evil.*

B. How important is the environment to human nature? Do living conditions determine what happens to people? If so, the reader is to believe that those of Dickens's people who are deprived of good influences are doomed, while those who enjoy love and economic wealth are good. Respond to this view.

Answer: *Answers will vary. Certainly this author feels that all have sinned and fallen short of the kingdom and glory of God.*

C. Love is a powerful theme in this novel. Explain.

Answer: *Love is a ubiquitous theme in* Oliver Twist. *Whether between man and woman, or parent and child, it always produces life and hope in Dickens's characters. Brownlow's love saves Oliver. Rose and Henry find love and wholeness together after all their suffering. But love is not successful if it is not returned. For instance, Nancy's love for Bill fails because it is not returned and therefore does not ameliorate (improve) her condition.*

D. Discuss the use of coincidence in this novel. Was its use excessive?

Answer: *It is excessive but probably appropriate for this particular genre. Remember, Dickens is writing when coincidence was expected and tolerated by his readers. There are many examples. Look at chapter 41: The Maylies happened to be in London. Nancy coincidentally knows where to find Rose. And how coincidental that Oliver spots Mr. Brownlow in the street the very next day.*

E. What was the narrative point of view? Why did Dickens choose this narrative technique?

Answer: *Third-person omniscient narration, where the reader sees into the mind of each character. The narrator can move things along this way—a necessity in a plot as complicated as Dickens creates.*

F. Respond to the following by critic Arnold Kettle:

> The plot of *Oliver Twist* is very complicated and very unsatisfactory. It is a conventional plot about a wronged woman, an illegitimate baby, a destroyed will, a death-bed secret, a locket thrown into the river, a wicked elder brother and the restoration to the hero of name and property. That it should depend on a number of extraordinary coincidences (the only two robberies in which Oliver is called upon to participate are perpetrated, fortuitously, on his father's best friend and his mother's sister's guardian!) is the least of its shortcomings. Literal probability is not an essential quality of an adequate plot. Nor is it a criticism that Dickens should have used his plot for the purposes of serial-publication, i.e., to provide a climax at the end of each instalment and the necessary twists and manoeuvres which popular serialization invited. (It is not a fault in a dramatist that he should provide a climax to each act of his play, and the serial instalment is no more or less artificial a convention than the act of a play.) What we may legitimately object to in the plot of *Oliver Twist* is the very substance of that plot in its relation to the essential pattern of the novel.

Answer: *Answers will vary. The rags-to-riches theme does depend on coincidences rather than on self-improvement and achievement (as in the Horatio Alger Jr. stories). Nevertheless, this reader feels that Kettle is too hard on Dickens.*

The Pearl

John Steinbeck

Objective Test

__A__ Kino originally decides to pray for a great pearl because (A) his son was bitten by a scorpion and he needs money for medicine, (B) he needs money for the dentist, (C) he is tired of living so poorly, or (D) his son has a chance to attend the university and he needs money to send him.

__C__ Who suggests that the pearl be abandoned? (A) Kino, (B) the son, (C) Juana, or (D) the doctor.

__B__ While escaping from his pursuers, (A) Juana is killed, (B) Coyotito is killed, (C) Kino loses the pearl, or (D) Kino falls and is drowned.

__A__ The only friends Kino seems to have are (A) Juan and Apolonia, (B) the priest and his housekeeper, (C) Jose and Maria, and (D) the doctor and his wife.

__D__ This story is (A) an epic, (B) a narrative poem, (C) a fable, or (D) a parable.

Suggested Vocabulary Words

A. If this story is a parable [short, moral story] everyone takes his own meaning from it. (epilogue)

B. Kino watched with the detachment [indifference; aloofness] of God while a dusty ant frantically [with desperation] tried to escape the sand trap an ant lion had dug for him. (ch. 1)

C. Kino looked at his neighbors fiercely [with violent passion]. . . . Kino's face shone with prophecy [inspired prediction]. (ch. 3)

D. And once some large animal lumbered [moved ponderously] away, crackling the undergrowth as it went. (ch. 6)

255

Discussion Questions

A. How did you feel when Kino throws the pearl back into the ocean? Would you have found a better way to handle this situation?
Answer: *Answers will vary.*

B. Why does Kino throw the pearl into the ocean?
Answer: *He recognizes that he is alienated from everyone, everything that is dear to him. As valuable as the pearl might be, it is less valuable than his relationships with people.*

C. How does Steinbeck use foreshadowing in his book?
Answer: *Juana suggests that the pearl is evil long before it has visited its full measure of evil upon them. Near the end of chapter 3, Juana even suggests that the pearl will destroy their son, as it ultimately does. Ironically, this was the very reason Kino prayed for the pearl.*

D. How does Steinbeck use ants to make some points?
Answer: *Human beings, like ants, work very hard to advance themselves but often to no avail.*

E. How does Steinbeck present the priest in *The Pearl*?
Answer: *The priest is selfish, manipulative, and perhaps even dishonest. This gives the reader insight into Steinbeck's views against clergymen and even Christianity.*

F. Even though Juana knows that the pearl will cause disaster, she returns it to her husband after it was lost. Why would she do this?
Answer: *Answers will vary, but perhaps she loves him too much to see him suffer. Later, no doubt, she wishes she had not returned it.*

G. What does this book tell you about the way the Naturalist Steinbeck sees God?
Answer: *God is not remotely interested in the affairs of humans except to hurt them.*

The Prince

Niccolò Machiavelli

Objective Test

__A__ *The Prince is* concerned with (A) totalitarian regimes,
(B) democracies, (C) representative democracies, or (D) socialist governments.

__A__ Personal virtue makes (A) bad government, (B) good government, (C) strong governments, or (D) sensitive governments.

__D__ Likewise, immoral behavior may be necessary to (A) satisfy the
majority, (B) stop enemies from taking over the state, (C) rule
generously, or (D) rule effectively.

__B__ The appearance of virtue may be more important, therefore, than
(A) actual evil, (B) actual virtue, (C) a good prime minister, or
(D) a strong parliament.

__B__ Machiavelli offers advice on (A) how to choose a leader,
(B) how to run a military, (C) how to fight a battle, or (D) how
to destroy enemies.

Suggested Vocabulary Words

A. But the difficulties occur in a new principality [small kingdom].
And firstly, if it be not entirely new, but is, as it were, a member of a
state which, taken collectively, may be called composite [made up of
parts], the changes arise chiefly from an inherent [involved in the essential character] difficulty which there is in all new principalities [prince-
doms; small kingdoms]; for men change their rulers willingly, hoping to
better themselves, and this hope induces them to take up arms against
him who rules: wherein they are deceived, because they afterwards find
by experience they have gone from bad to worse. This follows also on
another natural and common necessity, which always causes a new
prince to burden those who have submitted to him with his soldiery [mil-
itary personnel] and with infinite [without limit] other hardships which
he must put upon his new acquisition. (ch. 3)

257

B. Therefore it is unnecessary for a prince to have all the good qualities I have _enumerated_ [listed; numbered], but it is very necessary to appear to have them. And I shall dare to say this also, that to have them and always to observe them is _injurious_ [harmful], and that to appear to have them is useful; to appear merciful, faithful, _humane_ [compassionate], religious, upright, and to be so, but with a mind so framed that should you require not to be so, you may be able and know how to change to the opposite. (ch. 18)

C. I do not wish to leave out an important branch of this subject, for it is a danger from which princes are with difficulty preserved, unless they are very careful and _discriminating_ [able to discern differences]. It is that of _flatterers_ [sycophants; those giving excessive praise for their own advantage], of whom courts are full, because men are so _self-complacent_ [self-satisfied] in their own affairs, and in a way so deceived in them, that they are preserved with difficulty from this pest, and if they wish to defend themselves they run the danger of falling into _contempt_ [being mocked]. Because there is no other way of guarding oneself from flatterers except letting men understand that to tell you the truth does not offend you; but when every one may tell you the truth, respect for you _abates_ [stops]. (ch. 23)

D. But confining myself more to the particular, I say that a prince may be seen happy to-day and ruined to-morrow without having shown any change of _disposition_ [mood; temperament] or character. This, I believe, arises firstly from causes that have already been discussed at length, namely, that the prince who relies entirely on fortune is lost when it changes. I believe also that he will be successful who directs his actions according to the spirit of the times, and that he whose actions do not accord with the times will not be successful. Because men are seen, in affairs that lead to the end which every man has before him, namely, glory and riches, to get there by various methods; one with caution, another with haste; one by force, another by skill; one by patience, another by its opposite; and each one succeeds in reaching the goal by a different method. One can also see of two cautious men the one _attain_ [obtain] his end, the other fail; and similarly, two men by different observances are equally successful, the one being cautious, the other _impetuous_ [acting without deep thought]; all this arises from nothing else than whether or not they conform in their methods to the spirit of the times. This follows from what I have said, that two men working differently bring about the same effect, and of two working similarly, one attains his object and the other does not. (ch. 25)

Discussion Questions

A. Contrast Machiavelli's view of leadership with biblical views of leadership.

Answer: *Machiavelli calls for a form of pragmatism that is unknown in the Bible: he argues that might makes right. The Bible, however, calls its leaders to lay down their lives for their flock.*

B. Does Machiavelli think that history makes rulers, or that rulers make history?

Answer: *Machiavelli strongly feels that rulers make history.*

C. Machiavelli values stability and productivity above virtue. Respond.

Answer: *Machiavellian principles call for cunning, duplicity, or bad faith to accomplish the ruler's chosen goals. In Christian morality, the results never justify the means. People's lives are more important than outcomes.*

D. Machiavelli, in effect, argues for a secular government separate from a religious government. Explain.

Answer: *The ruler's agenda is secular, not religious, and morality is not a critical consideration for Machiavelli. In this sense, Machiavelli is arguing for a modern, secular state, disconnected from religious establishments.*

E. Why was Machiavelli popular in Germany during 1932–45?

Answer: *This was when Adolf Hitler was chancellor and Führer of Germany, and the state was ubiquitous and totalitarian, trying to bend everything to its purposes.*

Pygmalion

George Bernard Shaw

Objective Test

__C__ The names of the two gentlemen who make a bet are (A) Freddy and Alfred, (B) Mark and David, or (C) Professor Higgins and Colonel Pickerings.

__B__ Professor Higgins plans to use what to ameliorate (improve) his subject? (A) Poise training, (B) phonetics, or (C) behavior modification.

__C__ The subject is (A) Mary, (B) Susan, or (C) Eliza.

__A__ The problem is (A) what to do with the subject when the experiment is over, (B) how to change the subject, or (C) how to keep the subject from spending too much money.

__B__ At the end of the play Eliza (A) goes back to her former life, (B) is rich, or (C) marries Freddy.

Suggested Vocabulary Words

A. She sits down on the plinth [subbase] of the column, sorting her flowers, on the lady's right. She is not at all an attractive person. She is perhaps eighteen, perhaps twenty, hardly older. She wears a little sailor hat of black straw that has long been exposed to the dust and soot of London and has seldom if ever been brushed. Her hair needs washing rather badly: its mousy [grayish brown] color can hardly be natural. She wears a shoddy [worn] black coat that reaches nearly to her knees and is shaped to her waist. She has a brown skirt with a coarse [rough] apron. Her boots are much the worse for wear. She is no doubt as clean as she can afford to be; but compared to the ladies she is very dirty. Her features are no worse than theirs; but their condition leaves something to be desired; and she needs the services of a dentist. (act 1)

B. We're all intimidated [frightened; fearful]. Intimidated, maam: thats what we are. What is there for me if I chuck it but the workhouse in my old age? I have to dye my hair already to keep my job as a dust-man. If I was one of the deserving poor, and had put by a bit, I could chuck it; but then why should I, acause the deserving poor might as well be millionaires for all the happiness they ever has. They dont know what happiness is. But I, as one of the undeserving poor, have nothing between me and the pauper's [poor people's] uniform but this here blast-ed three thousand a year that shoves me into the middle class. (act 5)

C. Complications [special problems] ensued [occurred]; but they were economic, not romantic. Freddy had no money and no occupation. His mother's jointure [settlement], a last relic of the opulence [extrava-gant wealth] of Largelady Park, had enabled her to struggle along in Earlscourt with an air of gentility [high social status; poise; propriety], but not to procure any serious secondary education for her children, much less give the boy a profession. A clerkship at thirty shillings a week was beneath Freddy's dignity, and extremely distasteful [unappe-tizing] to him besides. (sequel)

Discussion Questions

A. Eliza Doolittle is a dynamic character who changes significantly through the play. How?

Answer: *Eliza changes from a shy, unselfish, humble woman to an outgoing, articulate person. Her roots, her humility, however, appeal to everyone.*

B. If you were to write another act to *Pygmalion*, what would it be?
Answer: *Answers will vary.*

C. Do you think Eliza marries Fred?
Answer: *Answers will vary.*

D. Compare the Audrey Hepburn film version called *My Fair Lady* (1956) with *Pygmalion*.
Answer: *Answers will vary.*

A Raisin in the Sun

Lorraine Hansberry

Objective Test

__B__ *A Raisin in the Sun* shows a few weeks in the life of the
Youngers, an African-American family living (A) in South
Carolina; (B) on the South Side of Chicago in the 1950s;
(C) in Little Rock, Arkansas, in the 1950s; or (D) on the North
Side of Pittsburgh in the 1960s.

__A__ The family is receiving $10,000 from (A) a life insurance policy,
(B) the lottery, (C) an inheritance, or (D) a rich uncle.

__C__ The family decides to (A) go to Nigeria, (B) send a member to
medical school, (C) buy a house in a white suburb, or
(D) invest the money in the stock market.

__D__ Their new white neighbors (A) welcome them with open arms,
(B) burn a cross in their yard, (C) refuse to let them move, or
(D) offer to buy the house from them.

__B__ The plays ends with (A) the family members going their separate ways, (B) the family finding strength within itself,
(C) the mother dying, or (D) a youthful family member going
to Harvard.

Suggested Vocabulary Words

A. No, thank you very much. Please. Well—to get right to the point
I—I am sure you people must be aware of some of the incidents which
have happened in various [several] parts of the city when colored people have moved into certain areas—Well—because we have what I
think is going to be a unique [singular] type of organization in
American community life—not only do we deplore that kind of thing—
but we are trying to do something about it. We feel—we feel that most
of the trouble in this world, when you come right down to it—most of
the trouble exists because people just don't sit down and talk to each
other. (act 2)

262

B. You are looking at what a well-dressed Nigerian woman wears—Isn't it beautiful? Enough of this <u>assimilationist</u> [absorbing the dominant culture] junk! (act 2)

C. Be on my side for once! You saw what he just did, Mama! You saw him—down on his knees. Wasn't it you who taught me—to <u>despise</u> [hate] any man who would do that[?] Do what he's going to do. (act 3)

Discussion Questions

A. What statement is the author making about the importance of race?

Answer: *Race is critical to the author. In fact, its recognition and maintenance are crucial.*

B. How credible are the characters in the play?
Answer: *They are fairly typical of the 1960s.*

C. How significant is the setting for this play?

Answer: *The setting is important in that redlining (keeping African Americans from locating in certain areas of real estate) was more common in the 1960s. In various forms racism and discrimination are still prevalent in America today. The American dream is yet to be fulfilled.*

The Return of the Native

Thomas Hardy

Objective Test

__B__ The novel opens with the plot already underway: (A) Diggory Venn has brought Clym Yeobright home; (B) Diggory Venn rides onto the heath with Thomasin Yeobright, whose marriage to Damon Wildeve has been delayed by an error in the marriage certificate; or (C) Diggory Venn is attacked by robbers.

__A__ Clym marries (A) Eustacia, (B) Thomasin, (C) Penelope, or (D) Daria.

__D__ Eustacia's dreams of moving to Paris are rejected by Clym, who wants to (A) move to Warsaw, (B) enter the priesthood, (C) open a country store, or (D) start a school in his native country.

__A__ Evil Eusticia (A) begins an affair with another man, (B) kills Clym, (C) runs away, or (D) burns down their house.

__B__ Clym's mother, Mrs. Yeobright, tries to visit Eustacia and Clym and is not allowed to enter. Feeling rejected by her son, she (A) leaves in anger, (B) succumbs to heat and snakebite on the walk home and dies, or (C) disinherits Clym.

__C__ Blaming himself for the death of his mother, Clym (A) buys a nice gravestone, (B) resolves to be a better husband, (C) separates from Eustacia when he learns of her role in Mrs. Yeobright's death and of her continued relations with Wildeve, or (D) murders Eustacia.

__D__ Wildeve and Eustacia try to leave town but (A) are struck by lightning, (B) change their minds, (C) commit suicide, or (D) both drown.

__A__ Meanwhile, (A) Thomasin and Diggory marry, (B) Clym finds that his mother did not really die, or (C) the stock market crashes.

__C__ Clym becomes a (A) miller, (B) captain, (C) preacher, or (D) farmer.

Suggested Vocabulary Words

A. Her reason for standing so dead still as the <u>pivot</u> [center] of this circle of heath-country was just as <u>obscure</u> [vague]. Her extraordinary <u>fixity</u> [singleness of purpose], her <u>conspicuous</u> [obvious] loneliness, her <u>heedlessness</u> [disregard] of night, <u>betokened</u> [expressed] among other things an <u>utter</u> [complete] absence of fear. A tract of country <u>unaltered</u> [unchanged] from that <u>sinister</u> [evil] condition which made Caesar anxious every year to get clear of its glooms before the autumnal <u>equinox</u> [days equaling nights in length], a kind of landscape and weather which leads travellers from the South to describe our island as Homer's Cimmerian land, was not, on the face of it, friendly to women. (book 1, ch. 6)

B. Venn felt much astonishment at this <u>avowal</u> [open declaration], though he did not show it clearly; that exhibition may greet remarks which are one remove from expectation, but it is usually withheld in complicated cases of two removes and upwards. "Indeed, miss," he replied. (book 2, ch. 7)

C. At length Clym reached the margin of a fir and beech plantation that had been enclosed from heath land in the year of his birth. Here the trees, laden heavily with their new and humid leaves, were now suffering more damage than during the highest winds of winter, when the boughs are especially disencumbered to do battle with the storm. The wet young beeches were undergoing <u>amputations</u> [removal of limbs], bruises, <u>cripplings</u> [damage to a limb], and harsh <u>lacerations</u> [savage cuts], from which the wasting sap would bleed for many a day to come, and which would leave scars visible till the day of their burning. Each stem was <u>wrenched</u> [yanked] at the root, where it moved like a bone in its socket, and at every onset of the gale <u>convulsive</u> [violently disturbing] sounds came from the branches, as if pain were felt. In a neighbouring <u>brake</u> [rough overgrown land; thicket] a finch was trying to sing; but the wind blew under his feathers till they stood on end, twisted round his little tail, and made him give up his song. (book 3, ch. 6)

D. The lad was in good spirits that day, for the Fifth of November had again come round, and he was planning yet another scheme to <u>divert</u> [distract] her from her too absorbing thoughts. For two <u>successive</u> [back-to-back] years his mistress had seemed to take pleasure in lighting a bonfire on the bank overlooking the valley; but this year she had apparently quite forgotten the day and the <u>customary</u> [commonly practiced] deed. He was careful not to remind her, and went on with his secret preparations for a cheerful surprise, the more <u>zealously</u> [with zeal, enthusiasm] that he had been absent last time and unable to assist. At every vacant minute he hastened to gather furze-stumps, thorn-tree roots, and other solid materials from the <u>adjacent</u> [contiguous; neighboring] slopes, hiding them from <u>cursory</u> [casual; brief] view. (book 5, ch. 5)

Discussion Questions

A. Discuss how Hardy uses coincidence to advance his plot. Is it appropriate?

Answer: *There are many coincidences. Just outside the inn, Mrs. Yeobright runs into Diggory Venn. It turns out that Thomasin is the woman asleep in his cart. She later becomes a key component of the plot. By another coincidence, Eustacia in the darkness encounters Clym and his two relatives. They apparently don't recognize her, but Clym says, "Good night!" It is truly a "little sound," but to Eustacia, "no event could have been more exciting."*

B. Is there a clear-cut villain or hero in this novel?

Answer: *It is hard to say. Eustacia certainly fits the role of villainess. I would see Diggory and Thomasin as a hero and heroine.*

C. What narrative technique does Hardy employ?

Answer: *Omniscient narration.*

D. At the end of *The Return of the Native,* Hardy writes in a footnote that the marriage of Thomasin and Diggory Venn was not the originally planned ending to the novel. He asks the reader to choose the best ending. What do you think is the best ending?

Answer: *Answers will vary.*

E. Does Clem get what he deserves?

Answer: *Answers will vary. This reader feels that Clem was not all that bad and probably deserved a second chance. I would have liked to see him remarry with a nicer person.*

Sister Carrie

Theodore Dreiser

Objective Test

__A__ Sister Carrie tells the story of two characters: (A) Carrie Meeber and George Hurstwood, (B) Sister Carrie and Margaret Thurber, (C) Raymond Beale and Upton Sinclair, or (D) Bob Jones and Agnes Traylor.

__D__ Carrie becomes a (A) bag lady, (B) mayor, (C) housewife, or (D) professional actress.

A George Hurstwood moves from (A) upper-middle-class prosperity to poverty, (B) poverty to upper-middle-class prosperity, (C) Oak Park to Wheaton, or (D) poverty to unbelievable riches.

__D__ What makes all this incredible is that (A) they are both weak people, (B) they both are from Boston, (C) they both were poor at the beginning, or (D) they have no personal virtue that commends them to their fate.

__C__ Hurstwood (A) is saved by Carrie, (B) joins the army, (C) commits suicide, or (D) regains his fortune.

Suggested Vocabulary Words

A. Carrie was certainly better than this man, as she was <u>superior</u> [better than], mentally, to Drouet. She came fresh from the air of the village, the light of the country still in her eye. Here was neither <u>guile</u> [deceit] nor <u>rapacity</u> [covetousness; grasping]. There were slight inherited traits of both in her, but they were <u>rudimentary</u> [basic]. She was too full of wonder and desire to be greedy. She still looked about her upon the great maze of the city without understanding. Hurstwood felt the bloom and the youth. He picked her as he would the fresh fruit of a tree. He felt as fresh in her presence as one who is taken out of the flash of summer to the first cool breath of spring. (ch. 13)

B. When Carrie reached her own room she had already fallen a <u>prey</u> [victim] to those doubts and misgivings which are ever the result of a lack of decision. She could not <u>persuade</u> [convince] herself as to the <u>advisability</u> [wisdom] of her promise, or that now, having given her word, she ought to keep it. She went over the whole ground in Hurstwood's absence, and discovered little objections that had not occurred to her in the warmth of the manager's argument. She saw where she had put herself in a <u>peculiar</u> [distinctive] light, namely, that of agreeing to marry when she was already supposedly married. She remembered a few things Drouet had done, and now that it came to walking away from him without a word, she felt as if she were doing wrong. Now, she was comfortably situated, and to one who is more or less afraid of the world, this is an urgent matter, and one which puts up strange, <u>uncanny</u> [eerie; mysterious] arguments. "You do not know what will come. There are miserable things outside. People go a-begging. Women are <u>wretched</u> [distressed; miserable]. You never can tell what will happen. Remember the time you were hungry. Stick to what you have." (ch. 23)

C. Oh, Carrie, Carrie! Oh, blind <u>strivings</u> [struggles for something] of the human heart! Onward, onward, it saith, and where beauty leads, there it follows. Whether it be the tinkle of a lone sheep bell o'er some quiet landscape, or the <u>glimmer</u> [glimpse] of beauty in <u>sylvan</u> [wooded] places, or the show of soul in some passing eye, the heart knows and makes answer, following. It is when the feet weary and hope seems vain that the heartaches and the longings arise. Know, then, that for you is neither <u>surfeit</u> [satisfaction] nor content. In your rocking-chair, by your window dreaming, shall you long, alone. In your rocking-chair, by your window, shall you dream such happiness as you may never feel. (ch. 47)

Discussion Questions

A. The main characters in this novel normally do not control their own fate. Neither Carrie nor Hurstwood live their lives through random circumstance. Their successes and failures have no moral value; this is a departure from the conventional literature of the period (such as *Wuthering Heights*). There seems to be an insidious, even evil power that is determining their fate. This is part of a Naturalistic worldview. What is Naturalism?

Answer: *Naturalism as a social and artistic movement was popular in the late-nineteenth and early-twentieth centuries. It argues that scien-*

tific laws determine things, and that there is no benevolent force in control of the universe—thus making God a unnecessary hypothesis. Hence, humankind is at the mercy of uninterested or even malevolent forces.

B. In what ways does Naturalism contradict the Bible?

Answer: *The God of the Old and New Testaments is intimately involved in the affairs of humanity and loves humans so much that he sent his only begotten Son to bring the good news of God's reign and to die for their sins (John 3:16).*

C. What is the significance of this passage:

> And now Carrie had attained that which in the beginning seemed life's object, or at least, such fraction of it as human beings ever attain of their original desires. She could look about on her gowns and carriage, her furniture and bank account. Friends there were, as the world takes it—those who would bow and smile in acknowledgment of her success. For these she had once craved. Applause there was, and publicity—once far off, essential things, but now grown trivial and indifferent. Beauty also—her type of loveliness—and yet she was lonely. In her rocking-chair she sat, when not otherwise engaged—singing and dreaming. (ch. 47)

Answer: *Carrie is dreaming of her old life and what could have been and wasn't. In a way, Carrie has committed spiritual suicide.*

D. In what ways is the Captain the most moral person in the novel?

Answer: *He begs for money for his friends and unselfishly takes care of others. Yet the Captain is a sterile and homeless person, like most of the people in the novel.*

The Song of Roland

Turoldus (?)

Objective Test

A   The epic poem begins with Charlemagne's army fighting the (A) Saracens, (B) English, (C) Germans, or (D) French.

D   Terrified of the might of Charlemagne's army of Franks, the Saracen leader Marsilla sends out messengers to Charlemagne, (A) asking for terms of surrender, (B) bearing his daughter as a ransom, (C) promising to kill Charlemagne and his army, or (D) promising treasure and Marsilla's conversion to Christianity if the Franks will go back to France.

B   Charlemagne and his men (A) refuse, (B) are tired of fighting and decide to accept this peace offer, (C) surrender, or (D) attack anyway.

C   Ganelon, Roland's father-in-law, (A) dies to protect his king, (B) flees to Italy, (C) betrays Charlemagne, or (D) kills Roland.

A   The Saracen army attacks Charlemagne's army, and the Frankish counterattack is led by (A) Roland, (B) Ganelon, (C) Charlemagne, or (D) Marsilla.

Suggested Vocabulary Words

A. The Emperor Karl of gentle France / Hither hath come for our <u>dire</u> [dismal] <u>mischance</u> [misfortune]. / Nor host to meet him in battle line, / or power to shatter his power, is mine. / Speak, my sages; your counsel lend. (2)

B. And he said to the king, "Be not <u>dismayed</u> [discouraged]: / Proffer to Karl, the <u>haughty</u> [disdainfully proud] and high, / Lowly friendship and <u>fealty</u> [fidelity; keeping agreements with another]; / Ample <u>largess</u> [generosity; liberal giving] lay at his feet, / Bear and lion and greyhound fleet. (3)

C. With them many a <u>gallant</u> [brave] lance, / Full fifteen thousand of gentle France. / The cavaliers [knights] sit upon carpets white, / Playing at tables for their delight: / The older and sager [wiser ones] sit at the chess, / The bachelors fence with a light address. (8)

D. Ganelon rides under olives high, / And comes the Saracen envoys nigh. / Blancandrin lingers [remains] until they meet, / And in cunning [clever] converse [conversation] each other greet. (19)

E. I will not sound on mine ivory horn: / It shall never be spoken of me in scorn [disrespect], / That for heathen [non-Christian] felons [criminals] one blast I blew; / I may not dishonor [violate] my lineage [ancestors; inheritance] true. (88)

Discussion Questions

A. How does Oliver function in this poem?

Answer: *He is the quintessential foil, contrasting with Roland. "Roland is brave, Oliver is wise" (37).*

B. How does the author build suspense?

Answer: *Through dialogue between Oliver and Roland as they struggle over whether or not to blow the horn.*

C. How convincing a villain is Ganelon?

Answer: *Ganelon is quite effective. He boldly claims that he did not commit treason—that he only wanted revenge against Roland.*

D. Is Roland's death necessary to the overall purpose of the epic poem?

Answer: *Epics require the death of a hero.*

20,000 Leagues under the Sea

Jules Verne

Objective Test

_C_ The novel begins in (A) 1966, (B) 1876, (C) 1866, or
(D) 1820.

_A_ For some time past, vessels have been met by (A) a fast-moving
object that destroys ships, (B) more hurricanes, (C) a deadly
whale, or (D) a new warship.

_A_ Captain Nemo is the captain of (A) the amazing submarine
Nautilus, (B) a frigate, or (C) a new airplane.

_C_ Nemo has advanced science significantly in the area of
(A) astrophysics, (B) biological science, or (C) oceanic science.

_A_ Nemo is motivated by (A) revenge, (B) pacifism, or (C) nationalism.

Suggested Vocabulary Words

A. For some time past vessels had been met by "an enormous
thing," a long object, spindle-shaped, occasionally <u>phosphorescent</u> [con-
centrated light], and <u>infinitely</u> [grossly] larger and more rapid in its
movements than a whale. (part 1, ch. 1)

B. At that moment Commander Farragut was ordering the last
<u>moorings</u> [anchorages; tying-up lines/chains] to be cast loose which
held the *Abraham Lincoln* to the pier of Brooklyn. So in a quarter of an
hour, perhaps less, the <u>frigate</u> [small warship] would have sailed without
me. I should have missed this <u>extraordinary</u> [beyond the ordinary],
<u>supernatural</u> [not natural], and <u>incredible</u> [beyond belief] expedition, the
recital of which may well meet with some suspicion. (part 1, ch. 4)

C. We had now arrived on the first platform, where other surprises
awaited me. Before us lay some picturesque ruins, which betrayed the
hand of man and not that of the Creator. There were vast heaps of stone,

amongst which might be traced the vague and shadowy forms of castles and temples, clothed with a world of blossoming zoophytes [invertebrate animals], and over which, instead of ivy, sea-weed and fucus [brown algae] threw a thick vegetable mantle. But what was this portion of the globe which had been swallowed by cataclysms [violent upheavals]? Who had placed those rocks and stones like cromlechs [circle of monoliths, monster stones, like Stonehenge] of prehistoric times? Where was I? Whither had Captain Nemo's fancy hurried me? (part 2, ch. 9)

D. He had made me, if not an accomplice [a participant], at least a witness of his vengeance [revenge; retribution]. (part 2, ch. 22)

Discussion Questions
A. Is Nemo an antagonist or the protagonist?
Answer: *Verne creates a sympathetic antagonist, but he is still an antagonist.*

B. How important are the lengthy scientific explanations to this novel?
Answer: *They make Nemo a more credible and sympathetic character, and in their own way these explanations add to the suspense. They also enhance the journey motif that is a pilgrimage in time and space.*

C. Compare this book to the Walt Disney movie version.
Answer: *The movie follows the book rather closely.*

D. What contemporary actor would you have play Captain Nemo?
Answer: *Answers will vary.*

E. Is Nemo justified in his quest to destroy ships?
Answer: *The Bible teaches that one should leave vengeance to God, never try to overcome evil with evil, and overcome evil with good.*

Two Years before the Mast

Henry Dana

Objective Test

__A__ The narrator is (A) a wealthy Harvard boy, (B) a poor New England farmer, (C) an English castaway, or (D) the cousin of the Captain.

__B__ One of the final insults inflicted on the sailors is (A) removing their rum rations, (B) excessive flogging, (C) depriving them of Sundays off work, or (D) half rations.

__B__ The narrator (A) kills a Kanaka (Hawaiian) by mistake, (B) befriends a native of Hawaii who later saves his life, or (C) falls sick and nearly dies in Hawaii.

__A__ The narrator (A) returns to Harvard and becomes a renowned lawyer and antislavery activist, (B) becomes a sea captain, or (C) resolves never to sail again.

__D__ After the California Gold Rush of 1849, he (A) joins the Union army, (B) revisits British Columbia, (C) becomes a first mate on a ship, or (D) revisits California, seeing old friends and commenting on drastic changes.

Suggested Vocabulary Words

A. Before I end my explanations, it may be well to define a *day's work,* and to correct a mistake <u>prevalent</u> [widespread] among landsmen about a sailor's life. (ch. 3)

B. But all these little <u>vexations</u> [irritations] and labors would have been nothing. (ch. 14)

C. Each one knew that he must be a man, and show himself smart when at his duty, yet everyone was satisfied with the usage; and a <u>contented</u> [satisfied] crew, agreeing with one another, and finding no fault, was a contrast indeed with the small, hard-used, dissatisfied, grumbling, <u>desponding</u> [feeling hopeless] crew of the Pilgrim. (ch. 23)

D. We hove them overboard with a good will; for there is nothing like being quit of the very last <u>appendages</u> [subordinate parts; attachments] and <u>remnants</u> [what remains] of our evil fortune. (ch. 36)

E. I would not wish to have the power of the captain diminished an <u>iota</u> [a tiny amount]. . . . One would expect that the master who would abuse and impose upon a man under his power, would be the most <u>compliant</u> [submissive] and <u>deferential</u> [respectful] to his employers at home. (ch. 37)

Discussion Questions

A. The narrator begins as a Harvard boy, seasick and without sea legs, one who has never really done a hard day's work in his life. Yet through it all, he is able to survive, and he is a stronger and better man because of the many ordeals. That is one interpretation. What would be an alternative interpretation?

Answer: *That he is a spoiled, self-centered boy who did not have the strength and fortitude to persevere through a difficult situation.*

B. How reliable a narrator is this young, inexperienced, pampered Harvard College dropout?

Answer: *Dana goes to great lengths to convince the reader that he is a reliable narrator. For instance, the narrator admits that the skipper should have absolute power—under some situations.*

C. Would the story be significantly different if the cruel Captain had written the book?

Answer: *Yes. We expect that he would have whitewashed or justified his cruel behavior.*

D. The book has a strong journey motif. Explain.

Answer: *In the midst of the unfolding plot, the whole crew is traveling around most of the known world. This greatly enhances the novel and, in its own way, heightens suspense.*

E. Why does this book appeal to people who have never been to sea?

Answer: *The themes of endurance and fortitude supersede the set-*

ting [such as the sea] and have universal application and value.

F. In your opinion, when is it appropriate to break the law?

Answer: *Only when human law violates God's law. Then the disobedience must be on the grounds of conscience and principle. The perpetrators must be willing to accept the consequences for their actions and be ready to make a defense when asked for an accounting (Acts 5:29; 1 Peter 3:15).*

Up from Slavery

Booker T. Washington

Objective Test

__A__ Washington is born a slave in (A) Virginia, (B) North Carolina, (C) Alabama, or (D) Arkansas.

__D__ Washington is greatly encouraged by descriptions fellow coal miners give of a place called (A) the Tuskegee Institute, (B) Howard University, (C) Virginia Tech, or (D) the Hampton Institute.

__C__ While taking corn to the mill, Washington is terrified that the corn would fall off his horse because (A) he would lose time, (B) the corn would be spoiled, (C) if he is late he would be beaten, or (D) he is so tired.

__B__ Washington finds it difficult to work with Native Americans because (A) they hate African Americans, (B) they feel they are superior to African Americans because they were never slaves, or (C) Washington does not personally like them.

__B__ Washington opens the Tuskegee Institute (A) with a federal grant; (B) by invitation from a man in Tuskegee, Alabama; (C) with support from the University of Alabama; or (D) with no support.

__A__ Tuskegee seems ideal for the school because (A) it is amid the bulk of the Negro population and secluded, with a five-mile branch line connecting it to the railroad; (B) it is in a beautiful place; or (C) it is in a region with a great climate for agriculture.

__C__ Washington realizes early that he cannot (A) speak negatively about whites, (B) make enough money, or (C) duplicate education that he has seen in other parts of the country.

__B__ When Washington begins to teach at Tuskegee, he sees (A) hungry and sad children; (B) a young man who has attended some high school, sitting in a one-room cabin, with grease on his clothing and filth around him, yet studying a French grammar; (C) young people staying away from church on Sunday morning.

__A__ One of the greatest honors that Washington experiences is (A) to be given an honorary doctorate from Harvard University, (B) to see his grandchildren attend Tuskegee, (C) to be given an NAACP award, or (D) to return to his home in Virginia.

__C__ While Washington is president of Tuskegee, the only U.S. president to visit there is (A) Grant, (B) Garfield, (C) McKinley, or (D) Wilson.

Suggested Vocabulary Words

A. I was awakened by my mother kneeling over her children and fervently [with passion] praying that Lincoln and his armies might be successful, and that one day she and her children might be free. (ch. 1)

B. Finally the war closed, and the day of freedom came. It was a momentous [important] and eventful day to all upon our plantation [an agricultural estate worked by resident labor]. (ch. 1)

C. He seemed to me to be the one young man in all the world who ought to be satisfied with his attainments [accomplishments]. (ch. 2)

D. They were so much in earnest [fervent; zealous] that only the ringing of the retiring-bell would make them stop studying. (ch. 6)

E. Mr. Campbell is a merchant and banker, and had had little experience in dealing with matters pertaining [relating] to education. (ch. 8)

F. The school was constantly growing in numbers, so much so that, after we had got the farm paid for, the <u>cultivation</u> [preparation; tilling] of the land begun, and the old cabins which we had found on the place somewhat repaired, we turned our attention toward providing a large, <u>substantial</u> [sturdy] building. (ch. 9)

Discussion Questions

A. From the Armageddon of the Civil War rose this Moses, Booker T. Washington, who was born in 1856 or 1859 in Virginia, of a slave mother and a white father he never knew. But he gave no indication in his autobiography of the pain this parentage almost certainly caused him: "I do not even know his name. I have heard reports to the effect that he was a white man who lived on one of the nearby plantations. But I do not find especial fault with him. He was simply another unfortunate victim of the institution which the nation unhappily had engrafted upon it at that time." How could Washington apparently have no rancor in his heart toward his biological father?

Answer: *Washington was able to forgive his tormenters—even though they did not ask to be forgiven.*

B. After Emancipation, Washington went to the Hampton Normal Agricultural Institute in Virginia. When he arrived, he was allowed to work as the school's janitor in return for his board and part of his tuition. After graduating from Hampton, Washington was selected to head a new school at Tuskegee, Alabama, where he taught the virtues of hard work and sound morality as the best way for his race to advance. How was Washington able to overcome so many obstacles?

Answer: *He worked very hard and did so with industry and compassion.*

C. At the end of this autobiography Washington writes:

> Despite superficial and temporary signs which might lead one to entertain a contrary opinion, there was never a time when I felt more hopeful for the race than I do at the present. The great human law that in the end recognizes and rewards merit is everlasting and universal. The outside world does not know, neither can it appreciate, the struggle that is constantly going on in the

hearts of both the Southern white people and their former slaves to free themselves from racial prejudice; and while both races are thus struggling they should have the sympathy, the support, and the forbearance of the rest of the world.

Yet, at the time, racism and prejudice were dominating the lives of millions of African-Americans. How could Washington write this?

Answer: *Washington believed in a God who would bring justice and hope in the midst of adversity. He believed, too, that African Americans would ultimately find their lives changed as they worked hard.*

D. Do you agree with critics who say that Washington was too passive in his relationship with white racism?

Answer: *Most of these critics lived in the 1960s and did not know what it was like to live in the 1880s. Besides, Booker T. Washington and the later Martin Luther King, with their nonviolence, did more for the Civil Rights movement than any other persons.*

Utopia

Sir Thomas More

Objective Test

__B__ As an ambassador for England and King Henry VIII, More travels to (A) Barcelona, Spain; (B) Antwerp, the Netherlands; (C) New York, United States; or (D) Florence, Italy.

__A__ More discusses philosophy with his friend (A) Peter Giles, (B) Henry VIII, (C) William Shakespeare, and (D) David Hume.

__C__ Giles soon introduces More to (A) David Jones, (B) Descartes, (C) Raphael Hythloday, or (D) Morley Smith.

__D__ Hythloday describes a mythological country called (A) Atlantis, (B) Cairo, (C) Timbuktu, or (D) Utopia.

__B__   More laments that Utopia (A) is too warlike, (B) will probably never impact England, (C) is too large, or (D) is a poor country.

Suggested Vocabulary Words

A. Their council is concerning the commonwealth [a loose confederation of democracies with a monarch]. If there be any controversies [disputes] among the commoners, which be very few, they despatch [dispose of rapidly/efficiently] and end them by-and-by. (book 2)

B. But either such as among themselves for heinous [hateful] offences be punished with bondage, or else such as in the cities of other lands for great trespasses [transgressions] be condemned to death. (book 2)

C. But after they heard us speak of the name of Christ, of his doctrine, laws, miracles, and of the no less wonderful constancy [steadfastness; faithfulness] of so many martyrs [religious victims of violence], whose blood willingly shed brought a great number of nations throughout all parts of the world into their sect; you will not believe with how glad minds, they agreed unto the same: whether it were by the secret inspiration [divine influence] of God, or else for that they thought it next unto that opinion, which among them is counted the chiefest. (book 2)

Discussion Questions

A. What form does More employ to write his philosophical treatise?
Answer: *More uses a prose narrative. There is virtually no action— merely a series of conversations.*

B. What is the status of women in Utopia?
Answer: *Women are considered equal in every way to men.*

C. Compare More's *Utopia* with Plato's *The Republic*.
Answer: *Both books present conversations among friends.* The Republic *purports to be a perfect, attainable society.* Utopia *describes an unattainable, perfect society whose parts—rather than the whole— might be implemented. In fact, More concedes that there are absurd components of Utopia.*

D. Is Utopia a perfect society or a society full of perfect people?

Answer: *Utopia is a potentially perfect society full of imperfect people.
Calvin similarly had a goal to create, at Geneva, what J. S. Neale calls a
"godly society in actual working order"—though Calvin would not approve
of various arrangements and customs in the Utopia that More describes.*

Walden

Henry David Thoreau

Objective Test

__A__ Thoreau spends two years (A) beside Walden Pond; (B) in
Worcester, Massachusetts; or (C) on the Boston Commons.

__D__ Local townspeople (A) admire his adventure, (B) help him out,
(C) nearly kill him, or (D) think he is strange.

__D__ The land on which he lives belongs to (A) Robert Louis
Stevenson, (B) Franklin Pierce, (C) Nathaniel Hawthorne, or
(D) Ralph Waldo Emerson.

__B__ He stays (A) two years; (B) two years, two months, two days;
(C) three years, three days; or (D) four months.

__A__ Thoreau discovers that Walden Pond is (A) only a hundred feet
deep, (B) bottomless, (C) salt water, or (D) full of trout.

Suggested Vocabulary Words

With a little more <u>deliberation</u> [forethought; planning] in the choice
of their <u>pursuits</u> [endeavors], all men would perhaps become <u>essentially</u>
[basically] students and observers, for certainly their nature and destiny
are interesting to all alike. In accumulating property for ourselves or our
<u>posterity</u> [descendants], in founding a family or a state, or acquiring
fame even, we are mortal; but in dealing with truth we are immortal,
and need fear no change nor accident. The oldest Egyptian or Hindoo
philosopher raised a corner of the veil from the statue of the divinity;
and still the <u>trembling</u> [shaking] robe remains raised, and I gaze upon as

fresh a glory as he did, since it was I in him that was then so bold, and it is he in me that now reviews the vision. No dust has settled on that robe; no time has elapsed since that divinity was revealed. That time which we really improve, or which is improvable, is neither past, present, nor future.

My residence was more favorable, not only to thought, but to serious reading, than a university; and though I was beyond the range of the ordinary circulating library, I had more than ever come within the influence of those books which circulate round the world, whose sentences were first written on bark, and are now merely copied from time to time on to linen paper. Says the poet Mr Udd, "Being seated, to run through the region of the spiritual world; I have had this advantage in books. To be intoxicated [inebriated] by a single glass of wine; I have experienced this pleasure when I have drunk the liquor of the esoteric doctrines." I kept Homer's *Iliad* on my table through the summer, though I looked at his page only now and then. Incessant labor with my hands, at first, for I had my house to finish and my beans to hoe at the same time, made more study impossible. Yet I sustained [supported; encouraged] myself by the prospect of such reading in future. I read one or two shallow books of travel in the intervals of my work, till that employment made me ashamed of myself, and I asked where it was then that I lived.

The student may read Homer or Aeschylus in the Greek without danger of dissipation [weakening; waste] or luxuriousness [excessive indulgence], for it implies that he in some measure emulate [imitate; copy] their heroes, and consecrate [dedicate; reserve as sacred] morning hours to their pages. The heroic books, even if printed in the character of our mother tongue, will always be in a language dead to degenerate times; and we must laboriously [industriously; by hard work] seek the meaning of each word and line, conjecturing [guessing; projecting] a larger sense than common use permits out of what wisdom and valor and generosity we have. The modern cheap and fertile press, with all its translations, has done little to bring us nearer to the heroic writers of antiquity [ancient times]. They seem as solitary, and the letter in which they are printed as rare and curious, as ever. It is worth the expense of youthful days and costly hours, if you learn only some words of an ancient language, which are raised out of the trivialness [smallness; unimportance] of the street, to be perpetual [permanent; ongoing] suggestions and provocations [incitements]. It is not in vain that the farmer remembers and repeats the few Latin words which he has heard. Men sometimes speak as if the study of the classics would at length make way for more modern and practical studies; but the adventurous student will always study classics, in whatever language they may be written and however ancient they may be. For what are the classics but the noblest recorded thoughts of man? They are the only oracles which are not decayed, and there are such answers to the most modern inquiry in them as Delphi and Dodona never gave. We might as well omit to study Nature because she is old. To read well, that is, to read true books in a true spirit, is a noble exercise, and one that will task the reader more than any exercise which the customs of the day esteem. It requires a training such as the athletes underwent, the steady intention almost of the whole life to this object. Books must be read as deliberately and reservedly as they were written. It is not enough even to be able to speak the language of that nation by which they are written, for there is a memorable interval between the spoken and the written language, the language heard and the language read. The one is commonly transitory [passing; temporary], a sound, a tongue, a dialect merely, almost brutish [crude], and we learn it unconsciously, like the brutes, of our mothers. The other is the maturity and experience of that; if that is our mother tongue, this is our father tongue, a reserved and select expression, too significant to be heard by the ear, which we must be born again in order to speak. The crowds of men who merely spoke the Greek and Latin tongues in the Middle Ages were not entitled by the accident of birth to read the works of genius written in those languages; for these were not written in that Greek or Latin which they knew, but in the select language of literature. They had not learned the nobler dialects of Greece and Rome, but the very materials on which they were written were waste paper to them, and they prized instead a cheap contemporary [present-day] literature. But when the several nations of Europe had acquired distinct though rude written languages of their own, sufficient for the purposes of their rising literatures, then first learning revived, and scholars were enabled to discern from that remoteness [distance in time or space] the treasures of antiquity [ancient times]. What the Roman and Grecian multitude could not hear, after the lapse of ages a few scholars read, and a few scholars only are still reading it. (ch. 3)

Discussion Questions

A. The poet Ezra Pound said that Thoreau wrote *Walden* as the "first intellectual reaction to mere approach of industrialization: Thoreau tried to see how little he need bother about other humanity." Agree or disagree with this statement and explain your opinion.

Answer: *Answers will vary.*

B. Thoreau extols the working poor. Although he worked on his house and hoed his beans, as mentioned above, there is no evidence that he ever held a regular job with the working poor. Does this hurt his credibility?

Answer: *In my opinion, yes. It makes his appealing rhetoric somewhat pedantic and academic rather than genuine and applicable.*

C. State some of the aphorisms, truths, or generalizations that he is promoting in his book.

Answer: *I went to the woods because I wished to live deliberately, to front only the essential facts of life, and see if I could not learn what it had to teach, and not, when I came to die, discover that I had not lived.*

It is not worth the while to go round the world to count the cats in Zanzibar.

D. Compare the worldview of Thoreau with the worldview of his friend Emerson.

Answer: *Both Thoreau and Emerson were Transcendentalists/ Romantics who celebrated the subjective, the empathic. They worshipped at the altar of Nature.*

Watership Down

Richard Adams

Objective Test

__A__ Fiver has a special gift of being (A) able to tell the future, (B) able to feel water under the ground, or (C) able to fly.

__C__ Fiver tells everyone but is unable to convince the head rabbit (A) Hazel, (B) Rocky, or (C) Threarah.

__A__ The warren finds a wonderful place to stay, but it is full of death because it is (A) a breeding ground for men to harvest rabbits, (B) over a volcano, or (C) full of diseased rabbits.

__B__ Helping the rabbits is a wounded bird named (A) Robert, (B) Kehaar, or (C) Hazel.

__C__ The warren has to fight to preserve (A) their leader, (B) Hazel, or (C) Watership Down.

Suggested Vocabulary Words

A. The rabbits became strange in many ways, different from other rabbits. They knew well enough what was happening. But even to themselves they <u>pretended</u> [gave a false appearance] that all was well, for the food was good, they were protected, they had nothing to fear but the one fear; and that struck here and there, never enough at a time to drive them away.

B. "Did you see his body? No. Did anyone? No. Nothing could kill him. He made rabbits bigger than they've ever been—braver, more skillful, more <u>cunning</u> [clever]. I know we paid for it. Some gave their lives. It was worth it, to feel we were Efrafans. For the first time ever, rabbits didn't go <u>scurrying</u> [running rapidly] away."

Discussion Questions

A. The search for home is a major theme of this novel. Discuss how Adams develops it.

Answer: *Home is more than a place; home, the rabbits discover, is an alive, vital community in a safe place.*

B. What makes Hazel such a good leader?
Answer: *Besides being courageous and strong, he also is compassionate. He is a servant-leader.*

C. Why do you think Adams chooses to tell his story by using rabbits?
Answer: *Rabbits by nature are peaceful animals who do not naturally betray violent natures. If they survive, it is by their wits and by working together.*

D. How do humans fare in this novel?
Answer: *Humans are destructive animals. They are the antagonists in this novel.*

White Fang

Jack London

Objective Test

__A__ Bill and Henry are attacked by (A) wolves, (B) Native Americans, (C) grizzly bears, or (D) robbers.

__B__ The protagonist is (A) Thornton, (B) White Fang, (C) Klondike Kelly, or (D) Theodore Roosevelt.

__D__ White Fang is sold to (A) Marcus, (B) Thornton, (C) Seward, or (D) Beauty Smith.

__B__ White Fang is saved by a man named (A) Thornton, (B) Scott, (C) Marcus, or (D) Beauty Smith.

__C__ White Fang and Scott return to (A) South Dakota, (B) Minnesota, (C) California, or (D) Arizona.

Suggested Vocabulary Words

A. Dark spruce forest frowned on either side the frozen waterway. The trees had been stripped by a recent wind of their white covering of frost, and they seemed to lean towards each other, black and ominous [foreboding], in the fading light. A vast silence reigned [dominated] over the land. The land itself was a desolation [empty; without life], lifeless, without movement, so lone and cold that the spirit of it was not even that of sadness. There was a hint in it of laughter, but of a laughter more terrible than any sadness—a laughter that was mirthless [without joy] as the smile of the sphinx [Egyptian god of death], a laughter cold as the frost and partaking of the grimness [sternness; gloominess] of infallibility [perfection; without fault]. It was the masterful and incommunicable [unspoken] wisdom of eternity laughing at the futility [uselessness; purposelessness] of life and the effort of life. (part 1, ch. 1)

B. Henry grunted with an intonation [sound; utterance] that was not all sympathy, and for a quarter of an hour they sat on in silence, Henry staring at the fire, and Bill at the circle of eyes that burned in the darkness just beyond the firelight. (part 1, ch. 2)

C. At such times, confronted [blocked forcefully] by three sets of savage teeth, the young wolf stopped precipitately [quickly], throwing himself back on his haunches [back legs], with fore-legs stiff, mouth menacing, and mane bristling. This confusion in the front of the moving pack always caused confusion in the rear. The wolves behind collided [ran/crashed into] with the young wolf and expressed their displeasure [unhappiness] by administering [giving; dispensing as punishment] sharp nips on his hind-legs and flanks. He was laying up trouble for himself, for lack of food and short tempers went together; but with the boundless [without limit] faith of youth he persisted [doggedly continued] in repeating the manoeuver [movement] every little while, though it never succeeded in gaining anything for him but discomfiture [frustration]. (part 2, ch. 1)

D. In San Quentin prison he had proved incorrigible [stubborn; not to be reformed]. Punishment failed to break his spirit. He could die dumb-mad and fighting to the last, but he could not live and be beaten.

The more fiercely he fought, the more <u>harshly</u> [roughly] society handled him, and the only effect of harshness was to make him fiercer. (part 2, ch. 5)

Discussion Questions

A. Why is London subtly comparing the prisoner (part 2) with White Fang?

Answer: *London strongly feels that human beings are no more than another animal species in the animal kingdom. According to London, people are not, therefore, created in the image of God but only as other creatures.*

B. Why do the animals seem more compassionate than the human beings?

Answer: *They are wild like men, but they are also natural and moved by instinct. Instinct is the currency of the land in London's universe. The more one gives in to instinct, the more pure and devoted one becomes.*

C. Why would pro-choice advocates admire London's worldview?

Answer: *To London—who never makes a statement about abortion—murdering a fetus would be no more onerous than killing any animal.*

D. What part do women play in *White Fang*?

Answer: *No part: he regards women as the "weaker sex" and anathema to the Darwinist North.*

Wuthering Heights

Emily Brontë

Objective Test

C This entire novel is (A) a journal, (B) a narrative epic, (C) a flashback, or (D) a poem.

A The narrator is actually (A) the servant girl Nellie, (B) Heathcliff, (C) Catherine, or (D) Mary.

B Mr. Earnshaw prefers to (A) live in the city; (B) have Heathcliff as a son instead of his biological son, Hindley; or (C) see Catherine marry in society circles.

B Catherine marries (A) Heathcliff, (B) Edgar, (C) Hindley, or (D) Charles.

D Heathcliff runs away because Catherine (A) marries someone else, (B) dies, (C) also runs away, or (D) says some regrettable things that Heathcliff overhears.

Suggested Vocabulary Words

A. He was not <u>insolent</u> [insulting; overbearing] to his <u>benefactor</u> [patron; one who gives gifts], he was simply <u>insensible</u> [unfeeling; lacking emotional response]; though knowing perfectly the hold he had on his heart, and conscious he had only to speak and all the house would be obliged to bend to his wishes. (ch. 4)

B. To be sure, one might have doubted, after the <u>wayward</u> [straying; unpredictable] and impatient existence she had led, whether she <u>merited</u> [was worthy of] a <u>haven</u> [place of safety] of peace at last. One might doubt in seasons of cold reflection; but not then, in the presence of her corpse. It asserted its own <u>tranquillity</u> [peacefulness], which seemed a pledge of equal quiet to its former <u>inhabitant</u> [someone occupying a place]. (ch. 16).

C. Yesterday was bright, calm, and frosty. I went to the Heights as I proposed: my housekeeper <u>entreated</u> [strongly urged; begged] me to

289

bear a little note from her to her young lady, and I did not refuse, for the worthy woman was not conscious of anything odd in her request. (ch. 31)

D. When Hareton was there, she generally paused in an interesting part, and left the book lying about: that she did repeatedly; but he was as <u>obstinate</u> [stubborn] as a mule, and, instead of snatching at her bait, in wet weather he took to smoking with Joseph; and they sat like <u>automatons</u> [robots; figures without will or purpose], one on each side of the fire. (ch. 32)

E. I <u>uttered</u> [spoke] an <u>ejaculation</u> [short emotional utterance] of <u>discontent</u> [dissatisfaction; hopelessness] at seeing the <u>dismal</u> [discouraging; gloomy] <u>grate</u> [fireplace], and <u>commenced</u> [began] shutting the <u>casements</u> (side-hinged windows], one after another, till I came to his. (ch. 34)

Discussion Questions

A. What do you think of this critic's comments?

> *Wuthering Heights,* which has long been one of the most popular and highly regarded novels in English literature, seemed to hold little promise when it was published in 1847, selling very poorly and receiving only a few mixed reviews. Victorian readers found the book shocking and inappropriate in its depiction of passionate, ungoverned love and cruelty (despite the fact that the novel portrays no sex or bloodshed), and the work was virtually ignored. Even Emily Brontë's sister Charlotte—an author whose works contained similar motifs of Gothic love and desolate landscapes—remained ambivalent toward the unapologetic intensity of her sister's novel. In a preface to the book, which she wrote shortly after Emily Brontë's death, Charlotte Brontë stated, "Whether it is right or advisable to create beings like Heathcliff, I do not know. I scarcely think it is."

Answer: *Answers will vary. Heathcliff is one of the most memorable villains of world literature; he represents the consequences of sin and refusal to forgive others. He is both a perpetrator and a victim.*

B. After Catherine offends Heathcliff, he leaves. Why? Is it to make himself worthy of her? To prepare for revenge?

Answer: *All answers are pure conjecture. I would say, "All of the above."*

C. Do you agree with critic Arnold Kettle in seeing Heathcliff as a hero?

> Heathcliff's revenge may involve a pathological condition of hatred, but it is not at bottom merely neurotic. It has a moral force. For what Heathcliff does is to use against his enemies with complete ruthlessness their own weapons, to turn on them (stripped of their romantic veils) their own standards, to beat them at their own game. The weapons he uses against the Earnshaws and Lintons are their own weapons of money and arranged marriages. He gets power over them by the classic methods of the ruling class, expropriation and property deals.

Answer: *Heathcliff is more an antihero. In all of world literature, Heathcliff is a prime example of Attila the Hun ("the Scourge of God"), a purpose-driven, revenge-driven individual.*

D. Does this novel have a happy or a sad ending?

Answer: *Both. On one hand the cousins are happily married, but Cathy, Heathcliff, and others are all dead, with no hint of reconciliation.*

Appendixes

Credits, Permissions, and Sources

Efforts have been made to conform to U.S. Copyright Law. Any infringement is unintentional, and the author will remove any material that infringes copyright, and about which the copyright claimant informs the author, will be removed pending resolution. All artwork is from www.clipart.com, and the author has purchased the right to use this copyrighted material in this work. Most of the literature cited in this book is in the public domain. Much of it is available on the Internet, through the following sites:

Gutenberg Project (http://ibiblio.org/gutenberg/etext)
Willa Cather, *My Antonia*
F. Scott Fitzgerald, *The Great Gatsby*
Jack London, *White Fang*
George Orwell, *Animal Farm*

Great Books Online (www.bartleby.com)
Henry Dana, *Two Years before the Mast*
Sir Thomas More, *Utopia*
Turoldus (?), *The Song of Roland*

Infomotions, Inc. The Alex Catalogue of Electronic Texts (www.infomotions.com/alex/)

Stephane Theroux. Classic Reader (http://classicreader.com)
Jane Austen, *Emma*
Charlotte Brontë, *Jane Eyre*
Emily Brontë, *Wuthering Heights*
James Fenimore Cooper, *The Last of the Mohicans*
Charles Dickens, *David Copperfield* and *Hard Times* and *Oliver Twist*
Fyodor Dostoyevsky, *The Brothers Karamazov*
Alexandre Dumas, *The Count of Monte Cristo*
George Eliot, *Middlemarch*
Gustave Flaubert, *Madame Bovary*
Thomas Hardy, *The Return of the Native*
Nathaniel Hawthorne, *The House of the Seven Gables*

Victor Hugo, *Les Misérables*
Aldous Huxley, *Brave New World*
Niccolò Machiavelli, *The Prince*
Herman Melville, *Moby Dick*
William Shakespeare, *Julius Caesar*
Upton Sinclair, *The Jungle*
Robert Louis Stevenson, *Kidnapped*
Henry David Thoreau, *Walden*
Jules Verne, *20,000 Leagues Under the Sea*
Booker T. Washington, *Up from Slavery: An Autobiography*

University of Virginia. Browse E-Books by Author
(http://etext.lib.virginia.edu/ebooks/)
Miguel de Cervantes, *Don Quixote*
Theodore Dreiser, *Sister Carrie*
Benjamin Franklin, *The Autobiography of Benjamin Franklin*
H. G. Wells, *The Invisible Man*
Zitkala-"Sa, *Old Indian Legends*

Glossary of Literary Terms

Alliteration is the repetition of initial consonant sounds. The repetition can be juxtaposed, side by side as in "simply sad," or nearby as in this example:

> I looked over Jordan and what did I see,
> Comin' for to carry me home!
> A band of angels comin' after me,
> Comin' for to carry me home.
>
> ("Swing Low, Sweet Chariot")

Allusion is a casual, brief reference to a famous historical or literary figure or event. Here is an allusion to God creating the earth:

> Upon what base was fixed the lathe wherein
> He turned this globe and rigolled it so trim?
> Who blew the bellows of His Furnace vast?
> Or held the mold wherein the world was cast?
>
> ("Upon What Base?" Edward Taylor)

Characters in a narrative. The person with whom the main character has the most conflict is the *antagonist*, who is the enemy of the main character, the *protagonist*. Characters introduced with the sole purpose of developing and contrasting with the main character are called *foils*. In the old television series *The Lone Ranger*, Tonto's only purpose is to be a foil to the Lone Ranger. Likewise, in *Don Quixote*, Sancho is a perfect example of a foil.

Conflict that occurs within a character is called *internal conflict*. In the Old Testament book of Esther, for example, Esther experiences internal conflict as she decides whether or not to do what Mordecai asks her. An *external conflict* is normally an obvious dramatic struggle between the protagonist and antagonist(s). In the same story, Esther and her community have an external conflict with Haman and the enemies of Esther's people.

Crisis or climax is the moment or event in the *plot* in which the conflict is most directly addressed: the main character "wins" or "loses," and the secret is revealed. After the climax comes the *denouement*, or falling action. In Edgar Allan Poe's short story "Tell Tale Heart," the climax occurs at the end of the story when the mad perpetrator admits his crime.

Figures of speech. Metaphor is a comparison that creatively identifies one thing with a dissimilar thing, and transfers or ascribes to the first thing some of the qualities of the second. A metaphor asserts that one thing is another thing: "The Lord is my shepherd." Frequently a metaphor is invoked by the verb *to be* or *to become:*

> I become a transparent eyeball;
> I am nothing.
> I see all;
> The currents of the Universal Being circulate through me;
> I am part or particle of God.
>> ("I Become a Transparent Eyeball,"
>> Ralph Waldo Emerson)

A *simile* or *analogy* says that something is like or as another:

> The wrath of God is like great waters that are damned for the present; they increase more and more and rise higher and higher, till an outlet is given.
>> ("Sinners in the Hands of an Angry
>> God," Jonathan Edwards)

Narration refers to the way an author chooses to tell the story. *First-person narration* lets a character refer to himself or herself as "I." *Second-person narration* addresses the reader and/or the main character as "you" (and may also use first-person narration, but not necessarily). *Third-person narration* is not from a character in the story; the story refers to its characters as "he," "she," and "they." Since this is the most common form of narration, it does not need to be illustrated. *Limited Narration* means the story is only able to tell what one person is thinking or feeling. In most of his novels, Charles

Dickens employs *omniscient narration*, with the story presented from various characters' viewpoints. *Reliable Narration* means that everything this narration says is true, and the narrator knows everything necessary to the story. An *unreliable narrator* may not know all the relevant information, may be intoxicated or mentally ill, and/or may lie to the audience. For example, the objective narrator in *Ethan Frome*, Edith Wharton, is a nonparticipant in the plot and a reliable narrator.

Onomatopoeia means the use of words that in their pronunciation suggest their meaning, such as the following: boom, buzz, chime, clang, crash, gush, hiss, hush, kerplunk, mumble, purr, splash, tinkling, whirr, wow.

Plot includes the events of the story line, in the order the story gives them. A typical plot has five parts: *exposition, rising action, crisis* or *climax, falling action,* and *resolution.*

Setting is the place(s) and time(s) of the story, including the historical period, social milieu of the characters, geographical location, and descriptions of indoor and outdoor locales.

Theme is the one-sentence major purpose of a literary piece, rarely stated but certainly implied. A *thesis* statement is similar to the theme. A theme is different from a *moral*, which states the author's didactic purpose. A *précis* is a summary of the plot.

Tone is the mood of a literary piece. For instance, the tone or mood of James Thurber's short stories is inevitably humorous.

Books for Age Groups

Younger Readers

Autobiography of Benjamin Franklin, The, Benjamin Franklin
Chosen, The, Chaim Potok
Count of Monte Cristo, The, Alexandre Dumas
David Copperfield, Charles Dickens
Hard Times, Charles Dickens
House of the Seven Gables, The, Nathaniel Hawthorne
Invisible Man, The, H. G. Wells
Kidnapped, Robert Louis Stevenson
Last of the Mohicans, James Fenimore Cooper
Little Women, Louisa May Alcott
Old Indian Legends, Zitkala-"Sa
Oliver Twist, Charles Dickens
Pearl, The, John Steinbeck
Song of Roland, The, Turoldus (?)
20,000 Leagues under the Sea, Jules Verne
Two Years before the Mast, Henry Dana
Up from Slavery, Booker T. Washington
Watership Down, Richard Adams
White Fang, Jack London

More Mature Readers

Agamemnon, Aeschylus
And There Were None, Agatha Christie
Animal Farm, George Orwell
Brave New World, Aldous Huxley
Brothers Karamazov, The, Fyodor Dostoyevsky
Civil War, The, Shelby Foote
Crucible, The, Arthur Miller
Daisy Miller, Henry James
Don Quixote, Miguel de Cervantes

Emma, Jane Austen
Fairie Queen, The, Edmund Spenser
Giants in the Earth, O. E. Rølvaag
Grapes of Wrath, The, John Steinbeck
Great Gatsby, The, F. Scott Fitzgerald
Intruder in the Dust, William Faulkner
Jane Eyre, Charlotte Brontë
Julius Caesar, William Shakespeare
Jungle, The, Upton Sinclair
Madame Bovary, Gustave Flaubert
Middlemarch, George Eliot
Misérables, Les, Victor Hugo
Moby Dick, Herman Melville
My Antonia, Willa Cather
Prince, The, Niccolò Machiavelli
Pygmalion, George Bernard Shaw
Raisin in the Sun, A, Lorraine Hansberry
Return of the Native, The, Thomas Hardy
Sister Carrie, Theodore Dreiser
Utopia, Sir Thomas More
Walden, Henry David Thoreau
Wuthering Heights, Emily Brontë

Biographies of Authors

Adams, Richard (1920–)   British writer of fiction and folktales for both adults and children. His best-known work is the novel *Watership Down* (1972). This story about a community of rabbits and its search for a new warren is memorable for the power of its narration. The excellent writing and powerful thematic components make it a timeless classic that transcends juvenile literature and places this novel with serious fiction.

Aeschylus (525? –456 B.C.)   Aeschylus was the earliest of the great tragic poets of Greece. He was not the best Greek dramatist, but as the predecessor of Sophocles and Euripides, he is called the father of Greek tragedy. He was also a soldier. Aeschylus fought successfully against the Persians at Marathon in 490 B.C., and at Salamis in 480 B.C. Aeschylus wrote ninety plays. His tragedies, first performed about 500 B.C., were presented as trilogies, or groups of three, usually bound together by a common theme. This became the prototype for Greek drama for a thousand years.

Alcott, Louisa May (1832–1888)   American author, Universalist, and proponent of Transcendentalism, Alcott is considered one of the major writers of juvenile fiction. There is hardly anything profound in her works and nothing that approaches literary genius. Yet, Americans love her stories and read them with great alacrity today. Is there an American young lady who has not read Alcott? Alcott's best-known book is the novel *Little Women* (1868–69), which portrays the escapades of four sisters growing up in New England during the Civil War. *Little Women* and its sequels center on family relationships and promote virtues such as perseverance and unselfishness, with a decidedly Unitarian favor.

Austen, Jane (1775–1817)   Austen was famous for her insightful studies of early-nineteenth-century English society. Austen portrayed the common, day-to-day life of members of the upper-middle class. Her works were full of irony and social satire. Austen's characters inevitably mature as they correct their faults through lessons learned during tribulation.

Brontë, Charlotte (1816–1855) and Emily (1818–1848) No English family produced more talent than the Brontë sisters. The sisters Charlotte and Emily Jane wrote some of the best Victorian English fiction of the nineteenth century. They both were masterful storytellers and took the gothic romance to a new level. Their characters were memorable and timeless.

Cather, Willa (1873–1947) Cather was one of the country's best novelists, whose carefully crafted prose painted sketches of American people and their country as memorable as those from any writer. At times her images are surreal and even haunting. Her subject matter inevitably concerned the American pioneer.

Cervantes, Miguel de (1547–1616) Cervantes is arguably the greatest Spanish author. *Don Quixote* is one of the masterpieces of world literature. Cervantes, a Spanish nobleman yet prisoner of the Saracens, wrote with sophistication and insight that exceeded his age.

Christie, Agatha (1890–1976) This English novelist raised mystery stories to a new level. Under Christie's pen, whodunit novels became first-rate literature. Her mysteries created clever and surprising twists of plot. Christie also created the memorable protagonists Hercule Poirot and Miss Marple.

Cooper, James Fenimore (1789–1851) Cooper is one of the most famous and certainly one of the most read romantic authors of the nineteenth century. Perhaps Emerson and Hawthorne were better writers. But everyone read Cooper. He was the Clancy of his age! In 1823 Cooper wrote *The Pioneers*, the first of the five novels that make up the Leather Stocking Tales. The remaining four books—*The Last of the Mohicans* (1826), *The Prairie* (1827), *The Pathfinder* (1840), and *The Deerslayer* (1841)—continue the story of Natty Bumppo, one of the most famous characters in American fiction

Dana, Henry (1815–1882) American writer and lawyer, born in Cambridge, Massachusetts, Dana went to Harvard. An eye disease interrupted his education. While recovering, he worked on a sailing ship. His memoir *Two Years before the Mast* (1840) told the story of his voyage from Boston, Massachusetts, around Cape Horn to California and back.

Dickens, Charles (1812–1870)   Charles John Huffam Dickens, with the pseudonym Boz, arguably was a mediocre English novelist, but this in no way diminishes his fame. He was a prolific writer, one of the most popular in the history of English literature. In his enormous body of works, Dickens combined masterly storytelling, humor, and irony with sharp social criticism and acute observation of people. Critics accused him of being a master at creating bothersome coincidences, boring archetypes, and maudlin plots.

Dostoyevsky, Fyodor (1821–1881)   The Russian writer and humanitarian Fyodor Mikhaylovich Dostoyevsky was one of the world's greatest novelists of all time. Rivaled only by Leo (Count Lev Nikolayevich) Tolstoy and William Faulkner, his works explore religious, moral, political, and psychological issues to an unprecedented and profound level. Dostoyevsky and Tolstoy led the great Russian theistic revival of the nineteenth century.

Dreiser, Theodore (1871–1945)   American naturalist, novelist, and journalist, Dreiser was known for his predictable plots, lackluster characters, and shoddy settings. Yet, he was one of the most popular authors of the early twentieth century. Like most naturalists, Dreiser presented life honestly. He accomplished this through accurate detail, especially in his detailed if uninspiring descriptions of the urban settings of many of his stories. Dreiser's characters inevitably were victims of social and economic forces, and of fate or bad luck. There was no loving God in Dreiser's universe.

Dumas, Alexandre (1802–1870)   French novelist and playwright of the romantic period, Dumas nonetheless wrote theistic worldview novels. He is the most widely read of all French writers and is best remembered for his historical novels *The Three Musketeers* (1844) and *The Count of Monte Cristo* (1844).

Eliot, George (1819–1880)   Mary Ann (or Marian) Evans, using the pen name George Eliot, was an English novelist. Her books, with their inspiring portrayals of ordinary lives, made her one of the best novelists of the nineteenth century. Evans was raised in a strict Christian home, but in her adult years she rebelled against the Lord. Her antireligious feelings are abundantly present in her novels.

Faulkner, William (1897–1962)   A Nobel Prize winner, Faulkner was the greatest American novelist of all time. He is best remembered for his epic portrayal, in some twenty novels, of the tragic conflict between the old and the new South. He created the memorable Sartoris and Snopes families. Faulkner is so much better than any other American author that it is difficult to categorize him in any literary epoch. In Western literature, only Leo Tolstoy and Fyodor Dostoyevsky come close to matching Faulkner's talent.

Fitzgerald, F. Scott (1896–1940)   Fitzgerald's novels discuss changing social attitudes during the 1920s, a period dubbed the Jazz Age by the author. He is best known for his novels *The Great Gatsby* (1925) and *Tender Is the Night* (1934), both of which depict disillusion with the romantic American dream of self-betterment, wealth, and success through hard work and perseverance. In a sense, his life was a metaphor for the Roaring Twenties. While in basic training near Montgomery, Alabama, he met and later married a southern belle, the opinionated eighteen-year-old Zelda Sayre. Zelda became the model for many of the female characters in his fiction.

Flaubert, Gustave (1821–1880)   The nineteenth-century French writer Gustave Flaubert is known for his obsessive pursuit of literary perfection. His novels, written in the literary style known as realism, were nonetheless unique. Unfortunately, his pedantic pomposity is manifest in his prose, and the reader often finds his plots to be tedious. Flaubert's most famous novel, *Madame Bovary* (1857), is one of the most important works in French literature. Along with English author Daniel Defoe's *Robinson Crusoe*, it sets the standard for the early novel during the next century.

Foote, Shelby (1916–)   Foote is one of the greatest southern novelists of his century. Beginning in fiction, Foote soon took his career in a radical, new direction. Between 1954 and 1974 he composed the three-volume, 1.2-million-word *The Civil War: A Narrative*, the work for which he is now best known. In spite of these achievements, Foote remained relatively unknown before his role in Ken Burns's *The Civil War,* a documentary series released by the Public Broadcasting Service in 1990, which made him a cultural hero.

Franklin, Benjamin (1706–1790)   Called the "First American,"
Franklin was a newspaper editor, author, diplomat, philosopher, and scientist. He founded the first fire station in America, and reputedly the
world's first public lending library, in 1731 in Philadelphia. His life personified the era in which he lived. Franklin's many contributions to the
cause of the American Revolution (1775–1783) and the new American
federal government, have placed him among the country's greatest
statesmen.

Hansberry, Lorraine (1930–1965)   This American writer and civil-
rights activist is best known for her play *A Raisin in the Sun* (1959),
which was made into a motion picture in 1961. She was born in
Chicago, Illinois, and because her parents were well known in national
African-American cultural circles, she met many influential African
Americans during her childhood. In 1938 Hansberry's family chal-
lenged Chicago's segregation laws by moving to an all-white neighbor-
hood—generating the theme of *A Raisin in the Sun*.

Hardy, Thomas (1840–1928)   English novelist and poet of the naturalist movement, Hardy created some of the most memorable characters
in late-nineteenth century literature. His best novels are *The Return of
the Native* (1878), *The Mayor of Casterbridge* (1886), *Tess of the
d'Urbervilles* (1891), and *Jude the Obscure* (1895). All are pervaded by
belief in a universe dominated by the determinism associated with
Charles Darwin. Hardy depicts nature as a malevolent presence. He
often explores the theme of urbanity replacing rural England.

Hawthorne, Nathaniel (1804–1864)   Born in Salem, Massachusetts,
into an old Puritan family, Hawthorne explored his roots for the rest of
his life. His first major publishing success was *Twice-Told Tales* (1837).
These early works are largely historical sketches and allegorical tales
dealing with moral conflicts and the effects of Puritanism on American
history. In his work is an inherent tension between theistic Puritanism
and subjective romanticism. Hawthorne was probably the most gifted
romantic writer in this transitional period.

Hugo, Victor (1802–1885)   This French poet, novelist, and playwright
wrote some of the greatest romantic works in the nineteenth century.
However, like the American author Nathaniel Hawthorne, he wrote with

a theistic worldview and in a romantic style. Hugo was more than an author; like Dickens and Lewis, he also championed social causes.

Huxley, Aldous (1894–1963) English novelist, essayist, critic, and poet, Huxley published four books of poetry before the appearance of his first novel, *Crome Yellow* (1921). His novels *Antic Hay* (1923) and *Point Counter Point* (1928) illustrate the materialism of the 1920s. *Brave New World* (1932), an ironic vision of a future utopia, placed Huxley among premier twentieth-century authors.

James, Henry (1843–1916) The American writer Henry James skillfully juxtaposed American and European ethos. He took the quintessential Victorian parlor scene to another level. James's work is characterized by subtle development of character rather than by complicated plots. His books move slowly and carefully pyschoanalyze the characters

London, Jack London (1876–1916) London was one of the best naturalist authors in American literature. During his brief life, London wrote more than fifty books and experienced enormous popular success as an author. Many of his stories, including his masterpiece *The Call of the Wild* (1903), deal with the reversion of a tame pet to the primitive wild.

Machiavelli, Niccolò (1469–1527) Italian historian, statesman, and political philosopher, Machiavelli entered public life as a clerk and left it as one of the greatest political philosophers of all time. His own multiple public service duties informed his most famous of political works, *The Prince.* That effectively established his reputation as a political philosopher of the first order. In this seminal work, he established a theory of political ideology that transformed all future discussions about political power.

Melville, Herman (1819–1891) Melville was one of the most talented, but also confused, American novelists of the nineteenth century. Although he was a romantic, Melville's exploration of psychological and metaphysical themes foreshadowed twentieth-century realism. Besides the epic classic *Moby Dick*, Melville wrote many other powerful novels. Notably among them was *Billy Budd,* where for the first time Melville abandoned all Judeo-Christian salvation theology and embraced a form of romantic epistemology.

Miller, Arthur (1915–)   Miller's play *The Crucible* (1953), although concerned with the Salem witchcraft trials, was actually aimed at the then widespread congressional investigation of subversive activities in the United States. The drama won the 1953 Tony Award. Eugene O'Neill, Tennessee Williams, and Arthur Miller championed the world-view of realism in literature and drama.

More, Thomas, Sir (1478–1535)   This English statesman and writer is famous for his religious stance against King Henry VIII, which cost him his life. As a writer, More is known best for *Utopia* (1516), a satirical account of life on the fictitious island of Utopia. There the people subordinate individuals' interests to those of society, practice universal education and religious toleration, and own all land in common. *Utopia* became the prototype for similar books. Among the best known of these are *Candide* by Voltaire and *Erewhon* by Samuel Butler.

Orwell, George (1903–1950)   Orwell has joined Swift as one of England's greatest satirists. He expressed his condemnation of totalitarian society in the brilliantly witty allegorical fable *Animal Farm* (1945) and in the satirical novel *Nineteen Eighty-four* (1949).

Potok, Chaim (1929–)   Born Herman Harold Potok, he is the son of Polish immigrants and was reared in an Orthodox Jewish home. This background deeply affected his writings. Chaim Potok began his career as an author and novelist with *The Chosen* (1967), the first book from a major publisher to portray Orthodox Judaism in the United States. Two years later he presented a sequel, *The Promise*. Potok returned to the subject of Hasidism with *My Name Is Asher Lev* (1972) and its sequel *The Gift of Asher Lev* (1990), the story of a young artist and his conflict with the traditions of his family and community. In other novels Potok has continued to examine the conflict between secular and religious interests: *In the Beginning* (1975), *The Book of Lights* (1981), and *Davita's Harp* (1985). His most recent works include *I Am the Clay* (1992), The *Tree of Here* (1993), *The Sky of Now* (1995), and *The Gates of November* (1996).

Rølvaag, O. E. (1876–1931)   Norwegian-American novelist Ole Edvart Rølvaag lived most of the stories he wrote in his novels. Rölvaag insightfully explored immigrant adjustment to life in America. His two major novels, written in Norwegian, were translated together into English in 1927 as *Giants in the Earth*. This is a realistic portrayal of immigrant life. Rølvaag wrote two sequels: *Peder Victorius* (1929) and *Their Father's God* (1931).

Shakespeare, William (1564–1616)   English playwright and poet, Shakespeare is perhaps the greatest of all dramatists. No author has more insights into human character than Shakespeare. This Elizabethan poet-playwright was a prolific writer. Shakespeare was the most unique writer in world history and has left an indelible mark on literary history.

Shaw, George Bernard (1856–1950)   This Irish-born playwright was the most significant British dramatist since Shakespeare. In addition to being a prolific playwright (writing fifty stage plays), he was also the most vitriolic satirist since Jonathan Swift. At the same time, Shaw was the quintessential realist, and thus the antithesis of a romantic.

Sinclair, Upton (1878–1968)   American writer and social reformer, Sinclair merged literature and social criticism in a new way. As a satirist, however, he did not display the same talent as he did for social criticism. His books are interesting but not great literature. The author of ninety books, Sinclair became well known for his novel *The Jungle* (1906), which exposed the unsanitary and miserable working conditions in the Chicago stockyards and led to an investigation by the federal government and the passage of pure food laws.

Spenser, Edmund (1552–1599)   Spenser bridged the medieval and Elizabethan periods and is most famous for the longest epic narrative in the English language, *The Faerie Queene*. This epic combines religious and historical symbolism with late-medieval and chivalric romance.

Steinbeck, John (1902–1968)   Steinbeck's most widely known work is *The Grapes of Wrath* (1939), for which he won a Pulitzer Prize (1940). The controversial novel, along the line of Upton Sinclair's *The Jungle*, took social protest to a new height. It was superb fiction in its own right. Steinbeck's other works include *The Moon Is Down* (1942), *Cannery Row* (1945), *The Wayward Bus* (1947), *East of Eden* (1952), *The Winter of Our Discontent* (1961), and *America and Americans* (1966). In 1962 he released *Travels with Charley*, an autobiographical account of a trip across the United States accompanied by a pet dog. Steinbeck was awarded the 1962 Nobel Prize in literature.

Stevenson, Robert Louis (1850–1894)   The Scottish novelist Stevenson wrote juvenile literature and serious adult literature. Stevenson suffered from tuberculosis and often traveled in search of warm climates to ease his illness. His adventure stories reflect his travels. *Treasure Island* (1883) is an action-packed search for buried gold involving the boy hero Jim Hawkins and the memorable Long John Silver. *The Strange Case of Dr. Jekyll and Mr. Hyde* (1886) is a theistic study of naturalistic themes.

Thoreau, Henry David (1817–1862)   Thoreau was one of the most gifted, if eccentric, writers of the nineteenth century and a strong proponent of Transcendentalism (the American form of Romanticism). He was a close friend of Ralph Waldo Emerson and Nathaniel Hawthorne, and he attended Harvard University—the "Berkeley" of the early nineteenth century. These influences led Thoreau to embrace individualism and the subjective as important, in a worldview that then permeated American intellectual society. His best-known work is *Walden, or, Life in the Woods* (1854); yet he wrote other intellectual pieces. In 1846 Thoreau chose to go to jail rather than to pay his poll tax and thus support the Mexican War (1846–1848). He clarified his position in his seminal and famous essay "Civil Disobedience" (1849), now widely referred to by its original title, "Resistance to Civil Government."

Turoldus (?)   There is a growing consensus that an obscure eleventh-century monk named Turoldus copied or even wrote *The Song of Roland*. The oldest surviving manuscript, the Oxford Digby 23, is signed "Turoldus" and written in Anglo-Norman, a language predominant in England following the Norman invasion from France in 1066. Since almost no one in eleventh-century France knew how to write, this document must have been written by a monk or some other clergy person. If Turoldus wrote this tale, he still probably acted chiefly as a recorder. The epic was no doubt popular in oral French folklore and used in celebrations long before Turoldus put it into writing. The legend, existing from the time of Charlemagne (died 814), was probably put into poetic form by a single individual. (http://www.enotes.com/chanson-de/12871)

Verne, Jules (1828–1905)   The French author Jules Verne was the earliest and most popular science fiction writer in Western literature. It was easy to be a science fiction writer at the end of the nineteenth century. People were fascinated with scientific progress and most felt that there was no limit to science's ability to improve the lives of people. With remarkable accuracy Verne anticipated spaceships, submarines, helicopters, and guided missiles long before they were developed. The *Nautilus*, for instance, is quite similar to World War I submarines invented fifty years later. Among Verne's most popular books are *Journey to the Center of the Earth* (1864), *From the Earth to the Moon* (1865), *20,000 Leagues Under the Sea* (1870), *Mysterious Island* (1870), and *Around the World in Eighty Days* (1873).

Washington, Booker T. (1856–1915)   As an American educator, Booker Taliaferro Washington urged African Americans to better themselves through education and diligence. He was born April 5, 1856, on a Virginia plantation, son of a slave mother and of a white father he never knew. Following the Civil War, his family moved to West Virginia, where he worked in coal mines. From 1872 to 1875 he attended a newly founded school for African-Americans, Hampton University. Later he was appointed principal of a black normal school in Alabama (now Tuskegee University). Washington made Tuskegee Institute into a major center for industrial and agricultural training and research.

Wells, Herbert George (1866–1946)   While Wells was not a Jules Verne, he was a first-class science fiction writer in his own right. His science fiction suffered from his naturalistic agenda, which became partisanship more than literature. He promoted the Darwinist-naturalistic position as fervently as Jack London (but without the literary talent of London). His novel *The Time Machine* (1895) mingled science, adventure, and political comment. Later works in this genre are *The Invisible Man* (1897), *The War of the Worlds* (1898), and *The Shape of Things to Come* (1933). All are prophetic visions of the twentieth century.

Zitkala-¨Sa (1876–1938)   Zitkala-¨Sa was born at the Yankton Reservation in South Dakota, where she was raised as a traditional Sioux. She attended a Quaker missionary school in Indiana, White's Manual Labor Institute. Later she attended Earlham College, 1895–1897, also in Indiana, then taught at Carlisle (Pa.) Indian Training

School. It was her passion to claim the folklore and heritage of her Native American peoples. Zitkala-"Sa is also known by the name Gertrude Simmons Bonnin, and her works are available online: http://guweb2.gonzaga.edu/faculty/campbell/enl311/zitkala.htm.

Index of Authors

The Author

James P. Stobaugh was a Merrill Fellow at Harvard University and holds a B.A. cum laude from Vanderbilt, an M.A. from Rutgers University, an M.Div. from Princeton Theological Seminary, and a D.Min. from Gordon-Conwell Theological Seminary.

An experienced teacher, he is a recognized leader in homeschooling and has published several books for students and teachers. Some are in the series Preparing Thoughtful Christians to be World Changers, with both student and teacher editions: *Skills for Literary Analysis*, *Skills for Rhetoric*, *World Literature*, *American Literature*, and *British Literature* (all in 2003).

Stobaugh has also published *Fire That Burns but Does Not Consume* (2003), and the highly valued *SAT and College Preparation Course for the Christian Student* (1998; revised edition, 2004).

He lives near Hollsopple, Pennsylvania, and travels widely to speak at conventions about literature, teaching, and education.

My Notes

My Notes

My Notes

My Notes